Social Network Analytics

Social Network Analytics
Computational Research Methods and Techniques

Nilanjan Dey
Samarjeet Borah
Rosalina Babo
Amira S. Ashour

ELSEVIER

ACADEMIC PRESS

An imprint of Elsevier

Academic Press is an imprint of Elsevier
125 London Wall, London EC2Y 5AS, United Kingdom
525 B Street, Suite 1650, San Diego, CA 92101, United States
50 Hampshire Street, 5th Floor, Cambridge, MA 02139, United States
The Boulevard, Langford Lane, Kidlington, Oxford OX5 1GB, United Kingdom

Notices
Knowledge and best practice in this field are constantly changing. As new research and experience
broaden our understanding, changes in research methods, professional practices, or medical
treatment may become necessary.

Practitioners and researchers must always rely on their own experience and knowledge in evaluating
and using any information, methods, compounds, or experiments described herein. In using such
information or methods they should be mindful of their own safety and the safety of others, including
parties for whom they have a professional responsibility.

To the fullest extent of the law, neither the Publisher nor the authors, contributors, or editors, assume
any liability for any injury and/or damage to persons or property as a matter of products liability,
negligence or otherwise, or from any use or operation of any methods, products, instructions, or ideas
contained in the material herein.

Library of Congress Cataloging-in-Publication Data
A catalog record for this book is available from the Library of Congress

British Library Cataloguing-in-Publication Data
A catalogue record for this book is available from the British Library

ISBN : 978-0-12-815458-8

For information on all Academic Press publications
visit our website at https://www.elsevier.com/books-and-journals

Working together
to grow libraries in
developing countries

www.elsevier.com • www.bookaid.org

Publisher: Mara Conner
Acquisition Editor: Chris Katsaropoulos
Editorial Project Manager: Joanna Collett
Production Project Manager: Kiruthika Govindaraju
Cover Designer: Victoria Pearson Esser

Typeset by SPi Global, India

Contents

Contributors

Rajib Bag Department of CSE, Supreme Knowledge Foundation Group of Institutions, Mankundu, India

Siddhartha Bhattacharyya Department of CA, RCC Institute of Information Technology, Kolkata, India

Samarjeet Borah Department of Computer Applications, Sikkim Manipal Institute of Technology, Sikkim Manipal University, Majitar, India

Surajit Borkotokey Department of Mathematics, Dibrugarh University, Dibrugarh, India

Koyel Chakraborty Department of CSE, Supreme Knowledge Foundation Group of Institutions, Mankundu, India

Isabel Dans-Álvarez-de-Sotomayor Department of Specific Didactics, University of Vigo, Pontevedra, Spain

J. Del Olmo Barbero King Juan Carlos University, Madrid, Spain

Pedro Henrique dos Reis Rezende School of Engineering and Architecture, FUMEC University, Belo Horizonte, Brazil

C. Fernández Muñoz Complutense University, Madrid, Spain

M.C. García-Galera King Juan Carlos University, Madrid, Spain

Anirban Ghatak Indian Institute of Management Visakhapatnam, Visakhapatnam, India

Sarada Prasad Gochhayat Department of Information Engineering, University of Padua, Padua, Italy

Loyimee Gogoi Department of Mathematics, Dibrugarh University, Dibrugarh; Sampling and Official Statistics Unit, Indian Statistical Institute (ISI), Kolkata, India

Mercedes González-Sanmamed Department of Pedagogy and Didactics, University of A Coruña, A Coruña, Spain

Malka N. Halgamuge School of Computing and Mathematics, Charles Sturt University, Melbourne, VIC, Australia

Aboul Alla Hassanien Faculty of Computers and Information Technology Department, Cairo University, Giza, Egypt

Leila Hedayatifar New England Complex Systems Institute, Cambridge, MA, United States

Sachin Kumar College of IBS, National University of Science and Technology MISiS, Moscow, Russia

Brojo Kishore Mishra C.V. Raman College of Engineering, Department of IT, Bhubaneswar, India

Beulah Moses School of Computing and Mathematics, Charles Sturt University, Melbourne, VIC, Australia

Diganta Mukherjee Sampling and Official Statistics Unit, Indian Statistical Institute (ISI), Kolkata, India

Pablo-César Muñoz-Carril Department of Pedagogy and Didactics, University of Santiago de Compostela, Lugo, Spain

Gia Nhu Nguyen Duy Tan University, Da Nang, Vietnam

Ranjit Panigrahi Department of Computer Applications, Sikkim Manipal Institute of Technology, Sikkim Manipal University, Majitar, India

Bibudhendu Pati Department of Computer Science, Rama Devi Women's University, Bhubaneswar, India

Binod Kumar Pattanayak Department of Computer Science and Engineering, Siksha 'O' Anusandhan (Deemed to be University), Bhubaneswar, India

Mukesh Prasad Centre for Artificial Intelligence, School of Software, FEIT, University of Technology Sydney, Sydney, NSW, Australia

Mamata Rath Department of Computer Science and Engineering, C.V. Raman College of Engineering, Bhubaneswar, India

Abhishek Ray BCS Technology, Gurgaon, India

Arif Mohaimin Sadri Moss School of Construction, Infrastructure, and Sustainability, Florida International University, Miami, FL, United States

Amandeep Singh School of Computing and Mathematics, Charles Sturt University, Melbourne, VIC, Australia

Jagendra Singh Associate Professor, Inderprastha Engineering College, Ghaziabad, India

Prayag Tiwari Department of Information Engineering, University of Padua, Padua, Italy

B.K. Tripathy School of Computer Science and Engineering, VIT, Vellore, India

Satish V. Ukkusuri Lyles School of Civil Engineering, Purdue University, West Lafayette, IN, United States

Pranay Yadav Research and Development Department, Ultra-Light Technology (ULT), Bhopal, India

Editors Biography

Samarjeet Borah is currently working as a professor in the Department of Computer Applications, Sikkim Manipal University (SMU), Sikkim, India. Dr. Borah handles various academics, research, and administrative activities. He is also involved in curriculum development activities, board of studies, doctoral research committee, IT infrastructure management, etc. along with various administrative activities under SMU. Dr. Borah is involved with three funded projects in the capacity of Principal Investigator/Coprincipal Investigator. The projects are sponsored by AICTE (Govt. of India), DST-CSRI (Govt. of India), and Dr. TMA Pai Endowment Fund, out of which one is completed and two are underway. He is associated with IEEE, ACM (CSTA), IAENG, and IACSIT. Dr. Borah organized various national and international conferences in SMU. Some of these events include ISRO Sponsored Training Program on Remote Sensing & GIS, NCWBCB 2014, NER-WNLP 2014, IC3-2016, ICACCP 2017, IC3-2018, etc. Dr. Borah is involved in the capacity of Editor/Guest Editor with various journals of repute such as *IJSE, IJHISI, IJGHPC, IJIM, IJVCSN, Journal of Intelligent Systems,* and *International Journal of Internet Protocol Technology.*

Nilanjan Dey is an assistant professor at the Department of Information Technology, Techno India College of Technology, Kolkata, W.B., India. He holds an honorary position of Visiting Scientist at Global Biomedical Technologies Inc., California, United States and a Research Scientist of Laboratory of Applied Mathematical Modeling in Human Physiology, Territorial Organization of Scientific and Engineering Unions, Bulgaria and Associate Researcher of Laboratoire RIADI, University of Manouba, Tunisia. His research topics include medical Imaging, soft computing, data mining, machine learning, rough set, computer-aided diagnosis, and atherosclerosis. He has 20 books and 300 international conferences and journal papers. He is the Editor-in-Chief of *International Journal of Ambient Computing and Intelligence* (IGI Global), United States; *International Journal of Rough Sets and Data Analysis* (IGI Global), United States; the *International Journal of Synthetic Emotions (IJSE)*; IGI Global, United States; and *International Journal of Natural Computing Research* (IGI Global), United States; Series Editor of *Advances in Geospatial Technologies* (AGT) Book Series (IGI Global), United States; Executive Editor of *International Journal of Image Mining (IJIM)*; Inderscience; and Associate Editor of IEEE Access Journal and the *International Journal of Service Science, Management, Engineering and Technology,* IGI Global. He is a life member of IE, UACEE, ISOC.

Rosalina Babo is a coordinator/professor at the School of Accounting and Administration of Porto/Polytechnic of Porto (ISCAP/IPP), Portugal. Since 2000 she is the head of Information Systems Department and was a member of the university scientific board for 12 years (2000–12). Rosalina Babowas is one of the founders (2006) of CEISE/STI Research Center and its director until 2011. Having several published papers in international conferences and books, her main areas of research are e-learning, usability, e-commerce, and social networks.

Amira S. Ashour is currently an assistant professor and Head of Department–EEC, Faculty of Engineering, Tanta University, Egypt. She has been the Vice Chair of the Computer Engineering Department, Computers and Information Technology College, Taif University, Kingdom of Saudi Arabia, for 1 year from 2015. She has been the Vice Chair of the CS Department, CIT College, Taif University, Kingdom of Saudi Arabia for 5 years. Her research interests are smart antennas, direction of arrival estimation, targets tracking, image processing, medical imaging, machine learning, signal/image/video processing, image analysis, computer vision, and optimization. She has 6 books and about 70 published journal papers to her credit. She is an Editor-in-Chief for the *International Journal of Synthetic Emotions* (*IJSE*), IGI Global, United States. She is an Associate Editor for the *IJRSDA*, IGI Global, United States as well as the *IJACI*, IGI Global, United States. She is an Editorial Board Member of the *International Journal of Image Mining* (*IJIM*), Inderscience.

Preface

Recently, social network data analysis is gaining more importance in various domains, such as business, crime analysis. It is rapidly gaining interest of the research community in various aspects, which is basically mapping and measuring of relationships and flows between people, groups, organizations, computers, URLs, and other connected information/knowledge entities. It is a difficult task due to the availability of huge amounts of data along with very complex structures. Therefore, a systematic discussion on various social network-related issues and challenges is always on demand. In addition, there are very limited numbers of books and resources available in this domain. In view of this, an edited volume focus on various technical concepts and aspects of social network analysis was planned. Contributions were received from across the globe on some emerging areas of research in this domain, such as social network patterns, social network models, visualizing and modeling, modeling social change, social network techniques, statistical models for social networks, SNA characteristics, social networking applications, various case studies, social networking challenges and future perspectives. Out of these, 13 contributory chapters were selected to develop a complete volume.

The book is segregated into three sections based on the nature of the contributions; that is, Introduction and Background, Social Network Analysis and Applications and Case Studies. Introduction and Background section comprises two chapters; three chapters form the Social Network Analysis section and we have eight chapters under Applications and Case Studies.

Social network and its various aspects are introduced by Panigrahi and Borah in the first chapter. They are also discussing classification, prediction, and analysis of social network data using Facebook metrics dataset as an example. Supervised classifiers are used for the analysis. Design, issues, emerging trends, and security of social network are elaborated in the second chapter by Rath et al. The chapter also exhibits an exhaustive review of various security and protection issues in social networks that directly or indirectly affect the individual member of the network. Furthermore, different threats in social networks have been focused that appear because of the sharing of interactive media content inside a social networking site.

Leila Hedayatifar puts forward a discussion on the emergence of stable and glassy states in the dynamics of social networks. This chapter is a part of the second section as it provides an analysis on the states of the social networks. It is followed by a discussion on the concept of de-anonymization of anonymized social networks by B.K. Tripathy. He also highlights the algorithms developed so far to achieve it by making an analysis of the effectiveness of these algorithms. Additionally, some problems in that direction, giving light on further research are discussed.

The third section contains the chapters that highlight the uses of social network and related data in various aspects. Singh, Halgamuge, and Moses provide an analysis of demographic and behavior trends using social media with reference to Facebook, Twitter, and Instagram. This chapter reviewed 30 research works on the topic of behavioral analysis using social media with a defined time frame. The authors have studied previous publications and analyzed the results, limitations, and number of users to draw conclusions. Rezende et al. put forward a discussion on social network influence on mode choice and carpooling during special events. They are analyzing the same with the help of a case study on Purdue game day. They present a multinomial logit model and a personal network research design (PNRD) 48 approach to explore the social network influence on mode choice decisions (car, walk, carpool, bus, 49 and other) during a special event held at a university campus. On the other hand, Chakraborty et al. put forward a discussion on sentiment analysis on a set of movie reviews using deep learning techniques. They have analyzed the sentiment of 50,000 IMDB movie reviews collected online. The authors have applied Google's Word2Vec and Doc2Vec algorithms for text classification of the reviews. Predictions are made by using clustering and classification techniques. Another discussion on sentiment analysis is provided by Tiwari et al. This analysis is for airline services based on twitter dataset. They present positive as well as negative sentiments and their correlation about customer tweets using the BIRCH algorithm and association rule mining techniques. Gogoi et al. propose an alternative allocation rule for multilateral interactions and isolation in middlemen-driven network games. They are replacing the axiom of efficiency by multilateral interactions to cover many possible networks and call this allocation rule as the network middlemen multilateral interaction value. The authors also provide numerical illustrations using international trade and internet server traffic data. Ghatak, Ray, and Mukherjee illustrate a methodological and empirical study on the interplay of identity and social network in their contribution. They attempt to understand the pattern of human social connection. The authors have observed that in the daily run of life, people always exercise a choice when it comes to determining the people with whom they connect. Carril et al. discuss on the use of social networks in the field of secondary education. The results achieved by the authors implicate that adolescents make use of social network systems for leisure, remaining these tools underutilized for academic issues. There are also significant differences in terms of gender, with women using social networks for a communicative purpose, oriented toward social relationships, while men use them for leisure and with a more hedonistic objective. NGOs have found in social networks a tool to reach their target groups more effectively. In their article, García Galera et al. address the role of digital communication in those organizations for the purpose of achieving their civic objectives.

This volume is aimed at bringing authors and researchers to a common platform to report the recent developments and findings in this emerging area of research. Contributions from various aspects of social network analysis are analyzed and incorporated. We hope, the volume will cater and help interested researchers and students to carry out further research in this area.

Classification and Analysis of Facebook Metrics Dataset Using Supervised Classifiers

Ranjit Panigrahi, Samarjeet Borah

Department of Computer Applications, Sikkim Manipal Institute of Technology, Sikkim Manipal University, Majitar, India

1 Introduction

The transition from static webpage to dynamic sharable webpages adds a new feather to the World Wide Web. This leads to the evolution of social media. Starting from simple communication to product marketing and election campaign, social networks play a crucial role as a fast broadcasting of information. It is the most popular communication medium and considered as the voice of common people, specifically among youths [1]. Social networks are not only considered to be the most important sources of information sharing [2–4], but also it is quite helpful for other activities such as blogging, discussions, news, remarks [5], reviews, and ratings [6, 7]. Many organizations felt about the potential of social network for attracting their target audiences for better brand building and [8] developing strategies to enhance their businesses by means of advertisements [9–11]. Due to such versatile use of social networks, social network analysis (SNA) becomes the center point of attraction among many researchers. SNA is the process of plotting and computing the relationships among people, organizations, and other entities as well as estimating their interests, patterns, and future course of action. In today's scenario, SNA has been adopted as a suggestive and as an analytic approach [2, 12].

Most of the researches focused on establishing the relationships between social network contents and the effect of such contents on the target audiences [13] and developing an effective system for prediction [9, 14] and better decision-making. From an organizational perspective, social media prediction is considered to be more effective as it is related to brand building [9, 15] and evaluating the market trends [16]. An effective prediction is possible by means of an accurate classification only [17, 18]. The challenge lies with accurate classification, that is, the selection of best classifier for the aforesaid tasks. In order to get a better prediction result, the classifier must be smart enough to classify accurately the underlying dataset. Once the dataset is classified accurately then the system can predict any future post about the user interests.

Social Network Analytics. https://doi.org/10.1016/B978-0-12-815458-8.00001-3

The objective of this study is to

- Analyze a Facebook metrics dataset understanding the characteristics of each features.
- Classify the dataset using 21 supervised classifiers of 7 popular groups and suggest the best classifier out of the classifier pool.
- Further analyze the classifiers across prediction probability to justify our claim about the best classifier at the previous step.

This article begins with an analysis of the Facebook metrics dataset provided by Moro et al. [9]. The dataset is further classified using 21 classifiers of 7 popular groups having 3 classifiers of each group. After a successful classification, the classifiers are considered for predicting unknown instances using 10 different test cases and the probability of prediction has been analyzed for individual test cases. The rest of the chapter is as follows. Section 2 describes the literature reviews, Section 3 focuses on dataset analysis, Section 4 is solely dedicated to results and discussion, followed by conclusion and future work in Section 5.

2 Literature Review

Social network classification approaches are most useful for grouping incoming instances based on some patterns and constraints [17–21]. It can be used to predict categorical class labels and classifies data based on training set and class labels and it can be used for classifying newly available data. A sum total of 21 classification techniques of 9 different groups are taken into consideration for the evaluation of best classifiers and subsequent prediction. These classification techniques have significant impact on social media classification and analysis. The classification techniques and their significance is presented further.

2.1 Bayes Classifiers

In a Bayesian classifier, the learning module constructs a probabilistic model of the features and uses that model to predict the classification of a new example [22]. The variations of Bayesian classifiers used here are:

A Bayesian network builds a model by establishing the relationships between features in a very general way. The Bayesian network is useful to classify the feature of any social network dataset if these feature relationships are known beforehand.

The classification task begins with classifying an arbitrary attribute $y=x_m$ called the class variable, where $y \in x{:}x=x_1, x_2, ..., x_n$ attribute variables. A classifier $h{:}\ x \rightarrow y$ is a Bayes net classifier that maps an instance of x to a value of y. The Bayes net algorithm [23] used in the literature assumes that all the variables are discrete in nature and no instances have missing values.

This Naïve Bayes classifier works in a supervised manner, in which the performance objective is to predict accurately an incoming test instance using the class label of training instance. It is a specialized form of Bayesian network where the attributes of the instances under prediction are conditionally independent and there should not be any hidden attributes present to influence the prediction process. Similar to Bayes Net, attributes under the Naïve Bayes should be discrete in nature. Naïve Bayes has a significant impact on social media analysis. Jiamthapthaksin et al. [24] presented a summarizing approach of user preferences based on user behaviors on Facebook page categories. The summarizing approach was created using the Naïve Bayes classifier along with other classification techniques. Further, Turdjai et al. [25] explored twitter data messages of top market palaces in Indonesia using five different supervised classifiers such as K-Nearest Neighbor, Logistic Regression, Naïve Bayes, Random Forest, and Support Vector Machine for analyzing marketplace customer satisfaction. Their analysis shows that the Support Vector Machine has an accuracy of 81.82% with 1000 sampling dataset and 85.4% with 2000 sampling dataset.

The hidden Markov model is an intelligent classifier for social network classification and analysis. The classifier is popular because of its tendency of sequence classification. Innovative modeling and detection techniques for Counter-Terror Social Network Analysis and Intent Recognition [26] have been proposed using the hidden Markov model (HMM). Similarly, a multidimensional hidden Markov model (MultiHMM) [27] was also proposed to analyze online network performance metrics using multiple traces from Twitter data, where original traces are analyzed and compared with the MultiHMM-generated traces. HMM was also used as an evolutionary model for ranking influence [28] of twitter by combining network centrality and influence observables.

2.2 Function Classifiers

The classifiers under this group are nonprobabilistic in nature, where the system tries to generalize the training data before the actual classification has taken place. Many variants of function classifiers have been proposed. The candidate classifiers that we consider under this group are the following.

Many literatures used LibSVM as a classification mechanism for social network analysis. The LibSVM was used for the term weighting method [29] for identifying emotions from the text content. The joint approach of SVM and LibSVM significantly improved the prediction accuracy.

Multilayer perceptron (MLP) has been used for Spam profile detection [30], sentiment analysis [31] in social networks, and classification of social network users [32]. Khadangi et al. [33] used MLP for measuring the relationship strength in online social networks based on users' activities and profile information, where MLP achieved a classification accuracy of 87%. Further, an MLP-based emotional context recognition system [34] was proposed for classifying online social network messages. In their research MLP achieves accuracy in a range of 59.03%–96.82% for various classes.

LibLinear [35] is an open-source library mostly used for large-scale linear classification. It uses logistic regression and linear support vector machines for the classification task. Many social network data were modeled using the LibLinear classification mechanism. For an instance, a target-oriented tweets monitoring system [36] was proposed to detect the messages that people updated during natural disasters into a social network. It provides the user the desired target information type automatically. Their approach achieved 75% classification accuracy.

2.3 Lazy Classifiers

All the classifiers under this group are termed as Lazy, because as the name suggests generalization beyond the training data is delayed until a query is made to the system. That is, it does not build a classifier until a new instance needs to be classified. Due to this reason, these classifiers are called instance based and consumes more computation time while building the model. The classifiers under consideration of lazy classifiers are Kstar [37], RseslibKnn [38], and locally weighted learning (LWL) [39, 40].

KStar [37] is a K-nearest neighbors classifier with various distance measures, which implements fast-neighbor search in large datasets and has the mode to work as RIONA [41] algorithm. KStar has a significant impact of classification and prediction. Due to its wide application [42–45], KStar becomes a potential candidate classifier for analysis.

LWL is another smart classifier which incorporate an instance-based mechanism to assign instance weights which are then used by a specified weighted instances handler for classification and prediction. Markines et al. [46] proposed a social spam detection method by evaluating many classification mechanisms. In their research work, LWL achieved a high detection rate of 97.68%. A reality mining-based social network analysis [47] was conducted using the LWL classifier along with other associate classifiers, where the accuracy rate of LWL was realized by an amount of 86.67%.

2.4 Metaclassifiers

Metaclassifiers are usually a proxy to the main classifier, used to provide additional data preprocessing. Three classifiers such as Decorate [46, 48, 49], Rotation Forest [50], and Ensemble Selection [51] are chosen here for analysis because of their wide acceptance.

A group of popular classifiers were examined for uncovering social spamming [52], where Decorate as a supervised classifier attracts 99.21% leaving its peers far behind. Similarly, characterizing automation of twitter spammer [53] was carried out on 31,808 twitter users using the Decorate classifier. Moving ahead, many social learning techniques including Rotation Forest were used for student exam scores' prediction by analyzing the social network data [54].

2.5 Rule Classifiers

Three rule-based classifiers are selected here for exploring Facebook metrics dataset. These are the Fuzzy Unordered Rule Induction Algorithm (FURIA) [55], Lazy Associative

Classifier (LAC) [56], and the Decision Table and Naïve Bayes (DTNB) [57]. Many performance analyses [58–61] were conducted using these classifiers.

2.6 Tree Classifiers

The principle of splitting criteria is behind the intelligence of any decision tree classifier.
Decision trees are presented similar to a flow chart, with a tree structure wherein instances
are classified according to their feature values. A node in a decision tree represents an
instance, outcomes of the test represented by branch, and the leaf node epitomized the
class label. Three variations of decision trees are explored here, viz., Best First Decision
Tree (BFTree) [62, 63], ForestPA [64], and SysFor [65] because of the fast model build time
and processing speed.

2.7 Other Classifiers

Many other classifiers such as CHIRP [66], FLR [67], and HyperPipes [68] are proved to be
efficient in many literatures. Researches have shown interests on these classifiers because
of the unique functionality they bear. This motivated us to consider these classifiers under
evaluation. As these classifiers do not exhibit the behavior of Bayes, Functions, Lazy, Meta,
Rules, and Trees, these classifiers are kept under the group "Others."

3 Dataset Analysis

The dataset considered here is the Facebook metrics dataset contributed by Moro et al. [9].
It is freely available at the UCI machine learning repository. The metrics are belonging to a
renowned cosmetic brand. The dataset holds 500 instances and 19 features including
13 continuous attributes, useful for performance analysis, and 6 categorical attributes
useful for classification and prediction. The characteristics of these attributes can be
external and internal. The external characteristics represent the data type and application
area whereas the internal characteristics deal with more detail specifications, which give
an idea of the possible impact of this dataset on the classifiers during classification and
prediction.

The attributes and their external characteristics are outlined in Table 1. In our experiment, the attribute *Type* is used for the classification of content type and prediction has
been carried out for any incoming unknown content type.

Further internal characteristics of all the attributes of Facebook metrics dataset are
outlined in Table 2, which represents whether the attributes are symmetrically or asym-
metrically distributed.

Observing the attributes internal characteristics, it is clear that most of the attributes
are not normally distributed among the class label. This can also be clearly visualized
through Fig. 1.

Before proceeding for classification, we must understand the dataset characteristics as
a whole. The dataset characteristics enlighten us about the class distribution, which is

Table 1 External Characteristics of Facebook Metrics Dataset

Attributes	Data Type	Application Area
Page total likes	Continuous	Performance analysis
Category (possible values: 1, action; 2, product; 3, inspiration)	Categorical	Classification
Post month	Categorical	Prediction
Post weekday	Categorical	Prediction
Post hour	Categorical	Prediction
Paid (possible values: 1, yes; 0, no)	Categorical	Classification
Post total reach	Continuous	Performance analysis
Post total impressions	Continuous	Performance analysis
Engaged users	Continuous	Performance analysis
Post consumers	Continuous	Performance analysis
Post consumptions	Continuous	Performance analysis
Post impressions by people who have liked your page	Continuous	Performance analysis
Post reach by people who like your page	Continuous	Performance analysis
People who have liked your page and engaged with the post	Continuous	Performance analysis
Comments	Continuous	Performance analysis
Likes	Continuous	Performance analysis
Shares	Continuous	Performance analysis
Total interactions	Continuous	Performance analysis
Type (possible values: *Link, photo, status, video*)	Categorical	Classification

Table 2 Internal Characteristics of Numeric Attributes of Facebook Metrics Dataset

Attributes	Minimum	Mean	Maximum	Standard Deviation
Page total likes	81,370	123,110.7	139,441	16,256.53
Category	1	1.878244	3	0.851822
Post month	1	7.025948	12	3.304626
Post weekday	1	4.143713	7	2.02867
Post hour	1	7.826347	23	4.364218
Paid (possible values: 1, yes; 0, no)	0	0.278	1	0.448289
Post total reach	238	13,876.08	180,480	22,718.04
Post total impressions	570	29,528.03	1,110,282	76,726.4
Engaged users	9	918.525	11,452	984.0311
Post consumers	9	797.1956	11,328	881.6221
Post consumptions	9	1412.323	19,779	1998.593
Post impressions by people who have liked your page	567	16,734.04	1,107,833	59,731.2
Post reach by people who like your page	236	6572.814	51,456	7674.324
People who have liked your page and engaged with the post	9	608.7864	4376	612.1126
Comments	0	7.467066	372	21.15972
Likes	0	177.59	5172	323.0745
Shares	0	27.21127	790	42.57031
Total interactions	0	211.6966	6334	379.8527

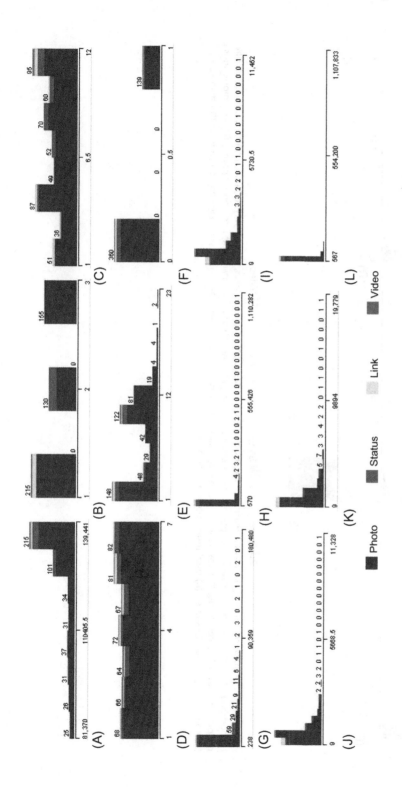

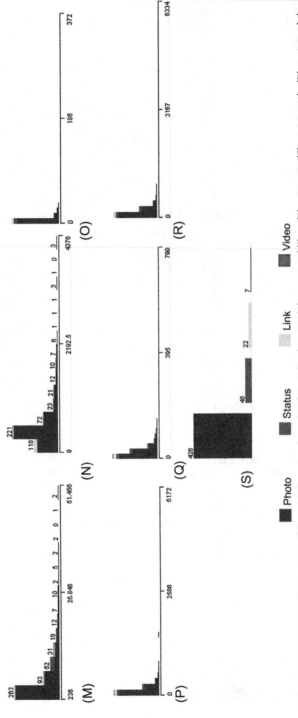

FIG. 1 Class wise instance distribution for each feature of Facebook metrics dataset: (A) page total likes, (B) category, (C) post month, (D) post weekday, (E) post hour, (F) paid, (G) post total reach, (H) post total impressions, (I) engaged users, (J) post consumptions, (K) post consumers, (L) post impressions by people who have liked your page, (M) post reach by people who like your page, (N) people who have liked your page and engaged with the post, (O) comment, (P) likes, (Q) shares, (R) total interactions, and (S) types.

Table 3   Facebook Metrics Dataset Characteristics

Characteristics		Description
Dataset name		Facebook metrics
Type of class		Multi class
Number of instances		500
Number of attributes		19
Number of distinct classes		4
Minority class	Class label	Video
	Instances	7
	%	1.4
Majority class	Class label	Photo
	Instances	426
	%	85.2

really a vital aspect for any classification approach. Table 3 and Fig. 1S represent the dataset class distribution. It is clearly visible that the dataset is prone to high class imbalance. Many classifiers may suffer during the classification of such dataset, which would be realized in the subsequent section. But it is worth mentioning that this is also a typical scenario where the best classifier can be figured out only if the chosen classifier is able to classify and predict the dataset with significant amount of accuracy and prediction probability.

4 Results and Discussion

Once every aspect of the dataset is taken into consideration, we are then in a position to classify the dataset. We are also not sure about an intelligent classifier which is able to classify the underlying dataset with significant amounts of accuracy and prediction probability. Therefore, 21 well-cited classifiers of 7 different groups such as Bayes', Functions, Lazy, Meta, Rules, Trees, and Others are taken into consideration for the classification and prediction task. The classifiers under consideration are summarized in Section 2.

The experiment is conducted in two broad phases. The classification phase and the prediction phase. At the former phase, the whole dataset is passed to the classifiers for the training purpose. The best classifier is presented thereon, and at the later stage the chosen classifier is considered for prediction.

The performance measures considered here are:

- **Accuracy (%):** This indicates the percentage of correctly classified instances during the course of classification. It is calculated as

$$\text{Accuracy} = \frac{\text{True positives} + \text{true negatives}}{\text{Total instances}} \times 100 \tag{1}$$

- **Misclassification rate (%):** The percentage of incorrectly classified instances are nothing, but the misclassification rate of the classifier and can be calculated as

$$\text{Misclassification rate} = \frac{\text{False positives} + \text{false negatives}}{\text{Total instances}} \qquad (2)$$

- **Root mean squared (RMS) error:** RMSE usually provides how far the model is from giving the right answer. It represents the average prediction error within the same scale (unit). It is calculated as

$$\text{RMS} = \sqrt{\frac{1}{n}\sum \epsilon_i^2} \qquad (3)$$

where, ϵ_i is calculated as $(\hat{x}_i - x_i)$

- **Precision:** Precision or positive predictive value (PPV) is calculated as

$$\text{Precision or PPV} = \frac{\text{TP}}{\text{TP} + \text{FP}} \qquad (4)$$

A classification technique with the highest accuracy and precision with the lowest misclassification rate and root mean squared error is considered to be the most intelligent classifier for prediction purposes.

Starting with the classification, the performance outcomes are recorded in terms of accuracy, misclassification rate, precision, and root mean squared error parameters. The detail outcomes are presented in Table 4 and through Figs. 2–8.

During the classification phase, it is found that Naïve Bayes seems to be a prominent classifier, which successfully classifies the Facebook dataset with 88.38% accuracy with very little misclassification rate of 11.61% in the Bayes group. With a low error rate of 0.24, it promises that Naïve Bayes is consistent in classification. Fig. 2 shows the performance outcome of all Naïve group of classifiers. The figure shows that Bayes Net lacks behind its peers in terms of classification and precision.

Considering the function group of classifiers, it is seen that the multilayer perception which employs the backpropagation neural network is far ahead than its counterparts. The accuracy and precision achieved is 93.93% and 0.892, which is really promising for carrying out a classification task. Multilayer perception also throws very less amount of error which makes this classifier more reliable in its group. Fig. 3 depicts the argument presented here.

Further employing the Lazy group of classifiers for the classification task, it can be seen that RseslibKnn wins the competition. It can be realized from Fig. 4 that RseslibKnn achieves the highest amount of classification accuracy in its group as well as across all other groups even for a high-class imbalance dataset. The root mean squared error throws by the classifier is minimum.

Table 4   Performance Outcomes of Supervised Classifies Using Facebook Metrics Dataset

Type	Classifiers Under Evaluation	Short Names	Accuracy	Mis Classification Rate	Precision	RMS Error
Bayes	Bayes net	BayesNet	84.8485	15.1515	0.923	0.2455
	Naïve Bayes	NaïveBayes	88.3838	11.6162	0.914	0.2335
	Hidden Markov model	HMM	85.8586	14.1414	0.737	0.433
Functions	Library for SVM	LibSVM	93.4343	6.5657	0.929	0.1812
	Multilayer perceptron	MP	93.9394	6.0606	0.892	0.1445
	LibLinear	LibLinear	87.8788	12.1212	0.859	0.2462
Lazy	Kstar	Kstar	92.4242	7.5758	0.919	0.2065
	RseslibKnn	RseslibKnn	97.9798	2.0202	0.97	0.1005
	Locally weighted learning	LWL	87.8788	12.1212	0.83	0.2097
Meta	Decorate	Decorate	95.4545	4.5455	0.954	0.1305
	Rotation forest	RotationF	94.9495	5.0505	0.938	0.1394
	Ensemble selection	EnsembleS	93.4343	6.5657	0.923	0.1567
Rules	Fuzzy unordered rule induction algorithm	FURIA	90.9091	9.0909	0.915	0.1787
	Lazy associative classifier	LAC	93.4343	6.5657	0.929	0.1797
	Decision table and Naïve Bayes	DTNB	90.9091	9.0909	0.915	0.2006
Trees	BFTree	BFTree	90.9091	9.0909	0.906	0.1981
	ForestPA	ForestPA	92.4242	7.5758	0.882	0.1696
	SysFor	SysFor	90.9091	9.0909	0.909	0.194
Others	CHIRP	CHIRP	92.4242	7.5758	0.915	0.1946
	FLR	FLR	90.404	9.596	0.863	0.219
	HyperPipes	HyperPipes	89.899	10.101	0.859	0.3555

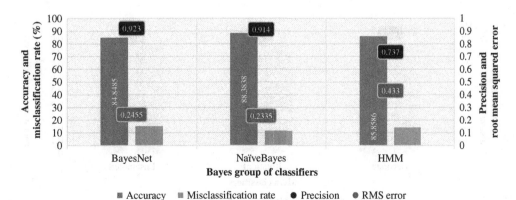

FIG. 2 Performance outcome of Bayes group of classifiers.

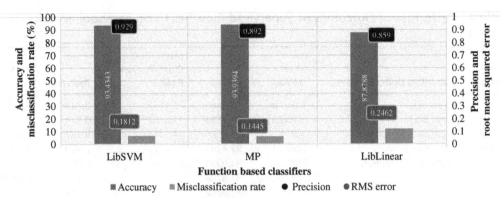

FIG. 3 Performance outcome of function based classifiers.

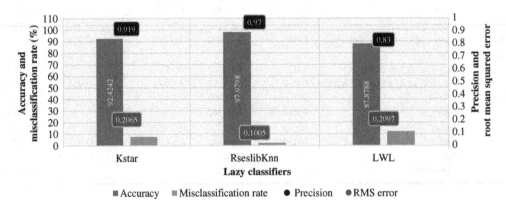

FIG. 4 Performance outcome of lazy classifiers.

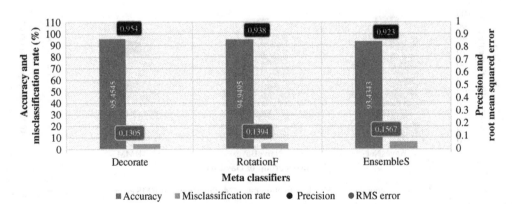

FIG. 5 Performance outcome of meta classifiers.

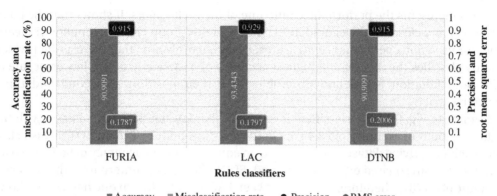

FIG. 6 Performance outcome of rules classifiers.

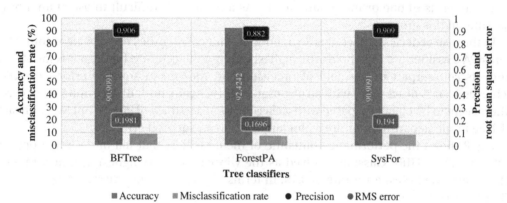

FIG. 7 Performance outcome of tree classifiers.

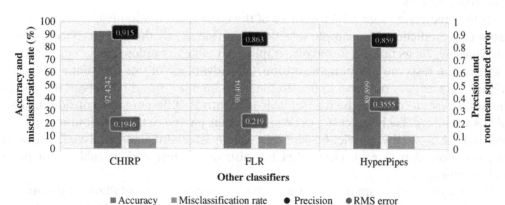

FIG. 8 Performance outcome of other classifiers.

Fig. 5 represents the performance outcome of meta-classifiers. It shows that the competition is very close. All the candidate classifiers of this group closely compete with each other for its various performance measures. Decorate evolves as the best classifier which smartly classifies the dataset at a highest accuracy of 95.45% and a very low error rate of 0.13. Both Rotation Forest and Ensembles take their position as second and third, respectively.

Coming to Fig. 6 of rule classifiers it is evident that LAC classifies the dataset with the highest amount of accuracy of 93.43%. On the contrary, both FURIA and DTNB also classifies their underlying datasets smartly with an equal amount of accuracy of 90.9 but so far as the root mean squared error is concerned, FURIA beats its counterpart with the lowest error rate of 0.1787. Therefore, it is a tie between LAC and FURIA. On one hand, LAC shows better accuracy and on the other hand FURIA beats its peer with the lowest error rate. Similarly, evaluating precision it is found that FURIA and DTNB scores equal amount of precision and thus a tie. This is a typical situation, where one classifier supersedes others in terms of one or more parameters. As a result, it is difficult to ascertain a best classifier in this group.

In the case of decision trees, it is an open-and-shut case for the ForestPA algorithm. The ForestPA classifier not only holds the highest amount of accuracy, but also it is far ahead from its counterpart in the field of precision and root mean squared error. ForestPA achieves 92.42% of accuracy with an error rate of 0.16. Again, both BFTree and SysFor classifiers seem to be equally capable with a classification accuracy of 90.9%, but SysFor beats BFTree in the department of precision and root mean squared error.

Fig. 8 shows the performance outcome of the classifiers that fall under the group of "Others." The CHIRP classifier evolved as the winner with the highest accuracy rate of 92.42% and the lowest error rate of 0.19. In terms of precision and misclassification rate, CHIRP beats its peers.

At the end, concluding the classification task it is found that overall RseslibKnn outperforms in all the field of performance metrics. Hence, this classifier has been proposed for the prediction task. On the prediction task we will evaluate the real capability of the RseslibKnn classifier.

At the prediction stage, 40% instances of the dataset are randomly chosen as the test dataset for prediction. The sample selection is carried out by the unsupervised reservoir sampling [69, 70] technique. Reservoir sampling generates a random subsample of a dataset using the reservoir sampling algorithm. The advantage of this technique is that the original dataset does not have to fit into the main memory, but the reservoir does. Once the test dataset is in hand, the dataset is divided into 10 different folds considering each fold as a test case. Each test case has been separately passed to the RseslibKnnfor prediction and the class label prediction accuracy will be ascertained and analyzed. The accuracy and precision of each class label has also been presented in Table 5 for better understanding.

While using RseslibKnn, it can be seen that instances with label Photo and status are smoothly predicted with an accuracy of 100%, whereas instances with Link and Video suffers the most with 75% and 0% accuracy.

Table 5 Performance Outcomes of RseslibKnn Using Facebook Metrics Dataset

Parameters/Class Label	Photo	Status	Link	Video
Accuracy	100%	100%	75%	0%
Precision	0.983	0.947	1	0

Table 6 Accuracy of RseslibKnn for Various Test Cases

Test Cases of RseslibKnn	Total Number of Instances	Correctly Classified Instances	Accuracy (%)	Incorrectly Classified Instances	Misclassification Rate
Test Case #01	20	19	95	1	5
Test Case #02	20	20	100	0	0
Test Case #03	20	20	100	0	0
Test Case #04	20	19	95	1	5
Test Case #05	20	20	100	0	0
Test Case #06	20	20	100	0	0
Test Case #07	20	19	95	1	5
Test Case #08	20	20	100	0	0
Test Case #09	19	19	100	0	0
Test Case #10	19	19	100	0	0
Average	198	195	98.4	3	1.6

Drilling down to the granular level, we even tried to predict each test cases and the results found are outlined in Table 6. The accuracy rate of the classifier is quite promising for all the test cases and in most cases, it achieves 100% of prediction rate.

5 Conclusion

A social network dataset called Facebook metrics dataset has been analyzed using the classification and prediction techniques. At the beginning of the research various characteristics and aspects of the dataset are explored. It was found that the dataset is highly class imbalanced, which provided a suitable platform to analyze the real capabilities of the classifier. Again, 21 widely used classifiers are taken into consideration for classification. RseslibKnn evolved as the best classifier with an accuracy of 97.98%. In the next step, test cases were prepared for prediction. A total of 40% random instances had been picked up from the dataset using the reservoir sampling algorithm. The 40% random data are equally divided into tenfolds of instances. Class labels of these test instances are removed to make these instances unknown to the classifier. Further, RseslibKnn was applied on these unknown instances to predict their classes. This time RseslibKnn predicts the instances with 98.4% accuracy, thus justifying our claim as the winner during the classification phase. As a future work the dataset can be treated for forecasting and its impact on the business domain.

References

[1] L. Johnson, A. Levine, R. Smith, The 2009 Horizon Report, The New Media Consortium, Austin, TX, 2009.

[2] J.B. Thompson, Media and Modernity: A Social Theory of the Media, John Wiley & Sons, 2013.

[3] C. Chelmis, V.K. Prasanna, in: Social networking analysis: a state of the art and the effect of semantics. Privacy, security, risk and trust (passat), 2011 ieee third international conference on and 2011 ieee third international conference on social computing (socialcom). IEEE, 2011.

[4] A.M. Kaplan, M. Haenlein, Users of the world unite! The challenges and opportunities of social media, Bus. Horiz. 53 (2010) 59–68.

[5] B. Pang, L. Lee, Opinion mining and sentiment analysis, Found. Trends Inform. Retrieval 2 (1–2) (2008) 1–135.

[6] E. Bakshy, J.M. Hofman, W.A. Mason, D.J. Watts, in: Identifying influencers on twitter, Fourth ACM International Conference on Web Seach and Data Mining (WSDM), 2011.

[7] B. Liu, Sentiment analysis and opinion Mining, AAAI-2011, San Francisco, USA, 2011.

[8] S. Edosomwan, S.K. Prakasan, D. Kouame, J. Watson, T. Seymour, The history of social media and its impact on business, J. Appl. Manag. Entrep. 16 (3) (2011) 79–91.

[9] S. Moro, et al., Predicting social media performance metrics and evaluation of the impact on brand building: a data mining approach, J. Bus. Res. (2016), https://doi.org/10.1016/j.jbusres.2016.02.010.

[10] R.W. Lariscy, E.J. Avery, K.D. Sweetser, P. Howes, Monitoring public opinion in cyberspace: how corporate public relations is facing the challenge, Publ. Relat. J. 3 (4) (2009) 1–17.

[11] K. Faizan, B. Samarjeet, P. Ashis, in: Mining consumption intent from social data: a survey, IJCA Proceedings on International Conference on Computing and Communication ICCC 2016(1), 2016, pp. 14–20.

[12] N. Dey, R. Babo, A. Ashour, V. Bhatnagar, M.S. Bouhlel (Eds.), Social Networks Science: Design, Implementation, Security, and Challenges: From Social Networks Analysis to Social Networks Intelligence, Springer International Publishing. ISBN: 978-3-319-90059-9, 2018.

[13] I.P. Cvijikj, E.D. Spiegler, F. Michahelles, in: The effect of post type, category and posting day on user interaction level on Facebook, Privacy, Security, Risk and Trust (PASSAT) and 2011 IEEE Third International Conference on Social Computing (SocialCom), 2011 IEEE Third International Conference on (pp. 810–813). IEEE, 2011.

[14] K. Singh, R. Kaur, D. Kumar, in: Comment volume prediction using neural networks and decision trees, Proceedings of the 2015 17th UKSIM-AMSS International Conference on Modelling and Simulation (UKSIM '15). IEEE Computer Society, Washington, DC, USA, 2015, pp. 15–20, https://doi.org/10.1109/UKSim.2015.20.

[15] S. Hudson, L. Huang, M.S. Roth, T.J. Madden, The influence of social media interactions on consumer–brand relationships: a three-country study of brand perceptions and marketing behaviors, Int. J. Res. Mark. 33 (1) (2015) 27–41.

[16] K.J. Trainor, J.M. Andzulis, A. Rapp, R. Agnihotri, Social media technology usage and customer relationship performance: a capabilities-based examination of social CRM, J. Bus. Res. 67 (6) (2014) 1201–1208, https://doi.org/10.1016/j.jbusres.2013.05.002.

[17] R. Ahuja, R. Gupta, S. Sharma, A. Govil, K. Venkataraman, in: Twitter based model for emotional state classification, 2017 4th International Conference on Signal Processing, Computing and Control (ISPCC), Solan, 2017, pp. 494–498, https://doi,org/10.1109/ISPCC.2017.8269729.

[18] R.G. Guimarães, R.L. Rosa, D. De Gaetano, D.Z. Rodríguez, G. Bressan, Age groups classification in social network using deep learning, IEEE Access 5 (2017) 10805–10816, https://doi.org/10.1109/ACCESS.2017.2706674.

[19] X. Li, Y. Rao, H. Xie, R.Y.K. Lau, J. Yin, F.L. Wang, Bootstrapping social emotion classification with semantically rich hybrid neural networks, IEEE Trans. Affect. Comput. 8 (4) (2017) 428–442, https://doi.org/10.1109/TAFFC.2017.2716930.

[20] N. Sever, L. Humski, J. Ilić, Z. Skočir, D. Pintar, M. Vranić, in: Applying the multiclass classification methods for the classification of online social network friends, 2017 25th International Conference on Software, Telecommunications and Computer Networks (SoftCOM), Split, 2017, pp. 1–6, https://doi,org/10.23919/SOFTCOM.2017.8115508.

[21] S. Desai, S.T. Patil, in: Efficient regression algorithms for classification of social media data, 2015 International Conference on Pervasive Computing (ICPC), Pune, 2015, pp. 1–5, https://doi.org/10.1109/PERVASIVE.2015.7087040.

[22] David L. Poole, Alan K. Mackworth, Artificial Intelligence: Foundations of Computational Agents, second ed., Cambridge University Press, India, 2010.

[23] R.R. Bouckaert, Bayesian Network Classifiers in Weka for Version 3-5-7, The University of Waikato, May 12, Available from: https://www.cs.waikato.ac.nz/~remco/weka.bn.pdf, 2008.

[24] R. Jiamthapthaksin, T.H. Aung, in: User preferences profiling based on user behaviors on Facebook page categories, 2017 9th International Conference on Knowledge and Smart Technology (KST), Chonburi, 2017, pp. 248–253, https://doi.org/10.1109/KST.2017.7886077.

[25] A.A. Turdjai, K. Mutijarsa, in: Simulation of marketplace customer satisfaction analysis based on machine learning algorithms, 2016 International Seminar on Application for Technology of Information and Communication (ISemantic), Semarang, 2016, pp. 157–162, https://doi.org/10.1109/ISEMANTIC.2016.7873830.

[26] C. Weinstein, W. Campbell, B. Delaney, G. O'Leary, in: Modeling and detection techniques for counter-terror social network analysis and intent recognition, 2009 IEEE Aerospace Conference, Big Sky, MT, 2009, pp. 1–16, https://doi.org/10.1109/AERO.2009.4839642.

[27] T. Chis, P.G. Harrison, in: Modeling multi-user behaviour in social networks, IEEE 22nd International Symposium On Modelling, Analysis & Simulation of Computer and Telecommunication Systems, Paris, 2014, pp. 168–173, https://doi.org/10.1109/MASCOTS.2014.29.

[28] D. Simmie, M.G. Vigliotti, C. Hankin, Ranking twitter influence by combining network centrality and influence observables in an evolutionary model, J. Complex Network. 2 (4) (2014) 495–517, https://doi.org/10.1093/comnet/cnu024.

[29] J. De Silva, P.S. Haddela, in: A term weighting method for identifying emotions from text content, 2013 IEEE 8th International Conference on Industrial and Information Systems, Peradeniya, 2013, pp. 381–386, https://doi.org/10.1109/ICIInfS.2013.6732014.

[30] A.M. Al-Zoubi, J. Alqatawna, H. Faris, in: Spam profile detection in social networks based on public features, 2017 8th International Conference on Information and Communication Systems (ICICS), Irbid, 2017, pp. 130–135, https://doi.org/10.1109/IACS.2017.7921959.

[31] D.A. Alboaneen, H. Tianfield, Y. Zhang, in: Sentiment analysis via multi-layer perceptron trained by meta-heuristic optimisation, 2017 IEEE International Conference on Big Data (Big Data), Boston, MA, 2017, pp. 4630–4635, https://doi.org/10.1109/BigData.2017.8258507.

[32] B.V.A. de Lima, V.P. Machado, in: Machine learning algorithms applied in automatic classification of social network users, 2012 Fourth International Conference on Computational Aspects of Social Networks (CASoN), Sao Carlos, 2012, pp. 58–62, https://doi.org/10.1109/CASoN.2012.6412378.

[33] E. Khadangi, A. Zarean, A. Bagheri, A. Bagheri Jafarabadi, in: Measuring relationship strength in online social networks based on users' activities and profile information, ICCKE 2013, Mashhad, 2013, pp. 461–465, https://doi.org/10.1109/ICCKE.2013.6682863.

[34] I. Ben Sassi, S. Ben Yahia, S. Mellouli, in: Fuzzy classification-based emotional context recognition from online social networks messages, 2017 IEEE International Conference on Fuzzy Systems (FUZZ-IEEE), Naples, 2017, pp. 1–6, https://doi.org/10.1109/FUZZ-IEEE.2017.8015678.

[35] R.-E. Fan, K.-W. Chang, C.-J. Hsieh, X.-R. Wang, C.-J. Lin, LIBLINEAR: a library for large linear classification, J. Mach. Learn. Res. (2017) 1871–1874.

[36] S.S.M. Win, T.N. Aung, in: Target oriented tweets monitoring system during natural disasters, 2017 IEEE/ACIS 16th International Conference on Computer and Information Science (ICIS), Wuhan, 2017, pp. 143–148, https://doi.org/10.1109/ICIS.2017.7959984.

[37] J.G. Cleary, L.E. Trigg, in: K*: an instance-based learner using an entropic distance measure, 12th International Conference on Machine Learning, 1995, pp. 108–114.

[38] A. Wojna, L. Kowalski, Rseslib: Programmer's Guide, http://rseslib.mimuw.edu.pl/rseslib.pdf, 2018.

[39] C.G. Atkeson, A.W. Moore, S. Schaal, Locally weighted learning, Artif. Intell. Rev. 11 (1997) 11, https://doi.org/10.1023/A:1006559212014.

[40] E. Frank, M. Hall, B. Pfahringer, in: Locally weighted Naive Bayes, 19th Conference in Uncertainty in Artificial Intelligence, 2003, pp. 249–256.

[41] G. Gora, A. Wojna, RIONA: a new classification system combining rule induction and instance-based learning, Fundamenta Informaticae XX (2002) 1–22. IOS Press.

[42] Y. Asim, A.R. Shahid, A.K. Malik, B. Raza, Significance of machine learning algorithms in professional blogger's classification, Comput. Electr. Eng. 65 (2018) 461–473. ISSN 0045-7906, https://doi.org/10.1016/j.compeleceng.2017.08.001.

[43] J. Alwidian, B.H. Hammo, N. Obeid, WCBA: weighted classification based on association rules algorithm for breast cancer disease, Appl. Soft Comput. 62 (2018) 536–549. ISSN 1568-4946, https://doi.org/10.1016/j.asoc.2017.11.013.

[44] G.W. Shin, J.-W. Juhn, G.I. Kwon, S.H. Son, S.H. Hahn, Automatic detection of L-H transition in KSTAR by support vector machine, Fusion Eng. Des. (2017). ISSN 0920-3796.

[45] P. Sameena, K. Gopalakrishna Prabhu, P.C. Siddalingaswamy, Techniques and algorithms for computer aided diagnosis of pigmented skin lesions—A review, Biomed. Signal Process. Control 39 (2018) 237–262. ISSN 1746-8094, https://doi.org/10.1016/j.bspc.2017.07.010.

[46] B. Markines, C. Cattuto, F. Menczer, in: D. Fetterly, Z. Gyöngyi (Eds.), Social spam detection, Proceedings of the 5th International Workshop on Adversarial Information Retrieval on the Web (AIRWeb '09), ACM, New York, NY, 2009, pp. 41–48, https://doi.org/10.1145/1531914.1531924.

[47] J.S. More, C. Lingam, in: Reality mining based on social network analysis, 2015 International Conference on Communication, Information & Computing Technology (ICCICT), Mumbai, 2015, pp. 1–6, https://doi.org/10.1109/ICCICT.2015.7045752.

[48] P. Melville, R.J. Mooney, in: Constructing diverse classifier ensembles using artificial training examples, Eighteenth International Joint Conference on Artificial Intelligence, 2003, , pp. 505–510.

[49] P. Melville, R.J. Mooney, Creating diversity in ensembles using artificial data, Inform. Fusion 6 (1) (2004) 99–111. Special Issue on Diversity in Multiclassifier Systems.

[50] J.J. Rodriguez, L.I. Kuncheva, C.J. Alonso, Rotation forest: a new classifier ensemble method, IEEE Trans. Pattern Anal. Mach. Intell. 28 (10) (2006) 1619–1630, https://doi.org/10.1109/TPAMI.2006.211.

[51] R. Caruana, A. Niculescu, G. Crew, A. Ksikes, in: Ensemble selection from libraries of models, The International Conference on Machine Learning (ICML'04), 2004.

[52] K. Lee, J. Caverlee, S. Webb, in: Uncovering social spammers: social honeypots + machine learning, Proceedings of the 33rd international ACM SIGIR conference on research and development in information retrieval (SIGIR '10), ACM, New York, NY, 2010, pp. 435–442, https://doi.org/10.1145/1835449.1835522.

[53] A. Amleshwaram, N. Reddy, S. Yadav, G. Guofei, C. Yang, in: CATS: characterizing automation of twitter spammers, Proceedings of 5th International Conference Communication Systems and Networks (COMSNETS), Bangalore, IEEE, 2013, pp. 1–10, https://doi.org/10.1109/COMSNETS.2013.6465541.

[54] M. Fire, G. Katz, Y. Elovici, B. Shapira, L. Rokach, Predicting student exam's scores by analyzing social network data, R. Huang, A.A. Ghorbani, G. Pasi, T. Yamaguchi, N.Y. Yen, B. Jin (Eds.), Active Media Technology. AMT 2012. Lecture Notes in Computer Science, vol. 7669, Springer, Berlin, Heidelberg, 2012.

[55] J. Hühn, E. Hüllermeier, FURIA: an algorithm for unordered fuzzy rule induction, Data Min. Knowl. Disc. 19 (2009) 293, https://doi.org/10.1007/s10618-009-0131-8.

[56] A. Veloso, W. Meira Jr., M.J. Zaki, Lazy associative classification, in: Sixth International Conference on Data Mining (ICDM'06), Hong Kong, 2006, pp. 645–654, https://doi.org/10.1109/ICDM.2006.96.

[57] M. Hall, E. Frank, in: Combining Naive Bayes and decision tables, Proceedings of the 21st Florida Artificial Intelligence Society Conference (FLAIRS), 2008, pp. 318–319.

[58] T. Sumathi, S. Karthik, M. Marikannan, Performance analysis of classification methods for opinion mining, Int. J. Innov. Eng. Technol. 2 (4) (2013).

[59] K. Zamani, G. Paliouras, D. Vogiatzis, Similarity-based user identification across social networks, A. Feragen, M. Pelillo, M. Loog (Eds.), Similarity-Based Pattern Recognition. Lecture Notes in Computer Science, vol. 9370, Springer, Cham, 2015.

[60] R.C.S.N.P. Souza, D.E.F. de Brito, R.L. Cardoso, D.M. de Oliveira, W. Meira, G.L. Pappa, An evolutionary methodology for handling data scarcity and noise in monitoring real events from social media data, A. Bazzan, K. Pichara (Eds.), Advances in Artificial Intelligence—IBERAMIA 2014, IBERAMIA 2014. Lecture Notes in Computer Science, vol. 8864, Springer, Cham, 2014.

[61] W. Yang, L. Kwok, in: Comparison study of email classifications for healthcare organizations, 2012 International Conference on Information Management, Innovation Management and Industrial Engineering, Sanya, 2012, pp. 468–473, https://doi.org/10.1109/ICIII.2012.6340020.

[62] H. Shi, Best-First Decision Tree Learning (thesis, master of science (MSc)), The University of Waikato, Hamilton, 2007. Retrieved from: https://hdl.handle.net/10289/2317.

[63] J. Friedman, T. Hastie, R. Tibshirani, Additive logistic regression: a statistical view of boosting, Ann. Stat. 28 (2) (2000) 337–407.

[64] M.N. Adnan, M.Z. Islam, Forest PA: constructing a decision forest by penalizing attributes used in previous trees, Expert Syst. Appl. 89 (2017) 389–403.

[65] M.Z. Islam, H. Giggins, in: Knowledge discovery through SysFor—a systematically developed forest of multiple decision trees, Ninth Australasian Data Mining Conference, 2011, pp. 195–204.

[66] L. Wilkinson, A. Anand, D.T. Nhon, in: CHIRP: a new classifier based on composite hypercubes on iterated random projections, Proceedings of the 17th ACM SIGKDD International Conference on Knowledge Discovery and Data Mining, San Diego, CA, USA, August 21–4, 2011, https://doi.org/10.1145/2020408.2020418.

[67] I.N. Athanasiadis, V.G. Kaburlasos, P.A. Mitkas, V. Petridis, in: Applying machine learning techniques on air quality data for real-time decision support, 1st Intl. NAISO Symposium on Information Technologies in Environmental Engineering (ITEE-2003), Gdansk, Poland, 2003.

[68] S. Webb, J. Caverlee, P. Calton, in: Predicting web spam with HTTP session information, Proceedings of the 17th ACM Conference on Information and Knowledge Management (CIKM '08). ACM, New York, NY, USA, 2008, pp. 339–348, https://doi.org/10.1145/1458082.1458129.

[69] J.S. Vitter, Random sampling with a reservoir, ACM Trans. Math. Softw. 11 (1) (1985) 37–57, https://doi.org/10.1145/3147.3165.

[70] Black, Paul E. (2015). "Reservoir Sampling". Dictionary of Algorithms and Data Structures. (Accessed 7 July 2017).

2

An Overview on Social Networking: Design, Issues, Emerging Trends, and Security

Mamata Rath*, Bibudhendu Pati[†], Binod Kumar Pattanayak[‡]

*Department of Computer Science and Engineering, C.V. Raman College of Engineering, Bhubaneswar, India [†]Department of Computer Science, Rama Devi Women's University, Bhubaneswar, India [‡]Department of Computer Science and Engineering, Siksha 'O' Anusandhan (Deemed to be University), Bhubaneswar, India

1 Introduction

From simple communication network currently social networks evolve, which are based on the emerging technologies that stand their base very strong with the formation of social sites with group members who have high influential capability to control and communicate the social networks as per their own strategies. Therefore, design issues are going to be very tedious by considering all the emerging challenges in such a magnificent network. Social networks such as Facebook have attracted millions of users in recent past and the members are increasing day by day. People use social networks to communicate information with other people located at different geographical distance within a fraction of time and to spread the relevant information globally, sometimes for marketing purposes too. Smart mobile devices and a large number of social mobile applications are currently emerging that encourage distinctive associations among the users of social networks. Although this is a developing collaborative force in digital social networks, privacy issue is a major concern among the clients. The expanding number of users of such applications is a challenge and threat for users as well as developers. This is because of the growing number of clients of such applications and the idea of setting up trust among such users. In this exploration, we address such protection concerns considering the clients' perspectives and their acknowledgment of such applications. The exploration will illustrate a portion of the recommended components to support clients' trust in social communications (Fig. 1).

A social network is an elucidation of the social structure involving members, mostly individuals or associations. It represents the ways in which they are connected throughout various social familiarities ranging from casual social contact to close familiar bonds. The informal organization is an entangled structure made out of social individuals and

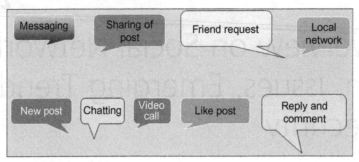

FIG. 1 General activities in a social network site.

connections between them. Vast scale online interpersonal organizations like Sina Weibo, Tencent Wechat, and Facebook have pulled in a large number of clients as of late people might want to utilize interpersonal organizations to convey or diffuse data. For instance, an organization builds up another item and they need to promote the item in a specific informal community. The organization has a restricted spending so they can just give free example items to few clients. They trust that the underlying clients could influence their companions to utilize the items, and their companions could impact their companions. Through the verbal impact, countless at last receive the products. Influence boost is an essential research issue in interpersonal organizations. It chooses an arrangement of k hubs as seeds with a specific end goal to boost the engendering of thoughts, conclusions, and items.

The chapter has been organized as follows. Section 2 presents a brief literature review on various application aspects of social network and utility tools used in social network development and maintenance such as big data perspective, soft computing techniques, etc. Section 3 presents the various dynamic issues and challenges in a social network. Section 4 focuses on the challenging factors during the design of social network-based application programs. Section 5 describes the static and dynamic social networks in brief. Section 6 depicts the factors that affect the design on social networks. Section 7 explains the security measures associated with social network groups and their proposed solution strategy. Section 8 illustrates a case study of Face book as a nominated social group. Here various functional aspects of Facebook are highlighted from a survey point of view. Section 9 concludes the chapter with future prospective of this emerging network.

2 Literature Review

This section of the chapter presents the study of some important contributions in the social networking area of researchers by eminent research people. Educational contribution to social networks between peer groups and members has been a challenge to researchers. Notwithstanding, the likelihood that associate gatherings ruled by either low-or high-accomplishing youth can have substantively extraordinary impacts on accomplishment has been to a great extent overlooked [1]. Social networks are exceptionally well known in this day and age. A large number of individuals utilize different types of social networks as they enable people to associate with their loved ones, and offer private data. Be that as it may, issues identified with keeping up the protection and security of a client's information [2] can happen, particularly when the client's transferred content is sight and sound, for example, photographs, recordings, and sounds. The transferred media content conveys data that can be transmitted virally and quickly inside a social networking site (SNS) and past. In such a manner Shailendra Rathore et al. [2] exhibit an exhaustive review of various security and protection dangers that object each client of social networking locales. The issue of influence maximization (IM) in a social system is to decide an arrangement of hubs that could amplify the spread of influence [3]. The IM issue has been indispensably connected to promoting, publicizing, and general supposition checking. Albeit late investigations have considered the IM issue, they are for the most part covetous or heuristic-based calculations, which are tedious for reasonable use in substantial scale social systems. As a moving hub in a city, a vehicle has its own dataset of directions. On every direction, remote connections can be worked between various clients and the vehicle [4]. Since every vehicle is related with a particular territory that covers certain potential client gatherings, such portable vehicles have turned into the premise of a vehicular social network (VSN) for prescribing items to potential clients in present day society. Crowdsourcing has turned into a well-known administration registering worldview for requesters to coordinate the omnipresent human-insight administrations for errands that are troublesome for PCs, however unimportant for people [5]. This concept concentrates on crowdsourcing complex assignments by group development in social networks where a requester associates with an expansive number of laborers. A decent pointer of proficient group coordinated effort is the social association among specialists.

In this section, some of the literature reassess have been placed that are reviewed to get some idea for associated concepts used in SNSs and during their design. Md. Sarwar Kamal of article [6] projects on a MapReduce framework toward metagenomic data classifier. Map reduce has been utilized in Big Data techniques for the refinement of extracted data from social network sites using various data mining methods. A new model of storage and access of big data and applications are presented in [7]. Data storage design and repository layout is another major critical task for handling the social network information. A competency-based behavioral interview has been designed in Ref. [8] that helps to review customers or members of social groups during conducting various survey on current security issues, political or elective issues. Medline text mining [9] and Unified Modeling Language (UML) generation technique for better project management has been proposed [10]. These act as a part of project design which may be helpful during the execution of some common projects, contest, or project layout design requirements. Statistical rough set computing [11] and Map reduce approach to decrease imbalanced parameters in big data is suggested [12]. Management of big data and their analysis using SNA techniques are more important as far as social polling or social nomination is concerned. These are carried out to perform survey on social issues, to select better choice in competitions, opinion mining, etc. Swarm intelligent technique for protein classification has been carried out and Exon separati on the process using neural skyline [13] has been planned. These techniques follow some important soft computing approaches for classification and problem solving techniques.

Individual-based computer models demonstrate that basic heuristic overseeing individuals' conduct may do the trick to create complex patterns of social conduct [14] at the gathering level, for example, those saw in creature social orders. "GrooFiWorld" is a case of such sort of computer models. In this model, self-association and straightforward behavioral principles produce complex patterns of social conduct like those depicted in tolerant and narrow-minded social orders of macaques. Social many-sided quality outcomes arise from the socio-spatial structure of the gathering, the nature of which is, thusly, a symptom of force of animosity. An informal organization model in Ref. [14] demonstrates that a comparable system may offer ascent to complex social structures in macaques. It is, in any case, obscure if the spatial structure of the model and that of macaques are surely comparable. In Ref. [14], the authors utilized informal organizations examination as an intermediary for spatial structure of the gathering.

The development of cooperation in social issues is a basic marvel for the working of various multilevel and complex frameworks [15]. The confirmation of cooperation ranges from the rudimentary natural living beings to the most modern human social orders. Despite the fact that the development of cooperation is broadly experienced, its advancement is not all around clarified, since the normal choice commonly advances egotistical practices which are frequently not socially ideal. In this chapter, the coevolution of system structure and rise of cooperation is contemplated in four classes of social situations, speaking to the detainee's problem, Hawk-Dove, snowdrift, and coordination classes of amusements, in organized populaces characterized by weighted complex systems. The quality of service [16], that is, interaction between two individuals is spoken to by organized (edge) weight, which changes as per individuals' inclination through the developmental system elements. Utilizing developmental dynamic system-based re-enactments of the recreations model on haphazardly weighted finish systems, Abhirup Bandyopadhyay and Samarjit Kar [15] presents a definite investigation of the advancement of dynamic complex systems through the development of the auxiliary properties of a system, for example, grouping coefficient, assortativity coefficient, entropy of degree appropriation, normal quality of interaction, and the advancement of agreeable conduct in each of the four classes of diversions. The impact of changing the cost-to-profit proportion on these system properties and development of cooperation is also shown.

The examination inspects the gendered talk patterns on a prominent online informal community, TheMarker Café, utilizing interpersonal organization investigation [17]. Generally, the discoveries reinforce past examinations that report confirmation of men's decisive and overwhelming talk style and social part versus ladies' more agreeable and strong talk style. Men composed more posts, while ladies remarked on other individuals' posts all the more regularly. Ladies' posts have obtained higher rankings than men's posts, fortifying the thought that ladies get more confirmations on online informal organizations. The investigation additionally inspected the exchange between the structure of the TheMarker Café organize and gendered talk patterns. Discoveries of Tsahi et al. [17] likewise affirmed a connection between action arrange structure and ladies content fame.

Receiving a socio-semantic point of view, this examination expects to check the connection between social impact and talk similitude organized in work groups and investigate its change over time [18]. Information comprises video transcripts of 45 3-h aggregate gatherings and week by week sociometric surveys. Connection between tie quality, performing artist centrality inside the impact organize, and shared components of talk between aggregate individuals are analyzed after some time. Watched connections bolster the theory of a connection between social impact and talk likeness. Changes after some time propose a closeness limit above which the connection among comparability and impact is turned around [18].

3 Promising Issues and Security Challenges in Social Networking

Social Network Analysis demonstrates that performance of a social network site can be measured by parameters such as degree centrality, between centrality, and closeness centrality. Degree centrality refers to direct connections as a member of social network has with other members. This is important to measure the influence of message passing from one source to many sources. Between centrality refers that a member or node is present in between two or more number of nodes. This factor has great influence in a social network to know what flows in the network and which node is the single point of failure. Closeness centrality is a measure of how close one member is to another in order to know the frequency of message transmission in a social network. Other important issues which have been technically analyzed and presented in this chapter are as follows.

3.1 Security Threat in Educational Social Network

Educational contribution to social networks between peer groups and members has been a challenge to researchers. Notwithstanding, the likelihood that associate gatherings ruled by either low-or high-accomplishing youth can have substantively extraordinary impacts on accomplishment has been to a great extent overlooked [1]. The research article in Ref. [1] demonstrates that while being implanted in a high-accomplishing system of companions is not related with expanded possess accomplishment, being installed in a low-accomplishing system is related with diminished claim accomplishment. In extra investigations, it presents prove that these affiliations are in any event to a limited extent because of impact, rather than just choice impacts or shared condition. It likewise looks at whether the structure of the system in which an understudy is inserted may influence their instructive accomplishment. This bit of research demonstrates that accomplishing at larger amounts decidedly predicts how halfway found does not foresee simultaneous accomplishment. This finding proposes that the conduct of people is influencing the development of system structure and not the switch.

3.2 Security, Issues, and Challenges in Social Network [2]

Social networks are exceptionally well known in this day and age. A large number of individuals utilize different types of social networks under wireless network [19] and as they enable people to associate with their loved ones, and offer private data. Be that as it may, issues identified with keeping up the protection and security of a client's information [20] can happen, particularly when the client's transferred content is sight and sound, for example, photographs, recordings, and sounds. The transferred media content conveys data that can be transmitted virally and quickly inside a SNS and past. In such manner [21, 22] exhibit an exhaustive review of various security and protection dangers that object each client of social networking locales. Also, it independently concentrates on different dangers that emerge because of the sharing of sight and sound substance inside a SNS [2]. Likewise talk about current cutting-edge resistance arrangements that can shield social network clients from these dangers.

3.3 Influence Maximization in Social Networks

The issue of IM in a social system is to decide an arrangement of hubs that could amplify the spread of influence [3]. The IM issue has been indispensably connected to promoting, publicizing, and general supposition checking. Albeit late investigations have considered the IM issue, they are for the most part covetous or heuristic-based calculations, which are tedious for reasonable use in substantial scale social systems. In light of the perception that auxiliary gap hubs for the most part are significantly more powerful than different hubs, in this paper, we build up a structure-gap based IM calculation (SHIM) with an accentuation on time effectiveness. The SHIM calculation uses structure gap data to altogether diminish the quantity of applicants of seed hubs. To gauge the structure significance of hubs, Zhu et al. [3] propose a structure gap esteem ascertain calculation to compute the basic gap estimation of hubs. The proposition in Ref. [3] demonstrates that the SHIM is NP hard and proposes a structure-based eager calculation to choose seeds with widespread influence and high basic opening worth. It conducts probes of genuine informational indexes to confirm calculation's chance effectiveness and precision, and the trial comes about demonstrate that contrasting and the current calculations, these calculations are considerably more proficient and versatile.

Fig. 2 shows the picture of a social network where people of different professions communicate in a social site for different activities. All the data are stored in a central computer called as a server.

FIG. 2 Communication among people in a social network.

3.4 Data Communication in VSN

As a moving hub in a city, a vehicle has its own dataset of directions. On every direction, remote connections can be worked between various clients and the vehicle [4]. Since every vehicle is related with a particular territory that covers certain potential client gatherings, such portable vehicles have turned into the premise of a VSN for prescribing items to potential clients in the present day society. However, little research has concentrated on publicizing through a VSN. For VSN-based publicizing, the advertiser normally situated in a remote Central Office (CO) chooses certain vehicles to go about as recommenders as indicated by their scope territories. Data about the vehicles' scope zones will be sent from the VSN to the advertiser working at the CO, that is, information backhauling. Moreover, the advertiser will sent the outcomes in regard to the picked recommenders to all vehicles [23] in the VSN, that is, information front hauling. Naturally, a compelling correspondence framework [24, 25] is desperately required to help information back-/front hauling among COs and VSNs.

3.5 Crowd Sourcing Complex Tasks

Crowd sourcing has turned into a well-known administration registering worldview for requesters to coordinate the omnipresent human-insight administrations for errands that are troublesome for PCs, however unimportant for people [5]. This concept concentrates on crowd sourcing complex assignments by group development in social networks, where a requester associates with an expansive number of labourers. A decent pointer of proficient group coordinated effort is the social association among specialists. Most past social group arrangement approaches, in any case, either expect that the requester can keep up data of all labourers and can straightforwardly speak with them to construct groups, or accept that the specialists are agreeable and join the particular group worked by the requester, both of which are unrealistic in numerous genuine circumstances. Wang et al. of article [5] models every specialist as a narrow-minded substance, where the requester wants to enlist modest laborers that require less installment and the specialists want to join the productive groups where they can increase high income. Inside the no cooperative social networks, a conveyed transaction-based group development component is intended for the requester to choose which specialist to employ and for the laborer to choose which group to join and what amount ought to be paid for his expertise benefit arrangement. The proposed social group development approach can simply construct communitarian groups by permitting colleagues to frame an associated chart with the end goal that they can cooperate proficiently. At long last, it leads to an arrangement of tests on genuine dataset of laborers to assess the viability of our approach. The trial comes about demonstrate that our approach can save impressive social welfare by looking at the benchmark concentrated methodologies and frame the beneficial groups inside less arrangement time by contrasting the customary conveyed approaches, making our approach a more financial alternative for certifiable applications.

3.6 Polar Opinion Dynamic in Social Network

The focal objective of Amelkin et al. [26] is in demonstrating the development of sentiments of a gathering of individuals, the specialists associated in a coordinated informal community [26]. Researchers accept that the target implies for conclusion assessment are restricted, and the specialists assess their sentiments by examination with the feelings of others. In this manner, the procedure of sentiment arrangement in a gathering is a system procedure, where every operator's supposition changes because of the specialist's connection with his or her neighbors in the system.

3.7 Privacy Preservation Location Sharing

A typical usefulness of numerous area-based long-range interpersonal communication applications is an area sharing administration that enables a gathering of companions to share their areas [27]. With a conceivably untrusted server, such an area sharing administration may debilitate the protection of clients. The existing answers for privacy-preserving location sharing services (PPLSS) require a trusted outsider that approaches the correct area of all clients in the framework or depend on costly calculations or conventions as far as computational or correspondence overhead is concerned. Different arrangements can just give rough questions and answers. To defeat these restrictions Schlegel et al. [27], propose another encryption thought, called order-retrievable encryption (ORE), for PPLSS for long-range informal communication applications. The recognizing attributes of PPLSS are that it: (1) enables a gathering of companions to share their correct areas without the need of any outsider or releasing any area data to any server or clients outside the gathering; (2) accomplishes low computational and correspondence cost by enabling clients to obtain correct area of their companions without requiring any immediate correspondence between clients or various rounds of correspondence between a client and a server, (3) gives proficient question handling by outlining a file structure for the ORE plot, (4) bolsters dynamic area updates, and (5) gives customized security assurance inside a gathering of companions by indicating a most extreme separation where a client will be situated by his/her companions. Exploratory outcomes demonstrate that the computational and correspondence cost of our PPLSS has vastly improved than the best in class arrangement.

3.8 Social Networking in Educational Networks

A most noticeable resource for universities is the information and must be shielded from security break. Joshi and Singh of article [28] examined the security dangers that particularly develop in a university's network, and with thought of these issues, proposed a data security structure for university network condition. The proposed structure decreases the danger of security rupture by supporting three-stage exercises; the primary stage surveys the dangers and vulnerabilities with a specific end goal to distinguish the frail point in instructive condition [28]; the second-stage concentrates on the most noteworthy hazard and make significant remediation design; the third period of hazard appraisal display perceives the helplessness administration consistence necessity so as to enhance a University's security position. The proposed structure is connected on Vikram University Ujjain India's processing condition and the assessment result demonstrated the proposed system upgrades the security level of university grounds network. This model can be utilized by the chance investigator and security administrator of the University to perform dependable and repeatable hazard examination in practical and reasonable ways.

3.9 The Role of Social Network in a Disaster Scenario

Social media, for example, Twitter and Facebook, assume a basic part in catastrophe administration by spreading crisis data to a fiasco-influenced community [29]. It positions as the fourth most prominent hotspot for getting to crisis data. Many investigations have investigated social media information to comprehend the networks and concentrate on basic data to build up a pre- and post-fiasco relief design. Focus in Ref. [29] applies social network examination to change over crisis social network information into learning [29].

Jooho Kim and Makarand Hastak investigate designs made by the collected associations of online clients on Facebook amid fiasco reactions. It gives bits of knowledge to comprehend the basic part of social media use for crisis data engendering. The examination comes about to show that social networks comprise three elements: people, crisis offices, and associations. The center of a social network comprises various people. They are effectively connected with to share data, speak with the city of Baton Rouge, and refresh data. Crisis offices and associations are on the fringe of the social network, interfacing a group with different groups. The aftereffects of this investigation will enable crisis offices to build up their social media operation techniques for a fiasco alleviation design.

3.10 Delegation Model in Social Networks

In spite of their huge development, current social networks do not have a methodical way to deal with assign rights [30] when an element approves another to get to the assets for its benefit. This paper proposes a designation shown in light of socio-specialized outline and hypothesis of participation and joint effort that best suits the prerequisites of social networks [30]. The model is figured through formal strategies, planned utilizing ontologies, and actualized through Facebook APIs. The model's expressiveness is inspected for covering approaches of various clients, its consistency is investigated for clashing and excess arrangements and client acknowledgment testing is performed for adequacy. For social legitimacy, the model is additionally contrasted and 27 past designation models concerning socio-specialized legitimacy parameters got from social standards effectively acknowledged in the human culture.

3.11 Social Network Formation Model

A dynamic model of social network formation [31] in which a settled number of operators connect in covering social gatherings. The researchers here infer a few outcomes on the arrangement of connections in such networks, including outcomes on the degree dispersion, on similar statics relating to degree and gathering size, and on the progression of homophily. Specifically, the authors infer near statics demonstrating that degree is regularly decidedly identified with social gathering size yet adversely identified with the measure of the cover over various social gatherings. This is bolstered by prove from a Facebook dataset. The paper demonstrates that homophily finished a specialist's life expectancy in the network can be nonmonotonic, achieving a worldwide most extreme in some period before in the end diminishing.

3.12 Financial Outcome of Social Networks

Scholastic research on whether social networks impact monetary results is as yet undeveloped. The writing [32] has commonly centered around three noteworthy inquiries—regardless of whether social networks influence financial specialist conduct, firm conduct, or middle person conduct. Since the hypothetical system in back is sorted out around an acknowledged arrangement of ideal models, and on the grounds that information on mediators and firms have been openly accessible for quite a while, the money-related financial aspects region has recently begun utilizing enormous information in its examination. This chapter portrays the surviving examination here and plots how the field is probably going to advance.

3.13 Pervasive Social Networking

In pervasive social networking crime scene investigation, cell phones are a run of the mill wellspring of evidence [33]. For instance, investigation from an Australian law requirement organization demonstrate the quantity of cell phones submitted for investigation expanding at a normal of 60% for each annum since 2006, and information from FBI territorial PC legal sciences lab demonstrating an expansion of 67% for every annum for cell phone examinations [33]. At the point when combined with the development in limit of memory card and gadget stockpiling, which pairs around at regular intervals, there is a progressing and expanding development in the volume of information accessible for confirmation and knowledge examination. There is a potential for data significant to a scope of violations inside the removed information, for example, psychological oppression and sorted out wrongdoing examinations, with potential cross-gadget and cross-case linkages. In Ref. [33], the creators propose the Digital Forensic Intelligence Analysis Cycle (DFIAC). Utilizing cell phone extricates from an Australian law requirement organization, this chapter shows the utility of DFIAC in finding data over an expanding volume of forensically removed information from cell phones, and a more prominent comprehension of the creating patterns in connection to cell phone measurable examination.

3.14 Security and Privacy in Wireless Body Area Network

Wireless body area network (WBAN) is another new technology in the innovation that gives remote system to screen and gather patient's well-being record information utilizing wearable sensors [34]. It is broadly perceived that an abnormal state of framework security and protection assume a key part in ensuring these information while being utilized by the human services experts and amid capacity to guarantee that patient's records are remained careful from interloper's threat. It is thus of awesome enthusiasm to talk about security and protection issues in WBANs. This chapter [34] evaluated WBAN correspondence engineering, security, and protection necessities and security dangers and the essential difficulties in WBANs to these frameworks in view of the most recent benchmarks and productions. The article [34] likewise covers the condition of-craftsmanship safety efforts and research in WBAN. At long last, open areas for future research and improvements are investigated.

3.15 Analysis of Social Networking Issues Related to Area of Focus

Table 1 shows the detailed information regarding various design and security-related issues in social networking which are studied in this chapter.

Table 1   Details of Social Networking Design and Focussed Issues in This Chapter

Sl. No	Literature	Year	Highlighted Topics
1	Bond et al. [1]	2017	Effect of social networks on academic outcomes
2	Rathore et al. [2]	2017	Survey of security and privacy threats of social network users
3	Zhu et al. [3]	2017	Influence maximization in social networks
4	Meng et al. [4]	2017	Data communication between vehicle social network
5	Wang et al. [5]	2017	Crowd sourcing complex tasks by team formation in social network
6	Amelkin et al. [26]	2017	Polar opinion dynamics in social network
7	Schlegel et al. [27]	2017	Privacy preservation location sharing
8	Joshi et al. [28]	2017	Security threats in educational social network
9	Kim et al. [29]	2018	Social network in disaster management
10	Ahmad et al. [30]	2017	Authentication of delegation of resource use in social networking
11	Tarbush et al. [31]	2017	Dynamic model of social network formation
12	Rau et al. [32]	2017	Financial outcome of social networks
13	Quick et al. [33]	2017	Pervasive social networking forensic
14	Janabi et al. [34]	2017	Privacy as a concern among social network users
15	Hua et al. [35]	2017	Cooperation among members of social network in VANET

3.16 Cooperation in Social Networking Members Under a VANET

Vehicular ad hoc network (VANET) is a subclass of mobile ad hoc networks (MANETs) where it is developed by moving vehicles [35]. VANET is getting progressively well known in rush hour gridlock administration particularly in a portion of the created nations. It can be ordered into well-being-related application where it can spare a large number of lives every day and non-security applications for business reason. Because of its erratic portability and discontinuous network availability, a solid end-to-end way among the source and the goal is relatively incomprehensible and consequently specially appointed steering conventions are connected in VANET [35]. Notwithstanding, the greatest test in VANET is not the steering issue, yet the collaboration between the hubs. Indeed, even the best directing convention would not be helpful when the hubs do not take part in sending the information. Hua et al. of article [35] introduced a far-reaching survey on the existing participation components in VANETs; especially, those based on versatile social networking. To start with, it investigates the current difficulties in VANET. Next, it talks about a scientific categorization for the existing collaboration instruments in VANETs and audits the proposed arrangements of every participation write. In addition, these clarify the collaboration arrangements that can be connected from the idea of Mobile Social Networking. At last this chapter provides a conclusion that the idea of mobile social networking could supplement the customary VANET collaboration instruments to empower hub participation. The future research course in VANET collaboration has been talked about also.

4 Challenging Aspects in Social Networking

Many challenging issues need to be addressed during the design of social network sites are as follows:

(i) Portrayal of education—Although different ontologies catch the rich social ideas, there is no need of several "argument" ontologies characterizing a similar idea. How might we push toward having few normal and thorough ontologies?

(ii) Control and administration of learning—Semantic Web is, relative the whole Web, genuinely associated at the RDF diagram level yet inadequately associated at the RDF report level. The open and disseminated nature of the Semantic Web additionally presents issues. How would we give proficient and compelling systems to getting to information, particularly social networks, on the Semantic Web?

(iii) Analysis, extraction, and integration of data from social network—Even with all around characterized ontologies for social ideas, extricating social networks effectively from the loud and inadequate learning on the (Semantic) Web is extremely troublesome. What are the heuristics for coordinating and intertwining social data and the measurements for the believability and utility of the outcomes?

(iv) Identity and honesty in circulated interference—Provenance partner's actualities with social elements which are between associated with social network and trust among social substances can be obtained from social networks. How to oversee and diminish the unpredictability of appropriated surmising by using provenance of learning with regard to a given confide in display?

In the present day work culture, most of the time people are busy with their mobile phones. Due to remaining always connected with social networks, they get new posts, messages, and current updated news at their finger tips instantly. This is the positive aspect of social networking that people always remain updated with latest news and technology. But at the same time there is also some adverse effect of the social networks as a result of which many accidents, crimes, attacks, fraud, etc. also take place due to high mental concentration on these up to date news and highly dynamic devoices. So this is very much important that during these types of problems, all possible communication channels must be used to alert people about such crimes through effective broadcasting of critical information. In paper [36] one such network model has been projected that performs emergency news communications to the public by using social network sites for the distribution of news. This concept presents a junction between Government Security Force and social websites through an application interface at the application level of the users.

5 Static and Dynamic Social Network Model

Social network clarifies the assembly of associations among people, where each individual is a social element. The gathering of ties among individuals and the energy of those ties is outlined by the social network. From a scientific perspective, this social system comprises of hubs (people or associations) and they are connected by single or various exact sorts of affiliation rules, for example, standards, dreams, certainties, budgetary trade, brotherhood, sexual connections, family relationship, abhorrence, struggle, or exchange are construed by methods for social network [37].

5.1 Static Network Model

In a run-of-the mill social network, people are spoken to by nodes, which are connected by edges on the off chance that they have cooperated. A "collaboration" might be immediate, for example, prepping, battling, having a telephone discussion, or sending an email. On the other hand, a "collaboration" can be a gathered roundabout relationship, for example, connection of an arrangement of highlights, purchasing propensities, likeness in the direction, or speak to a straightforward spatial nearness of being sufficiently close for a considerable length of time for an incredible discourse on the fittingness of vicinity networks when all is said and done and the traps of social network analysis in animal investigations and beyond [37]. These distinctive kinds of communications as mentioned in Refs. [25, 38] can be isolated into various networks [39, 40] for express correlation consolidated into one multimodal (otherwise called heterogeneous, multilayered, multiplex, multisocial) network, or just spoke to as one network, disposing of the data about the cooperation writes.

From a network point of view, static social network communities are approximately characterized as districts of a network with thick associations inside the area, in respect to its environment. As it were, a group is an arrangement of people more firmly associated with each other than with individuals from different communities. Various people group distinguishing proof techniques have been generally utilized as a part of humanism and science. With the current increment in the span of network datasets, there has been a blast in computational group distinguishing proof apparatuses. As specified over, a noteworthy inconvenience of these strategies is that the worldly part of associations is disposed of.

The concept of dynamic communities conquers this issue. A dynamic group is a gathering of people who communicate all the more much of the time, adjacently and determinedly among themselves than with different people. Mitra et al. of article [37] demonstrates that the concept of dynamic communities reveals heretofore shrouded examples and procedures in networks utilizing two equid species as illustrations. This technique is broadly important and could give more prominent bits of knowledge into animal sociality, particularly in situations where connections fluctuate with time, as happens generally crosswise over species. By expanding the customary static perspective of a group as an arrangement of people to now incorporate the people and their associations over a day and age, it is conceivable to better comprehend the structure and working of animal social orders (counting humans).

The inspiration for distinguishing communities and the supposition hidden group induction techniques is that communities are dormant structures that are showed by the watched connections. Computational dynamic communities derivation techniques adopt two conceptual strategies: transiently hanging static communities recognized at each time step or grouping collaborations after some time to streamline some target, for example, relative worldly thickness inside communities versus outside or to limit the adjustment in group membership.

5.2 Dynamic Social Network Model

Dynamic networks are essential in various situations. In the first place, if the network information are being contrasted with free procedures, for example, the spread of data or malady or natural changes; at that point dynamic networks will give more precise assessments of spreading rates. Second, if the network has unsurprising examples of progress, for instance, diel cycles or occasional changes, at that point dynamic networks ought to be utilized to catch the effect of these progressions. Third, dynamic networks [41, 42] are vital for investigations of spread through networks when the connection between edge weight and transmission likelihood is nonlinear. At last, dynamic social networks are additionally valuable in circumstances where communications among people are thick, for example, in investigations of hostage gatherings. The utilization of static versus dynamic network requires cautious thought, both from an exploration question point of view and from an information viewpoint, and this chapter gives a guide on the most proficient method to assess the relative significance of these.

Dynamic social networks may likewise be dynamic by nature. Ties are built; they may thrive and may create cozy connections, and they can likewise condense quietly, or unexpectedly go bad and run with a blast. These intelligent changes might be reflected in the result of the auxiliary areas of the on-screen characters encompassed by the network thinking about the case, when companions of companions move toward becoming companions, highlights of the performing artists, highlights of sets of on-screen characters, and persevering random effects keeping in mind the end goal to imply peculiar effects. A dynamic social network involves relations among on-screen characters that change with stage. An underlying hypothesis of a couple of the model which are given transiently in paper [37] suggests that the network associations are fleeting events, as well as can every now and again be considered as states with an inclination to persist with stage. Various affiliations generally examined in network investigation normally satisfy this need of predictable adjustment, for example, companionship, trust, and collaboration. Different networks all the more intensely look somewhat like the "occasion information"; an occurrence can be located as the arrangement of all phone calls middle a gathering of performing artists at any given time point, or the arrangement of all messages being pushed at

Table 2   Details of the Survey on Themes That Focus on Social Networking Issues

Sl. No	Literature	Year	Subject of discussion on social network
1	Davidekova et al. [36]	2017	Emergency social network approach that uses emergency posting through application program interface
2	Marche et al. [43]	2017	Object navigation in social network as per distance from one node to other
3	Merini et al. [44]	2017	Image tracing in social network using CNN approach
4	Santi et al. [45]	2012	Analysis of mobile social network based on mobility model for the purpose of next generation network
5	Nie et al. [46]	2016	Learning and teaching from multiple social networks
6	Hargitai et al. [47]	2016	Investigation on social network analysis based on big data, big problems, and internet log data
7	Zhao et al. [48]	2018	Recommendation of movie for social awareness through multi modal network learning
8	Mitra et al. [37]	2016	Analytical study of dynamic models in social network
9	Rachael et al. [49]	2017	Focus on positive aspects of social security measures
10	Md. Kamal et al. [50]	2016	An automated system for monitoring of Facebook data

any given time point. While it is expressive to derive these networks as needles of correspondence, it is not sensible to regard their connections as constant states, in spite of the fact that there lies the likelihood of gathering the force of an occasion over a specific period and after that view these totals as pointers of states. Table 2 describes the details of the survey on different themes that focus on social networking issues.

5.3 A Framework for Dynamic Social Model

The system allows the following of both group based and additionally the individual events. So as to depict occasions or rather the events a crisp time named as the group hail is alluded, which would cover all the conceivable advances inside the extent of a group [29]. Based on this concept, keeping in mind the end goal to shield every single plausible change of a group occasion definitions term has been advanced. In nature, it is watched that every one of the people inside the group have shared regular interests which frame the premise of their communication. Considering an illustration where individuals physically or essentially accumulate for a talk on a theme or for sharing a thought, this aids in the recognizable proof of individuals and nonindividuals. Albeit human communities are more sensible in this angle, yet at the same time manufactured communities are believed to have the same basic examples. Consequently, a self-ruling independence for a group can be accepted based on common interests. This character is being known as the group banner, and it envisions the arrangement of a group and its constituent partners. This people group hail is incomparable and cannot be isolated or copied. The lifecycle of a group banner can be divided as a couple of stages as follows. (1) A people group frames in a depiction: Flag has been raised. (2) It might be steady from a preview to another: Flag is still there. (3) It could draw in new individuals or lose a few individuals: Flag is waving. (4) It might consolidate another group: Dominant banner takes control. (5) It might separate into at least two littler communities, with each new part having its own freedom: The most critical part conveys the banner with itself. (6) At last it can break separated into pieces while no piece safeguards the character of the group: Flag has been vanished.

5.4 Use of Dynamic Social Network: Social-Aware Routing in MANET

This section will exhibit an application wherein the steering approaches in Mobile Ad Hoc Networks are recognized by the network group structures. A MANET can be characterized as a dynamic remote network where the key association might be available or missing. Here every hub can travel generously at any way, yet should bring about a composed irregular development. Attributable to the suppleness of the hubs and the nearness of a precarious connection in a MANET, the primary test lies on outlining a skilled directing plan. Most recent inquires about have exhibited that the effects of social networks and social-aware calculations are seen in MANETs, so it bears an incredible potential in network steering. The fundamental purpose for this lies on the reality of having a characteristic inclination of individuals in shaping little groups or communities inside the vast correspondence networks for visit correspondence than that with outside individuals. Through the presence of the group of hubs which are thickly associated, the social property is wonderfully imitated to the fundamental MANETs. With this the fundamental thought of group structure in mobile ad hoc networks is created. This additionally offers ascend to the numerous steering methodologies which have given extensive change over customary strategies. Because of the recomputation of the social structure because of network topology change, these group location techniques abuse those methodologies which were not germane for dynamic MANETs as this would bring about noteworthy computational charges and regulation time. In this manner, when a versatile group structure discovery calculation is utilized, the center of the network will accelerate alongside the change of the strength to steering approaches in MANETs.

6 Factors That Affect the Design of a Social Network

Social networking services are changing the way in which individuals utilize and draw in with the Internet and with each other. Youngsters, especially, rush to utilize the new innovation in ways that inexorably obscure the limits among on the web and offline exercises. Social networking services are additionally growing quickly as innovation changes with new mobile measurements and highlights. Kids and youngsters inside the United Kingdom, who have grown up underestimating the Internet and mobile innovations, make up a noteworthy fragment of the first to misuse the positive open doors and advantages of new and developing services, yet in addition the first to need to arrange suitable practices inside the new communities [51], and to need to distinguish and oversee chance. Social networking services are on the ascent all around, and this change is additionally clear in expanded United Kingdom engagement with locales. Ofcom's current International Communications Market 07 report (ii) discovered proof that more grown-ups utilize social networking locales in the United Kingdom than in some other of the European nations incorporated into the review. ComScore information from August 2007 (iii) proposes that United Kingdom Internet clients clock up a normal of 23 visits and 5.3 h on social networking destinations every month. Ofcom announced that 39% of all United Kingdom Internet clients utilize social networking services, while the ComScore figures indicate 24.9 million individual social networking service guests in August 2007. As per late Hitwise figures, the most prevalent committed social networking locales in the United Kingdom are MySpace, Facebook, and Beboiv. These kinds of social networking services are profile centered—movement bases on web pages that contain data about the exercises, interests, and likes (and aversions) of every part. While the quantity of guests to social networking locales is expanding, so too are the quantities of new services being propelled, alongside the quantity of longstanding (inside the generally short life expectancy of the Internet) websites that are including, creating or refining social networking service highlights or apparatuses. The manners by which we interface with social networking services are growing as well. Recreations based and mobile-telephone based social networking services that connect with the existing web-based stages or new mobile-centered communities are quickly creating territories.

6.1 Management of Relationship Among Users in a Social Network

Management connections on the web and dealing with online presence of users are critical to messing around with and utilizing social networks securely. Notwithstanding, the speed of the improvement of social networking services may imply that the youngsters will probably have created individual procedures or learnt from peers than from formal guideline and support from grown-ups. Social networking destinations shift in the sorts of apparatuses and usefulness, they give characterization of social networking locales as having three basic components: a part profile (in their definition this is dependably a web page), the capacity to add different individuals to a contact list, and bolstered collaboration between individuals from contact records (connection changes enormously, and there will ordinarily be some level of association encouraged between individuals who are not on each other's contacts lists) (vi.) Social networking locales are often seen by their clients as shut conditions, where individuals converse with other members. This impression of social networking services as giving a private space is probably going to represent conduct, dialect, and postings that do not interpret well outside their expected shut setting. While it is imperative that youngsters comprehend the general population nature of quite a bit of their action inside social networking services (and can utilize consents and protection controls to oversee individual data and interchanges), we likewise need to guarantee that online action is seen comprehensively, that is, as the aggregate of action of all the online locales and networks that an individual has a place with.

6.2 Profit by Social Network

Profile-based social networking services: Profile-based services are essentially sorted out around individuals' profile pages—pages that basically comprise data around an individual part, including the individual's photograph and subtle elements of interests, different preferences. Bebo, Facebook, and MySpace are for the most part great cases of profile-based services. Clients build up their spaces in different ways, and can often add to each other's spaces, normally leaving content, implanted substance, or connections to outer substance through message dividers, remark, or assessment devices. Clients often incorporate outsider substance (as gadgets) to upgrade their profiles or as a method for including data from other web services and social networking services.

6.3 Type of Content Floating in Social Networks

Content-based social networking services: In these services, the client's profile remains an essential method for sorting out associations; however it assumes an optional part to the posting of substance. Photograph sharing site Flickr is a case of this kind of service, one in which groups and remarks are based around pictures. Numerous individuals have discharge Flickr accounts and joined to the service to see their companions' or family's consent secured pictures. Shelfari is one of the present yield of book-centered locales, with the part's "bookshelf" being a point of convergence of every part's profile. Different cases of substance-based communities incorporate http://YouTube.com for video sharing and last.fm, in which the substance is orchestrated by software that screens and speaks to the music that clients tune in to. In last.fm, content is created by the client's action. The demonstration of tuning in to sound documents makes and updates profile data ("as of late tuned in to"). This thus creates information around an individual client's "neighbors"—individuals who have as of late tuned in to a similar sort of music.

6.4 Audience of Social Network Site

Youngsters and social network services are overwhelmingly gone for and intended for teenagers and grown-ups. Most services have a base participation age of 13 or 14 years, and numerous will unequivocally state they are intended for >18 year olds. There might be well-being limitations on the records of under 16–18-year olds—for instance, regardless of whether they can show up in broad daylight looks. There are destinations particularly intended for youngsters—for instance, both Teen Second Life and Habbo Hotel are gone for teenagers. http://Imbee.com is essentially a blogging service for tweens (youngsters matured 9–13 years), requiring a parent's consent to join. Both Disney and Nick.Com have devoted services for kids, Disney having as of late procured ClubPenguin, a virtual world SNS went for 6-to-14-year olds, in August 2007. Kids and tweens can make penguin symbols or online agents [52], for which they can "purchase" (with virtual cash earned in-world diversions) garments, extras, pets, homes, furniture, and so on. Services went for youngsters normally have stricter security settings, more prominent levels of balance and more constrained client cooperations. Some furthermore have parental controls—for instance, requiring join, as a rule with a Mastercard, and set inclinations, for example, the level of in-world correspondence permitted. Well-being impediments may well make kid-centered destinations less valuable for supporting instructive practices and activities than standard locales, which reach far less demanding—factors which achieve their own difficulties. The National School Boards Association (United States) as of late discharged research discoveries of an investigation into the online practices of United States 9–17-year olds. Their example included 2300 youngsters and parents. Nine-to-seventeen-year olds announced investing nearly as much energy in social networking and web destinations as they do sitting in front of the TV—around 9 h online contrasted with 10 h of TV. In all, 96% of the youngsters overviewed announced.

7 Security Prospective in Social Networking

For a newcomer to the Internet field, social networking locales are a perpetually prominent path for individuals to remain associated. Some may even dare to state that business openings are framed and lost on the web, as our web nearness turns into a fundamental piece of our own lives [49]. In a period where our online character eclipses our real character, as well as other key budgetary and individual frameworks too, the potential security dangers related with these social networks cannot be focused on enough. Throughout the years, scientists and programmers alike have distinguished a modest bunch of security dangers running from individuals, procedure to application. The reason for this investigation is to give a general diagram of the real security themes encompassing social networks today, and present the fundamental instruments behind each. Here, we catch up with some substantial results that each hazard may have, lastly give a course to take a gander at as far as arrangements are concerned.

7.1 Social Networking: Information Leakage and Theft Mechanism

The vast majority when asked will concur that not every person they know is their closest companion; there are the insignificant colleagues the distance to those with whom we share our most profound insider facts, alongside numerous shades in the middle. However, the boundless wonders of social networking destinations have added new significance to companions: two individuals are often "companions or not" [49]. While social networks may not really increment solid ties, it surely does almost no for feeble ties. One may have two or three dear companions and a large number of inaccessible companions, and a social network may essentially order them all as "companions." More contacts are not really an awful thing; the issue is who approaches our data? Social networking destinations give a specific level of access control, yet a great many people do not require the push to design these legitimately. To exacerbate the situation, oftentimes the data goes through a few jumps of "companions," and by the possibility of six degrees of division it appears to be outlandish to expect we are a long way from the terrible folks.

Utilization of Real Names and Personal Information—to really sweeten the deal, social networking destinations contain data that is either generally genuine or effortlessly distinguished as phony. For the sole motivation behind staying aware of companions in an apparently reliable space, individuals have almost no impetus to misrepresent data on Facebook.

7.2 Trust Relationship in Facebook

Without considering the mobilization necessity unwinding for Facebook in the most recent years, clients used to require a legitimate scholarly email deliver so as to enlist. The greater part of Facebook clients still work under this supposition (to the extent I can tell, the open Facebook does not trouble the newcomers either), and we naturally trust whoever is in our network. Most ground networks are open and picking up a mail address is not troublesome. In addition, numerous clients will readily acknowledge companion demands from individuals that are not even in their network. When an outsider interfaces with somebody in another network, he pretty much acquires his companion's qualifications with regard to managing others in a similar domain, giving him simple access to different clients. As a reward, this may enable a malevolent client to bypass domain-based security settings.

7.3 Phishing Technique of Attack in Facebook

As the name may recommend, phishing is the demonstration of taking sensitive data with a medium that has been intended to disguise an honest to goodness source. For instance, an evil client could profess to be a bank and convey mass messages requesting login accreditation confirmation. The client would undoubtedly be diverted to a website that seems like the real bank website that the programmer has developed and be incited to enter their accreditations. Refined phishes may use different systems inside social building and program/server deformity, to influence the plan to look more conceivable.

There are two key variables to a successful phishing plan: (1) appearance of authenticity and (2) reliability of the conveyance medium. Current phishing plans depend on detailed individual data for focused attack. Studies demonstrate that lance phishing, or phishing with focused individual data, can accomplish up to an 80% achievement rate [49]. For a while, we appeared to have this under control, with application level heuristic channels and network/firewall level area screening. Enter social network locales, for example, Facebook, MySpace, and LinkedIn. As expressed beforehand, at no other time has the online populace so energetically revealed their own data, for example, telephone numbers, locations, interests, and instruction history, that what used to be the true objective of major corporate secret activities operations would now be able to be gathered at the snap of a couple of catches. Because of their business esteem and far-reaching acknowledgment, these destinations are impenetrable to corporate firewalls. Joined with poor client instruction, effective APIs, and trashy protection settings, social network destinations give the ideal place to gather data and breed assault vectors.

There are some possible solutions to the above attack in social sites. Clients ought to be instructed about the conceivable outcomes that phishing brings. Not exclusively should clients be delicate about suspicious URLs and messages, they ought to take after strict approaches with respect to phishing site cautioning messages. Above all, clients should audit security settings in their social network applications and presentation. At the application level, one may consider upholding Microsoft Internet Explorer or Mozilla Firefox's phishing control. As an additional assurance, services like PhishTank and BlueCoat [49] give network and application level boycotting.

7.4 Source Identification of Spread Rumor in Social Networks

Recognizing rumor sources in interpersonal organizations assumes a basic part in constraining the harm caused by them through the auspicious isolate of the sources. In any case, the worldly variety in the topology of informal communities and the progressing dynamic procedures challenge our conventional source distinguishing proof strategies that are considered in static systems. Jiang et al. of article [53] presents a thought from criminology and proposes a novel technique to defeat the difficulties. First, it decreases the time-shifting systems to a progression of static systems by presenting a period incorporating window. Second, rather than assessing each individual in conventional systems, it embraces an invert dispersal technique to indicate an arrangement of suspects of the genuine talk source. This procedure tends to the adaptability issue of source-recognizable proof issues, and along these lines significantly advances the proficiency of talk source ID. Interpersonal organization information can help with getting important understanding into social practices and uncovering the basic advantages. New enormous information advances are rising to make it simpler to find significant social data from advertise investigation to counterterrorism [54]. Sadly, both different social datasets and huge information advancements raise stringent security concerns. Foes can dispatch derivation assaults to anticipate touchy inactive data, which is unwilling to be distributed by social clients. In this manner, there is a tradeoff between information advantages and protection concerns. In this chapter, we explore how to improve the trade-off between idle information security and modified information utility. He et al. of article [54] proposes an information disinfection methodology that does not incredibly diminish the advantages brought by interpersonal organization information, while touchy dormant data can even now be ensured. Notwithstanding considering intense enemies with ideal derivation assaults, the proposed information cleansing procedure can in any case safeguard the two information advantages and social structure, while ensuring ideal dormant information security.

8 Impact of SNSs—Facebook as a Case Study

There are numerous inquiries concerning the social impact of across-the-broad utilization of SNSs like Facebook, LinkedIn, MySpace, and Twitter [55]. Do these advancements confine individuals and truncate their connections? Or on the other hand are there benefits related with being associated with others along these lines? The Pew Research Center's Internet and American Life Project chose to inspect SNS in a survey that investigated individuals' general social networks and how utilization of these advances is identified with put stock in, resilience, social help, and group and political engagement.

The discoveries displayed in Ref. [55] paint a rich and complex photo of the part that advanced innovation plays in individuals' social universes. Wherever conceivable, the research [55] expected to unravel whether individuals' shifting social practices and states of mind are identified with the diverse ways they utilize SNSs, or to other pertinent statistic qualities, for example, age, sexual orientation, and social class.

8.1 Facebook Clients Are More Trusting Than Others

Sometimes when inquired as to whether they felt "that a great many people can be trusted." At the point when relapse examination was done to control for statistic factors, it was discovered that the run-of-the-mill web client is more than twice as likely as others to feel that individuals can be confided in Facebook. Further, it was discovered that Facebook clients are considerably more prone to be reliable. A relapse examination was done to control for different components and it was discovered that a Facebook client who utilizes the site numerous times each day is 43% more probable than other web clients and more than three times as likely as nonweb clients to feel that a great many people can be trusted.

8.2 Facebook Users Have All the More Pleasant Connections

A survey in Ref. [55] claims that the normal American has a little more than two discourse associates, that is, individuals with whom they talk about critical issues. This is an unobtrusive, however altogether bigger number than the normal of 1.93 center ties revealed when the survey [55] group asked this same inquiry in 2008. Controlling for different variables, it was discovered that somebody who utilizes Facebook a few times each day midpoints 9% all the more close, center ties in their general social network contrasted and other web clients.

8.3 Facebook Clients Get More Social Help Than Other Individuals

The research [55] took a gander at how much aggregate help, passionate help, fellowship, and instrumental guide grown-ups get. On a size of 100, the normal American scored 75/100 on a size of aggregate help, 75/100 on enthusiastic help (for example, accepting exhortation), 76/100 in brotherhood (e.g., having individuals to invest energy with), and 75/100 in instrumental guide. Web clients as a rule score 3 focuses higher in all out help, 6 focuses higher in camaraderie, and 4 focuses higher in instrumental help. A Facebook client who utilizes the site various times each day tends to score an extra 5 focuses higher in all out help, 5 focuses higher in passionate help, and 5 focuses higher in fellowship, than web clients of comparative statistic qualities. For Facebook clients, the extra lift is equal to about a large portion of the aggregate help that the normal American gets because of being hitched or cohabitating with an accomplice.

9 Conclusion

The offered chapter presents an extensive survey on various critical issues that have been considered and carefully identified during the review process. After observation in most of the contribution, it was found that the major challenges lie in the area of security and smart communication among members of the social network. The chief challenge lies in authentication of delegation for proper use of resources [56, 57] in social network and design of dynamic models for correct network formation. Similarly, where the role of financial outcome of the subnetworks under a social group is very significant, at the same time cooperation among members of the social network is considered equally important during the above study and analysis. The topic of how to maximize the influence of the social network system was discussed with few proposed models as well as the educational outcome of the social networks as a key part of educational improvement was also elaborated with problem solution. The above research piece of work reports most of the practical and social issues of the most recent and emergent technology of current age with their positive aspects with scope of further development for optimization.

References

[1] R.M. Bond, V. Chykina, J.J. Jones, Social network effects on academic achievement, Soc. Sci. J. 54 (4) (2017) 438–449. ISSN 0362-3319, https://doi.org/10.1016/j.soscij.2017.06.001.

[2] S. Rathore, P.K. Sharma, V. Loia, Y.-S. Jeong, J.H. Park, Social network security: issues, challenges, threats, and solutions, Inf. Sci. 421 (2017) 43–69. ISSN 0020-0255, https://doi.org/10.1016/j.ins.2017.08.063.

[3] J. Zhu, Y. Liu, X. Yin, A new structure-hole-based algorithm for influence maximization in large online social networks, IEEE Access 5 (2017) 23405–23412, https://doi.org/10.1109/ACCESS.2017.2758353.

[4] F. Meng, X. Gong, L. Guo, X. Cai, Q. Zhang, Software-reconfigurable system supporting point-to-point data communication between vehicle social networks and marketers, IEEE Access 5 (2017) 22796–22803.

[5] W. Wang, J. Jiang, B. An, Y. Jiang, B. Chen, Toward efficient team formation for crowdsourcing in non-cooperative social networks, IEEE Trans. Cybern. 47 (12) (2017) 4208–4222.

[6] M.S. Kamal, S. Parvin, A.S. Ashour Shi, N. Dey, De-Bruijn graph with Map Reduce framework towards metagenomic data classification, Int. J. Inf. Technol. 9 (1) (2017) 59–75.

[7] H. Matallah, G. Belalem, K. Bouamrane, Towards a new model of storage and access to data in big data and cloud computing, Int. J. Ambient Comput. Intell. 8 (4) (2017), https://doi.org/10.4018/IJACI.2017100103.

[8] D.V. Balas-Timar, V.E. Balas, M.A. Breaz, A.S. Ashour, N. Dey, Technique for scoring competency based behavioural interviews: a fuzzy approach, Congresului Internaţional, Cercetarea modernă în psihologie, May, 2016.

[9] W. Abdessalem, A.S. Ashour, D.B. Sassi, N. Dey, Medline text mining: An enhancement genetic algorithm based approach for document clustering, in: Applications of intelligent optimization in biology and medicine: Current trends and open problems, Springer, Vegas, 2015 (Chapter 10, March).

[10] W.B.A. Karaa, Z.B. Azzouz, A. Singh, N. Dey, A.S. Ashour, H.B. Ghazala, Automatic builder of class diagram (ABCD): an application of UML generation from functional requirements, Software Pract. Exper. 46 (11) (2015) 1443–1458.

[11] D.P. Acharjya, A. Anitha, A comparative study of statistical and rough computing models in predictive data analysis, Int. J. Ambient Comput. Intell. 8 (2) (2017) 32–51.

[12] M.S. Kamal, S.H. Ripon, N. Dey, V. Santhi, A map reduce approach to diminish imbalance parameters for big deoxyribonucleic acid dataset, Comput. Meth. Programs Biomed. 1 (2) (2016).

[13] M.S. Kamal, S.F. Nimmy, M.I. Hossain, N. Dey, A.S. Ashour, V. Sathi, in: ExSep: an exon separation process using neural skyline filter, International Conference on Electrical, Electronics, and Optimization Techniques (ICEEOT), Chennai, 2016.

[14] I. Puga-Gonzalez, C. Sueur, Emergence of complex social networks from spatial structure and rules of thumb: a modelling approach, Ecol. Complex. 31 (2017) 189–200. ISSN 1476-945X.

[15] A. Bandyopadhyay, S. Kar, Coevolution of cooperation and network structure in social dilemmas in evolutionary dynamic complex network, Appl. Math. Comput. 320 (2018) 710–730. ISSN 0096-3003.

[16] M. Rath, B. Pattanayak, MAQ: a mobile agent based QoS platform for MANETs, Int. J. Bus. Data Comm. Netw. 13 (1) (2017) 1–8.

[17] T.Z. Hayat, O. Lesser, T. Samuel-Azran, Gendered discourse patterns on online social networks: A social network analysis perspective, Comput. Hum. Behav. 77 (2017) 132–139. ISSN 0747-5632, https://doi.org/10.1016/j.chb.2017.08.041.

[18] J. Saint-Charles, P. Mongeau, Social influence and discourse similarity networks in workgroups, Soc. Netw. 52 (2018) 228–237. ISSN 0378-8733.

[19] M. Rath, in: Delay and power based network assessment of network layer protocols in MANET, 2015 International Conference on Control, Instrumentation, Communication and Computational Technologies (IEEE ICCICCT), Kumaracoil, India, 2015, , pp. 682–686.

[20] B.K. Pattanayak, M. Rath, A mobile agent based intrusion detection system architecture for mobile ad hoc networks, J. Comput. Sci. 10 (2014) 970–975.

[21] M. Rath, B.K. Pattanayak, Energy efficient MANET protocol using cross layer design for military applications, Def. Sci. J. 66 (2) (2016). DRDO Publication.

[22] M. Rath, B.K. Pattanayak, B. Pati, Comparative analysis of AODV routing protocols based on network performance parameters in mobile adhoc networks, in: Foundations and Frontiers in Computer, Communication and Electrical Engineering, CRC press, Taylor & Francis, 2016, pp. 461–466 ISBN: 978-1-138-02877-7. May.

[23] M. Rath, B.K. Pattanayak, SCICS: a soft computing based intelligent communication system in VANET, in: Smart Secure Systems—IoT and Analytics Perspective, Communications in Computer and Information Science, vol. 808, Springer, Cham, 2018.

[24] M. Rath, B.K. Pattanayak, B. Pati, QoS satisfaction in MANET based Real time applications, Int. J. Contr. Theor. Appl. 9 (7) (2016) 3069–3083.

[25] M. Rath, B.K. Pattanayak, Monitoring of QoS in MANET based real time applications, in: Smart Innovation, Systems and Technologies, vol. 84, Springer, Cham, 2018, pp. 579–586.

[26] V. Amelkin, F. Bullo, A.K. Singh, Polar opinion dynamics in social networks, IEEE Trans. Automat. Contr. 62 (11) (2017) 5650–5665, https://doi.org/10.1109/TAC.2017.2694341.

[27] R. Schlegel, C.Y. Chow, Q. Huang, D.S. Wong, Privacy-preserving location sharing services for social networks, IEEE Trans. Serv. Comput. 10 (5) (2017) 811–825.

[28] C. Joshi, U.K. Singh, Information security risks management framework—a step towards mitigating security risks in university network, J. Inform. Secur. Appl. 35 (2017) 128–137. ISSN 2214-2126.

[29] J. Kim, M. Hastak, Social network analysis: Characteristics of online social networks after a disaster, Int. J. Inform. Manag. 38 (1) (2018) 86–96. ISSN 0268-4012.

[30] A. Ahmad, B. Whitworth, F. Zeshan, E. Bertino, R. Friedman, Extending social networks with delegation, Comput. Secur. 70 (2017) 546–564.

[31] B. Tarbush, A. Teytelboym, Social groups and social network formation, Games Econ. Behav. 103 (2017) 286–312. ISSN 0899-8256.

[32] R. Rau, Social networks and financial outcomes, Curr. Opin. Behav. Sci. 18 (2017) 75–78. ISSN 2352-1546.

[33] D. Quick, K.-K.R. Choo, Pervasive social networking forensics: intelligence and evidence from mobile device extracts, J. Netw. Comput. Appl. 86 (2017) 24–33. ISSN 1084-8045, https://doi.org/10.1016/j.jnca.2016.11.018.

[34] S. Al-Janabi, I. Al-Shourbaji, M. Shojafar, S. Shamshirband, Survey of main challenges (security and privacy) in wireless body area networks for healthcare applications, Egyptian Inform. J. 18 (2) (2017) 113–122. ISSN 1110-8665.

[35] L.C. Hua, M.H. Anisi, P.L. Yee, M. Alam, Social networking-based cooperation mechanisms in vehicular ad-hoc network—a survey, Veh. Comm. 10 (2017) 57–73.

[36] M. Dávideková, M. Greguš, in: Social network types: an emergency social network approach—a concept of possible inclusion of emergency posts in social networks through an API, 2017 IEEE International Conference on Cognitive Computing (ICCC), Honolulu, HI, 2017, pp. 40–47, https://doi.org/10.1109/IEEE.ICCC.2017.13.

[37] A. Mitra, S. Paul, S. Panda, P. Padhi, A study on the representation of the various models for dynamic social networks, Procedia Comput. Sci. 79 (2016) 624–631. ISSN 1877-0509.

[38] M. Rath, B.K. Pattanayak, B. Pati, Energy competent routing protocol design in MANET with real time application provision, Int. J. Bus. Data Comm. Netw. 11 (1) (2015) 50–60.

[39] M. Rath, B. Pati, Load balanced routing scheme for MANETs with power and delay optimization, Int. J. Comm. Netw. Distr. Syst. 19 (4) (2017) 2017.

[40] M. Rath, Congestion control mechanism for real time traffic in mobile adhoc networks, in: Computer Communication, Networking and Internet Security. Lecture Notes in Networks and Systems, vol. 5, Springer, Singapore, 2017.

[41] M. Rath, B. Pati, B.K. Pattanayak, in: Inter-layer communication based QoS platform for real time multimedia applications in MANET, Wireless communications, signal processing and networking (IEEE WiSPNET) Chennai, India, 2016, pp. 613–617.

[42] M. Rath, B.K. Pattanayak, in: A methodical survey on real time applications in MANETS: focussing on key issues, International Conference on, High performance computing and applications (IEEE ICHPCA), Bhubaneswar, India, pp. 1-5, 22–24, 2014.

[43] C. Marche, L. Atzori, A. Iera, L. Militano, M. Nitti, in: Navigability in social networks of objects: the importance of friendship type and nodes' distance, 2017 IEEE Globecom Workshops (GC workshops), Singapore, 2017, pp. 1–6.

[44] I. Merini, T. Uricchio, R. Caldelli, in: Tracing images back to their social network of origin: a CNN-based approach, 2017 IEEE Workshop on Information Forensics and Security (WIFS), Rennes, France, 2017, pp. 1–6, https://doi.org/10.1109/WIFS.2017.8267660.

[45] P. Santi, Mobile social network analysis, in: Mobility Models for Next Generation Wireless Networks: Ad Hoc, Vehicular and Mesh Networks, Wiley Telecom, 2012, p. 448, https://doi.org/10.1002/9781118344774 1. (Chapter 19).

[46] L. Nie, X. Song, T.-S. Chua, Learning from multiple social networks, in: Learning from Multiple Social Networks, Morgan & Claypool, 2016. 1.

[47] E. Hargittai, C. Sandvig, Big data, big problems, big opportunities: using internet log data to conduct social network analysis research, in: Digital Research Confidential: The Secrets of Studying Behavior Online, MIT Press, 2016, p. 288. 1.

[48] Z. Zhao, et al., Social-aware movie recommendation via multimodal network learning, IEEE Trans. Multimedia 20 (2) (2018) 430–440.

[49] R.P. Mady, D.T. Blumstein, Social security: are socially connected individuals less vigilant? Anim. Behav. 134 (2017) 79–85. ISSN 0003-3472.

[50] M.S. Kamal, N. Dey, A.S. Ashour, V.E. Balas, FbMapping: an automated system for monitoring Facebook data, Neural Netw. World 5 (9) (2016).

[51] Creating and Connecting//Research and Guidelines on Online Social—and Educational—Networking, National School Boards Association, August 2007.

[52] M. Rath, M.R. Panda, in: MAQ system development in mobile ad-hoc networks using mobile agents, IEEE 2nd International Conference on Contemporary Computing and Informatics (IC3I), Noida, pp. 794–798. January, 2017.

[53] J. Jiang, S. Wen, S. Yu, Y. Xiang, W. Zhou, Rumor source identification in social networks with time-varying topology, IEEE Trans. Dependable Secure Comput. 15 (1) (2018) 166–179.

[54] Z. He, Z. Cai, J. Yu, Latent-data privacy preserving with customized data utility for social network data, IEEE Trans. Veh. Technol. 67 (1) (2018) 665–673.

[55] http://www.pewinternet.org/2011/06/16/social-networking-sites-and-our-lives/ (Accessed 30 January 2018).

[56] M. Rath, Resource provision and QoS support with added security for client side applications in cloud computing, Int. J. Inform. Technol. 9 (3) (2017) 1–8.

[57] M. Rath, B. Pati, B.K. Pattanayak, in: Cross layer based QoS platform for multimedia transmission in MANET, 2017 11th international conference on intelligent systems and control (ISCO), Coimbatore, 2017, pp. 402–407.

Further Reading

[58] M. Rath, B.K. Pattanayak, B. Pati, Resource reservation and improved QoS for real time applications in MANET, Indian J. Sci. Technol. 9 (36) (2016) 1–6.

[59] M. Rath, B.K. Pattanayak, B. Pati, A contemporary survey and analysis of delay and power based routing protocols in MANET, J. Eng. Appl. Sci. 11 (1) (2016) 536–540.

[60] M. Rath, C.R. Panigrahi, in: Prioritisation of security measures at the junction of MANET and IoT, Second International Conference on Information and Communication Technology for Competitive Strategies, ACM Publication, New York, ISBN: 978-1-4503-3962-9, 2016.

[61] M. Rath, B.K. Pattanayak, B. Pati, Energetic routing protocol design for real-time transmission in mobile adhoc network, in: Computing and Network Sustainability, Lecture Notes in Networks and Systems, vol. 12, Springer, Singapore, 2017.

3

Emergence of Stable and Glassy States in Dynamics of Social Networks

Leila Hedayatifar

New England Complex Systems Institute, Cambridge, MA, United States

1 Introduction

Human societies are in a state of continuous change. Over the years, societies grow up and as a consequence, their organizations and emerged communities are getting more complex. This complexity causes many challenges to understand, describe, and predict these systems. Based on the observations, having knowledge about the performance of the components separately does not give us all information about the whole system. Dynamics of societies is a sort of self-organized process in which individuals interact with their neighbors and modify their relations based on their benefits [1, 2]. Changes in the microscopic levels and small time scales give rise to the formation of patterns in macroscopic levels and at larger scales. In other words, the emergence of collective behaviors in complex phenomena is something more than interaction among components.

Social networks are examples of communication networks in which human communications happen face to face among people [3–5] or indirectly [6–12]. Direct contact between persons is the reason of the spreading of rumors, news, jokes, and many diseases and epidemics. In recent years, many concepts have been introduced such as centrality measures, and cliques and communities to study network structures. Studying and understanding the dynamics of these social networks are an important area that many scientists have worked on and have introduced some concepts such as small-world property and preferential attachment [13]. Many of real-world networks are open and in continuous growth by adding new nodes like WWW. On the contrary, many known networks are closed and a number of their nodes do not change over time like interaction between countries or students in classrooms. The dynamic of these networks is based on flipping of relations [14]. This chapter is assigned to study some dynamical properties of these systems based on Heider's balance theory. This theory was introduced to understand why individuals change their relations in different situations [3]. Changes in relations deform societies' topology to gain stability eventually. To investigate the dynamics of interactions in a society using Heider's balance theory several studies have been done on empirical data such as

Social Network Analytics. https://doi.org/10.1016/B978-0-12-815458-8.00003-7

the karate club and international conflicts [15, 16], as well as analytical [17, 18] and numerical models [4, 19–22]. In this chapter, we use this theory to study the dynamics of social networks and paths that end to local or global balanced states. How breaking symmetry of relations affects the frequency of balanced states and at the end, by considering humans ability to remember sequence of events, we address why balanced states do not appear frequently in real systems.

2 Current State and Historical Development

2.1 Heider Balanced Theory

A society consists of a collection of members and their relationships that influence each other. In this context, Heider [3] proposed the "cognitive balance theory" which quantifies the relation between two persons and their attitude toward a topic in a triadic configuration. Based on this theory, connections are rearranged to become stable [5]. As shown in Fig. 1, there are four possible triadic relations. These triangles can be classified into two balanced and unbalanced configurations. The first two triads are balanced and the two last ones in Fig. 1 refer to unbalanced triads. Tension in unbalanced relations stimulates individuals to modify and change their relation to reach a balanced configuration.

Later, Cartwright et al. [23] generalized Heider's approach by changing the "attitude" node with third person to study the interactions among individuals in triadic relations. In this sign graph, links can be positive or negative. Positive relations refer to friendship, cooperation, tolerance, etc., while negative links denote animosity, rivalry, or intolerance in social groups [24–27]. The relations change as to implement four rules: friend of my friend is my friend, friend of my enemy is my enemy, enemy of my friend is my enemy, enemy of my enemy is my friend.

2.2 Energy Reduction

Now how could one gain a physical insight into the structure and dynamics of such systems? One answer that can help us is the concept of Hamiltonian. A smart technique that could be implemented to study the evolution is to relate a Hamiltonian to the system [28]. If the relation or the link between the nodes i and j is represented by S_{ij}, for friendship it would be 1 and for enemy it would be -1. A Hamiltonian definition for a fully connected network with N nodes is provided as [28]

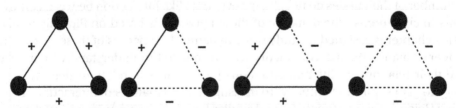

FIG. 1 Four possible states of triadic relations based on Heider's balance theory.

$$H = \frac{-1}{\binom{N}{3}} \sum S_{ij} S_{ik} S_{jk} \qquad (1)$$

According to this definition, energy of the balanced and unbalanced triangles of relations are, respectively, referred to as -1 and 1 energies. The total energy of the system is obtained by subtracting the number of unbalanced triangles from the number of balanced triangles. To have the energy in the range of $[1, -1]$, it is normalized by the total number of triangles. By evolution of relations to reduce tension in the whole of the system, the energy decreases to reach -1.

2.3 Evolving Networks

For a three-node system which shapes a triangle, a balanced triangle is formed only when the product of the values assigned for the links between each pair of nodes has a positive sign. The tendency is to have a balanced triangle, which implies that as the network evolves, the unbalanced triangles eventually become balanced. A study on the dynamics of social networks, considering balance theory, traces back to Antal et al. [29]. They proposed two models based on the evolution of links for fully connected networks: local triad dynamics (LTD) and constrained triad dynamics (CTD).

In the LTD model, in each time step, a triad is chosen randomly. If it is a balanced configuration nothing is changed. If the triad is unbalanced, on a randomly chosen of links, unbalanced triad modifies to a balanced one, as shown in Fig. 2. Modifying this unbalanced triad may lead to produce some unbalanced triads that share a link with the target triad. In the next steps, these triads will evolve and like a cascade all the triads will become balanced. It is shown that depending on the value of p, the final state of a society based on this model is "paradise" or "bipolar" states. Paradise state denotes a society in which all the relations are positive; bipolar state indicates a society with two groups that the relations inside each group are positive and the relations between groups are negative.

In the CTD model, in each time step, a link S_{ij} is chosen randomly. Then, individual i changes its relation with individual j if flipping their relation reduces the number of unbalanced triads or in other words it reduces the total energy in the whole system. Even if local energy for individual i increases during this process, the change is accepted. Therefore,

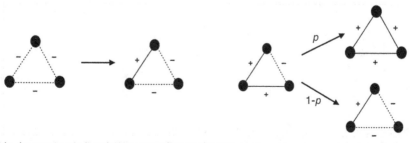

FIG. 2 Possible changes in triadic relations according to the LTD model.

evolution of links between each two nodes i and j is calculated by the sum over all pairs of links of that nodes with the thirds nodes k:

$$\frac{d}{dt}S_{ij} \equiv \sum_{j=1} S_{ik}S_{jk} \tag{2}$$

Links that do not change energy are flipped by probability 0.5. In the evolution of the society, according to this model two conditions happen at final states. If the process guides the system to its minimum global energy state, all triangles become balanced. In balanced state, the system could either attain "paradise" or "bipolar" states. Sometimes the system traps in local minimum energies or pseudo-stable states which are called "jammed" states. In jammed states, some triangles are still unbalanced, but changing of any link would increase the energy in the system.

3 Pseudo-Paths Toward Jammed States

It is worth noting that in the early stages, if dynamic starts from a totally antagonistic system, many links have the possibility to be changed. It seems that jammed states are not some sudden event that appears suddenly over the evolution of the system. Fig. 3 shows a schematic view of a system which evolves according to the CTD model. Light gray lines and their separations represent the various paths a system can go through. Dark gray circles refer to the jammed states and balanced states are shown at the end of the evolutions. The magnified part of the figure shows what happens near a jammed state. Evolution is

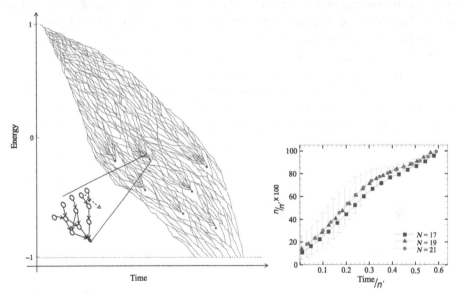

FIG. 3 The left panel represents a schematic view of the network evolution [14]. The right panel shows the percentage of links that are not possible to change as a system get close to jammed states.

shown from left to right during which the energy changes from 1 to −1. Changes in color of lines from light gray to dark gray show this process. In the dark gray line zone, any change guides the system toward jammed states which are shown by dark gray dots. As energy goes down, the number of allowable links decreases especially in the vicinity of local or global minimum energy states (see the right panel of the figure). In this panel, the results are shown for different sizes of networks (*N* refers to the number of nodes) and curves show the percentage of links that cannot be changed (*n*) to the total number of links (*n*′). Curves indicate the average values over all the appeared jammed states. By decreasing the number of possible links toward local minimum energy states, some paths seem to appear. These are called the pseudo-path toward jammed states. An interesting question can be how could one detect these paths in advance to encounter jammed states.

Although the Hamiltonian concept provides a platform to more easily trace the dynamic of the system [28, 30], because of the diversity of possible paths, it could draw a clear picture of the steps. One solution is to introduce an indicator to uncover the emergence of hidden pseudo-deterministic paths toward jammed states. Most of the times, when we talk about a system with high interaction among its members, the concept of collective behavior comes into play [13, 19, 30–32]. In fact, in the evolution of a system based on the CTD model, collectivity can be seen in the formation of communities [28]. Marvel et al. [28] showed that jammed states occur below the zero energy and there is a relation between the value of energy and the number of communities at jammed states. This means that at higher values of energy, the system is more complex and the number of communities is higher. It is shown that near the balanced and jammed states that communities form, participation of individuals increases [14].

3.1 Discussion

3.1.1 Role of Individuals' Participation

According to the Heider balance theory and CTD model, communities are a collection of agents that are mostly friend with each other and enemy with members of other groups. Now, we know that by the evolution of the society, paths toward the minimum tension states are selected by the system. And we are aware that some pseudo-paths guide the system to jammed or balanced states. It is shown that the collective behavior of individuals is responsible for this process [14]. In fact, in the vicinity of these special states, the participation of all individuals goes up. It is shown that there is a difference between the concept of participation and community [14]. The concept of community refers to the group of individuals that mostly communicate with each other or have the same attitude in the society. But the concept of participation refers to a situation that all the members have a mutual concern.

It is shown that on the paths toward jammed states, further away from jammed states, the possibility to avoid encountering to jammed states increases [14]. In fact, there is a characteristic length that greater than that the evolution is random and roots may not end up to a jammed state. It can be shown that in the vicinity of jammed states, the participation of individuals start to increase. This fact can be used as an indicator to detect these states in advance. Therefore, participation is directly proportional to the formation of communities and is a sign of community formation.

3.1.2 Inverse Participation Ratio

Regarding detecting jammed states in advance, it is worthy to study the behavior of participation ratio of the system over its evolution. This method uses eigenvalues and eigenvectors of the interaction matrix. Eigenvectors are usually used to detect communities [33–37]. It is also used as a measure of individual's participation [14]. In a network with two communities, positive and negative components of the eigenvector corresponding to the largest eigenvalue can be used to detect those communities [36, 38]. But when the number of communities exceeds two, we need to look at the patterns in other eigenvectors [36, 39]. In the case of detecting communities, only the sign of the components is important. But in the case of calculating node's participations, it is the magnitude of the components that is important. The greater value of eigenvector components refers to the greater participation of nodes. The name of the method is inverse participation ratio (IPR) and is obtained by [40–42].

$$IPR = \frac{1}{\sum_{i=1}^{N} V_i^4} \tag{3}$$

where V_i is the i component of the eigenvector. As the power is 4, the value of IPR only depends on the value of V_i either positive or negative. The minimum IPR is when except one component, all the others are zero. By deviation of the value of components from zero, IPR starts to increase. Maximum value of it is equal to the size of the system (number of nodes). The next step is to define eigenvalues that contain information.

As the network here is fully connected and undirected, the interaction matrix is symmetric and the diagonal components are zero. When a matrix is symmetric, its eigenvalues and eigenvectors are real. To find out the effective eigenvalues, it is worthy to compare eigenvalues of the jammed states with eigenvalues of an assembly of random networks with positive and negative links. As the random networks hardly possess any information, any deviation from a bulk random behavior contains a useful information [43]. Fig. 4 shows the results of this comparison for jammed states of networks with 35 nodes. The dark gray squares represent the eigenvalues of jammed states and the gray circles inside the black square indicate the eigenvalues random networks. To make the value of a jammed state more clear, one of them is shown in light gray squares. Eigenvalues of the other jammed states are also the same. From the figure it is clear that three of them are out of the black square, the lowest eigenvalue (λ_{min}), the greatest (λ_{max}), and the second greatest (λ_{max-1}) eigenvalues.

Hence, it is enough to study the evolution of IPR for these three eigenvalues (Fig. 5). From the figure, it is obvious that near the jammed states, the behavior of IPR is different from the balanced states and this deviation is more clear in λ_{min}. In the greatest

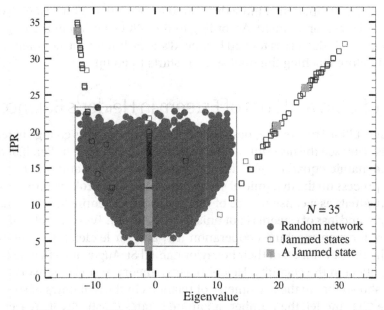

FIG. 4 The inverse participation ratio (IPR) vs the eigenvalues for jammed and random states [14]. The number of nodes in the networks is 35.

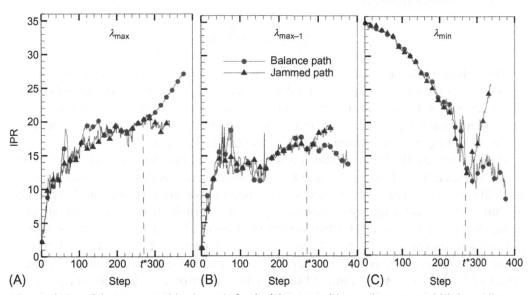

FIG. 5 Evolution of the inverse participation ratio for the (A) greatest, (B) second greatest, and (C) the smallest eigenvalues for a path toward jammed state and balanced state [14].

eigenvalue, λ_{max}, participation of individuals increase toward the final state irrespective of whether it is balanced or jammed. According to the IPR evolution in the λ_{min}, the participation of individuals decreases toward balanced states, but for the jammed states from a time interval before reaching the final state, it starts to go up.

4 Effect of Gain and Loss of Esteem in Heider's Balance Theory

A few years ago, Elliot Aronson [44] describes the effect of relations change in terms of gain and loss of esteem; see the description and literatures in Ref. [45]. In Ref. [20] by adding a term to the dynamic equation of Heider's balance theory, the authors investigated the effect of this process on the dynamic of social networks. They broke symmetry of relations between individuals as a consequence of this condition. Scientific discussions about the concept of gain and loss of esteem is not finished yet [46–50]. Two examples of considering this effect are for man-machine cooperation [51] and for leadership evaluations which depend on the time evolution of their behavior named St. Augustine effect [52]. It is worth studying the effect in the cognitive Heider balance theory of social networks. In the next section, it is shown that in the asymmetry of relations in the dynamics of social networks based on the CTD model, the number of jammed states drastically increases.

4.1 Balanced States

The simplest equation that can explain the dynamics of relations in a network based on the Heider balance theory is

$$\frac{dx_{ij}}{dt} = \Theta(x_{ij})\Theta(1 - x_{ij})\sum_{k}^{N-2} x_{ik}x_{kj} \tag{4}$$

The stability condition of a system in its final state is where all the links are $|x_{ij}| \approx 1$ and $x_{ij}\, dx_{ij}/dt > 0$; either x_{ij} increases to 1 or it decreases to -1. Fig. 5 represents a jammed state, where positive links are within a triad, and negative links are between different triads. Considering that products of Θ functions is one, the r.h.s. in Eq. (4) is +7 in positive links, and is -1 in negative links; therefore this configuration is stable.

We now explain the jammed states where relations are asymmetric [20, 53]. Choose node i and set all of its links $x_{ij} = 1$, and $x_{ji} = -1$ or vice versa. As this node can be selected in N different ways, we have $2N$ such states. Then choose another node and divide the remaining $N-1$ nodes into two nonempty groups, internally friend and mutually enemies. This state is balanced. The division can be done in $2^{N-2} - 1$ ways. Relations of node i with others are either $x_{ij} = 1, x_{ki} = 1, x_{ji} = -1, x_{ik} = -1$, or $x_{ij} = -1, x_{ki} = -1, x_{ji} = 1, x_{ik} = 1$. These two options mean that there are $2N(2^{N-2} - 1)$ jammed states and in summary, there are $2N + 2N(2^{N-2} - 1) = N2^{N-1}$ jammed states. The stability of these jammed states can be verified analytically. Consider part I includes a configuration of $N1$ nodes, part II includes $N2$ nodes, and node i is $i = 1$; so, $N = N1 + N2 + 1$. This system is balanced except node 1. Consider for $j \in$ I and $k \in$ II one has $x_{j1} = x_{1k} = 1$ and $x_{1j} = x_{k1} = -1$, as shown in Fig. 6. Stability can be checked by calculating the r.h.s. of Eq. (4).

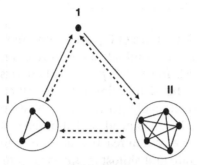

FIG. 6 A jammed state configuration by two internally friend and mutually hostile groups of nodes I, II, and also node 1 with asymmetric relations [20]. The *solid lines* represent positive or friendly relations and the *dashed lines* show negative or hostile relations.

There are also 2^{N-1} balanced states, including paradise states where all the links are positive. This means that the frequency of jammed states is at least N orders larger than the frequency of balanced states. The phrase "at least" is because numerical calculations are done for $N=5$. In larger systems in which we would see even more complex configurations, this number may increase.

4.2 Differential Equation

By adding the effect of gain and lose of steam into the conventional master equation of Heider balance, the time derivative of link x_{ij} varies as

$$\frac{dx_{ij}}{dt} = \left(1 - x_{ij}^2\right)\left[\alpha(x_{ji} - x_{ij}) + \frac{1-\alpha}{N-2}\sum_k^{N-2} x_{ik}x_{kj} + \gamma\frac{dx_{ij}}{dt}\right] \tag{5}$$

where α measures the intensity of the direct reciprocity process for the relations between i and j [20]. So, $1-\alpha$ is a measure of intensity of Heider's balance theory. Here α controls the rate of the two processes. In the conventional equation, the third term is zero. Coefficient γ measures the importance of x_{ij} dynamics and is kept independent of α. The role of prefactor $1-x^2$ is similar to the product of Θ functions in Eq. (4) to keep relations in the range $(-1, 1)$. After a short algebra process, one can obtain [20]

$$\frac{dx_{ij}}{dt} = \frac{\left(1 - x_{ij}^2\right)}{1 - \gamma^2\left(1 - x_{ij}^2\right)\left(1 - x_{ji}^2\right)}\left[\alpha\left(1 - \gamma\left(1 - x_{ij}^2\right)\right)(x_{ji} - x_{ij}) + \frac{1-\alpha}{N-2}\sum_k^{N-2}\left[x_{ik}x_{kj} + \gamma\left(1 - x_{ji}^2\right)x_{jk}x_{ki}\right]\right] \tag{6}$$

One can note that close to the stationary state, where $|x_{ij}| \approx 1$, the equation reduces to the situation that $\gamma=0$. Yet, as shown in Ref. [53], the direct reciprocity mechanism is to reduce the asymmetry of the relations before encountering jammed states. If the α coefficient is small, the process is slow and the Heider balance configuration is not attained.

4.3 Discussion

It is worthwhile to see the stable states of Eq. (6) for different values of α and γ as well as different probability distributions of initial values of relations. Distributions are chosen to be uniform and their range is in $(p-0.3, p+0.3)$, where p is the other parameter of the simulations and the width of the distribution is 0.6 for all calculations which guarantee asymmetries of relations. In each set of $x_{ij}(t)$, $i, j = 1, ..., N$, system experiences three phases of different stable states: paradise, balanced, and jammed states. After limited time steps, relations get close to ± 1 and the system reach a saturated situation. Exceptions from this process happens but is very rare and almost happens at $\alpha = 0$ [54]. These cases eliminate from the realizations.

In Fig. 7, simulations are performed for networks with $N = 20$ nodes, equivalent to have 380 equations of motion. The aim here is to draw a phase diagram of different final states for various sets of parameters, that is, p, α, and γ [55]. The number of realizations for each set of parameters is 200. The number of states in each phase is counted. Lines between

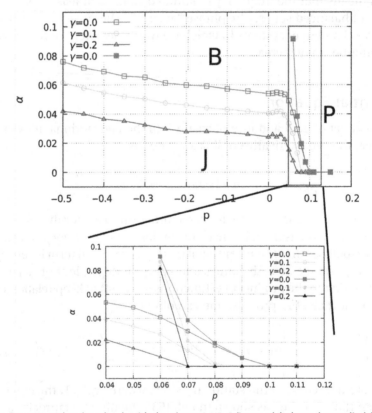

FIG. 7 The phase diagram on the plane (p, α), with the phases J, HB, P (jammed, balanced, paradise) (*upper plot*), and an inset (*lower plot*) [20]. The lines are for $\gamma = 0.0$, 0.1, and 0.2. Lines with filled symbols represent phase transition from balanced to paradise states and open symbols indicate phase transition from jammed to balanced states.

each two phases show the situation that the number of final states in the phases are the same. If we consider the value of α on the lines as αc; for $\alpha > \alpha c$, most of the final states are balanced ones and for $\alpha < \alpha c$ most of the final states are jammed states. This behavior depends on the value of p and for $p > 0.06$, the paradise states are dominant. Note that as γ coefficient increases, the phase transition from jammed states to balanced states appear in lower values of αc. Increasing γ has a small effect on phase transition from balanced states to paradise states by a slight shift into smaller values of p.

Empirically, relations are not mostly symmetric [53, 55] and according to the results of this work, in the case of asymmetric relations, many of the statuary states are jammed states with a few unbalanced triads. Recall that in the case of symmetric relations, jammed states are not generic. In Eq. (5), the term proportional to γ produces another mechanism to even the asymmetric relations out, because an increase of x_{ij} is correlated with an increase of x_{ji}. In the presence of this term, the asymmetry is removed by two mechanisms and not only by one. Therefore, to gain the balance, a smaller value of α is necessary; hence, the critical value of α decreases with γ, as shown in Fig. 7.

5 Glassy States in Aging Social Networks

"Yesterdays' friend (enemy) rarely becomes tomorrows' enemy (friend)." It seems that the history of relations play a pivotal role in the dynamic of social networks. As human beings have the ability to remember sequence of events even unconsciously, some concepts emerge over time in social interactions such as commitment and allegiance. These concepts lead to the formation of cultural communities, alliances, and political communities [56–58]. In terms of psychology, the more time a relation do not change over time, the more powerful the commitment is. There are some people, like family members, business partners or even friends (or enemies), with whom most persons have no tendency to change their relationships at least for a long time. History of relations can be a good reason for the resistance of changing that can be appeared by two parameters: "weight of links" and "age of links." In general terms, it depends on the weight or age of links, modifying or breaking them up among individuals eventually become difficult. In fact, young relations have more chance to change than aged ones. Some works have tried to mimic the strength of relationships through some models that consider a lifetime of relations and their emotional intensity [59, 60]. Fig. 8 shows that social networks are very complex with some important parameters for links.

Thanks to our ability to collect empirical data about human interactions, it is currently shown that social interactions act as a series of correlated events. Each decision depends on the local environment and previous decisions. In this context, based on the evolution of in-cluster and out-cluster relations [32, 61–64], scientists have found that the heterogeneous dynamics are a consequence of memory. Some examples of these efforts are studies on face-to-face contacts [65], cellphone users [66], rumor-spreading processes [67, 68], individuals' web browsing patterns [69], Boolean networks [70], or prisoner's dilemma

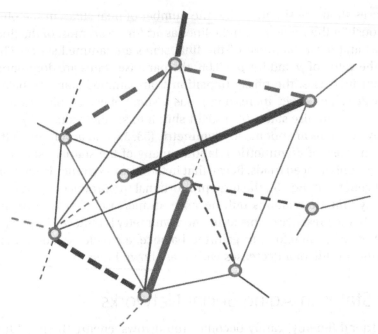

FIG. 8 In social network dynamics, links can represent various information such as age, strength, and type of relations [60]. This figure shows part of a network. Links indicate two types of relations for instance, friendship and animosity are denoted by *solid* and *dashed lines*. Gradients of age are displayed by colors from *light gray* (young) to *dark gray* (old) and line thickness represents the weight of links.

games [71, 72]. Age of links decreases the probability of relation changes [73]. The Gallos et al. [74] observations on real social networks explored that younger persons have less closure in their relations by getting elder. In terms of modeling the social network dynamics, it is useful to develop models to understand how memory or history has global consequences on social system evolutions.

According to the nature of memory aspects in real systems [75–77], authors at [60] mimicked the aging process of social relations using a kernel function in which age of the relationships grows from past to present like a power law. They generalized the order of the derivative in the conventional equation of balance theory [17, 78–80] to a noninteger order. Their results showed the emergence of some long-lived states, named *glassy* states. It can be informative to compare the concepts of glassy and jammed states. Although both of them are not global minimum tension states, they have a characteristic that makes them distinguishable. According to the tension-reduction process, social networks tend to move toward lower tension or energy levels and reach the global minimum tension states either paradise or bipolar states. Over this evolution, the system can be trapped in some local minimum tension states called jammed states. In that situation, there is no possibility to alter a relation and reduce tension or energy within the system. It has been shown that jammed states occur with negative energies. In contrast, in glassy states, individuals resist to modify the quality of their relations to reduce the stress that keep the system in unstable states. Although there are some links that changing them can guide the system toward lower tension states, thanks to the resistance of aged links to change, the probability of change is low.

5.1 Evolution of Aging Networks

Considering the CTD model, to study the effects of memory on the evolution of a social network, the following assumptions are needed: although changes in relationships guide the system toward lower tension states, due to a history of relations, individuals show less tendency to alter their connections. This approach results in aged networks. In previous studies, the authors did not consider any difference between age and strength of relations in terms of weighted networks [81–83].

To study the effects of past events on the present ones, some works (e.g., Refs. [84–88]) have studied the fractional derivatives or integrals as a generalization of ordinary differential integral equations to non-integer ones. A similar approach of the fractional calculus is considered for the conventional balance differential equation [60]:

$$ {}_{t_0}^{c}D_t^{\alpha} \equiv \sum_{j=1} x_{kj}(t)x_{ji}(t) \tag{7} $$

The left-hand side of this equation is Caputo fractional differential operator by order α [89], where $0 < \alpha < 1$. The fractional order of derivation, α, represents the significance of the memory. Where $\alpha = 1$ refers to the nonmemory balance theory master equation [17, 78–80]. Eq. (7) can be written in the form of Volterra integral [90, 91]:

$$ x_{ki} = x_{ki0} + \frac{1}{\Gamma(\alpha)} \int_{t_0}^{t} dt'(t-t')^{(\alpha-1)} \left[\sum_{l=1} x_{kl}(t')x_{li}(t') \right] \tag{8} $$

This form of scale invariant time-dependent kernel lets us to consider historical effects. In fact, due to the time lag-dependency nature of these operators, past events appear as "non-Markovian" process on the dynamics. This mathematical approach practically means that past events that are further from the present less contribute to the current state.

The authors used the predictor-corrector algorithm [91–93] to find a numerical solution for the integral of Eq. (8). They used the product rectangle rule [91] in which time is divided into equispaced grids $t_j = t_0 + h_j$ with equal space h. Therefore, Eq. (8) becomes [60].

$$ x_{ki} = x_{ki0} + h^{\alpha} \sum_{j=0}^{n-1} b_{n-j-1} \left[\sum_{l=1} (x_{kl}x_{li})_j \right] \tag{9} $$

In this equation, $b_n = \frac{(n+1)^{\alpha} - (n)^{\alpha}}{\Gamma(\alpha+1)}$ coefficients control the effect of the past events.

5.2 Discussion

5.2.1 Simulation Model

In the simulation part [60], the authors worked with networks that are fully connected and include N nodes where all individuals are connected with each other. They start from an antagonistic network that all the links are -1. During the evolution at each time step, links must fulfill two conditions. The first condition: links are selected randomly and are allowed to switch their signs if the number of unbalanced triangles is reduced. The second condition: there is a competition between inclination of a link to reduce tension and the insistence to keep the past relation because of the memory effect. To do this, a random number is chosen from a uniform distribution over $(0, 1)$. If the number is less than $A_{ij}^{(\alpha-1)}$, the sign of the link (s_{ij}) switches into its opposite (± 1). The magnitude of A_{ij} is equivalent to the link's age, where α shows the strength of memory on relations. The value of α changes over $(0, 1)$. Lower values of A_{ij} or higher values of α lead to higher probability of changing a link. In any N steps, the age of links (A_{ij}) that do not change increases by one unit. N is the number of nodes. According to these conditions, the system in various paths toward reaching minimum tension states stays unchanged for some time intervals. If the system stays static for a period of order of the number of links, it traps in some states called *glassy* states.

5.2.2 Formation of Aged Networks

In the conventional Heider balance theory, the dynamics is a Markovian process in which past incidents play no role in rearrangements of link. Thus, when individuals decide to modify their relations, independent from past, they only check the quality of relations at the present moment. Converting the conventional time equation of balance theory [53, 94] to the fractional form allows adding memory effects. Thus, interactions become time dependent and the system experiences a non-Markovian process. Considering fractional space only rescales the evolution time and has no impact on the phase space and the dynamics of the system. In other words, memory prolongs time intervals between changes become longer. Fig. 9 illustrates the largest time interval between changes in various realizations of network dynamics before reaching a balanced state. This figure shows the results of 10,000 realizations for networks with 21 nodes and $\alpha = 0.7$. In the study of network dynamics based on the CTD model, Antal et al. [29] showed that systems move through various paths to reach stable states either paradise or bipolar and that all triangles are balanced. They also showed that there are some local minima called jammed states in which the system is divided into several communities (>2).

Adding memory effect into the CTD model [60] leads to the formation of aged networks. Depending on the significance of memory which shows with α, links can gain age with probability $A^{(\alpha-1)}$. The larger value of α shows the less effects of past events on individuals' decision and $\alpha = 1$ reflects a memoryless system. In the presence of memory, before reaching global or local equilibrium, the system may be trapped into glassy states, where individuals do not forget their long-lasting friendships or animosities. For networks with 21 nodes and $\alpha = 0.7$, Fig. 8 illustrates the longest periods that a system remains unchanged. The number of realizations is 10,000. These time intervals follow a

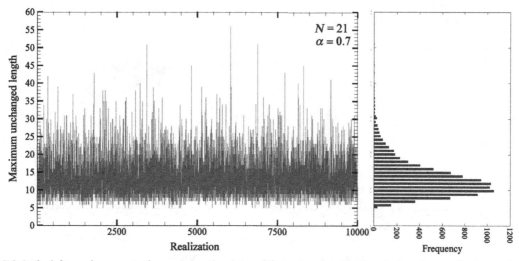

FIG. 9 The left panel represents the maximum time interval that networks with 21 nodes in various realizations resist against changes [60]. The left panel shows the frequency of the maximum time intervals which follow a Poisson distribution.

Poisson distribution function. Deviation of distribution from the normal one shows inhomogeneity in the time intervals. As α decreases, time intervals that the system do not change increases.

Fig. 10 illustrates frequency of final states based on the energy and the mean value links, Where networks have 45 nodes and simulation is repeated for 10,000 realizations. In lower values of α, the system in all realizations is trapped in glassy states. Interestingly, these glassy states can occur even in positive energies, which represent an instability within the system. In these cases, systems tolerate high tension conditions. In larger values of α, the system has more flexibility and biased relationships form later, let the system has the opportunity to reach lower energy states. The bottom-right panel of this figure displays the number of glassy states versus the number of realizations in different values of α. Accordingly, when the members of a society are more flexible, the chance to reach lower energy states increases. In contrast, when a society contains biased or stubborn people, it becomes stuck in intermediate long-lived states.

6 Conclusion

In social networks based on the Heider balanced theory, interactions among individuals are governed by the tension reduction mechanism. During the evolution of societies, they get stuck in stable states either there are no tension, called balanced states or a few tension remains in the system, called jammed states. In jammed states, tension cannot be reduced except with an external force. It seems that the number of possible changeable links near the jammed states decreases drastically. It is shown that the participation of individuals is responsible for the emergence of pseudo-paths toward reaching jammed states. In this

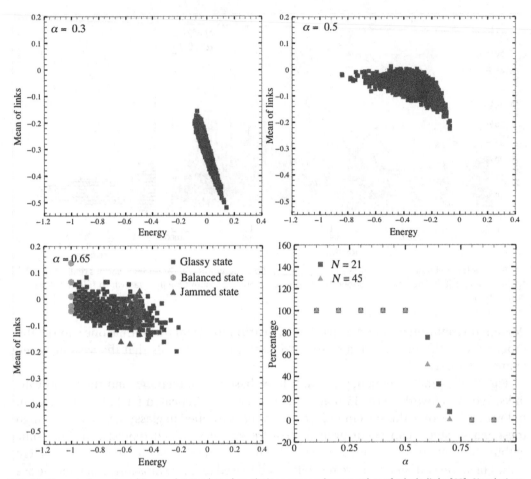

FIG. 10 Glassy, balanced, and jammed states based on their energy and mean value of whole links [60]. Simulations are done for 10,000 realizations networks with 45 nodes and for different values of α. There are a phase transition in the density of glassy states to balanced states at about $\alpha \sim 0.6$.

regard, IPR can be used as an indicator to recognize these states in advance. However, in a system with symmetric relations, the number of jammed states is rare, breaking symmetry, which is more realistic, increasing the frequency of the jammed states. Introducing the effect of gain and loss of esteem into the time evolution equations of social relations gives rise to asymmetric relations. The other important and influential process on the evolution of relations in social networks is the ability of human beings to remember the sequence of events. In real systems, most of the links have a limited lifetime which can be due to feedbacks, internal or external forces and controls. Aging process of links leads to the emergence of aged networks that is a good language to describe the dynamic of many temporal networks. It is shown that in the dynamic of aging social networks, some long-life states appear and that, however changing of relations can reduce tension, there is no inclination in old relations to be changed.

References

[1] L. Leydesdorff, Is society a self-organizing system? Journal of Social and Evolutionary Systems 16 (1993) 331–349.

[2] R. Hegselmann, Thomas C. Schelling and James M. Sakoda: the intellectual, technical, and social history of a model, J. Artif. Soc. Soc. Simul. 20 (3) (2017).

[3] F. Heider, Attitudes and cognitive organization, J. Psychol. 21 (1946) 107–112. F. Heider, The Psychology of Interpersonal Relations, Wiley, New York, 1958.

[4] F. Odella, Technology studies and the sociological debate on monitoring of social interactions, Int. J. Ambient Comput. Intell. 7 (1) (2016) 1–26. Web 3 February 2018, https://doi.org/10.4018/IJACI.2016010101.

[5] T.M. Newcomb, R.H. Turner, P.E. Converse, Social Psychology: The Study of Human Interaction, Holt, Rinehart and Winston, New York, NY, 1965.

[6] P. Roy, N. Patra, A. Mukherjee, A.S. Ashour, N. Dey, S.P. Biswas, Intelligent traffic monitoring system through auto and manual controlling using PC and android application, Applied Video Processing in Surveillance and Monitoring Systems, IGI Global, 2017, pp. 244–262. Web 3 February 2018, https://doi.org/10.4018/978-1-5225-1022-2.ch011.

[7] A. Mukherjee, N. Dey, N. Kausar, A.S. Ashour, R. Taiar, A.E. Hassanien, A disaster management specific mobility model for flying ad-hoc network, Int. J. Rough Sets Data Anal. 3 (3) (2016) 72–103. Web 3 February 2018, https://doi.org/10.4018/IJRSDA.2016070106.

[8] S.P. Biswas, P. Roy, N. Patra, A. Mukherjee, N. Dey, Intelligent traffic monitoring system, S. Satapathy, K. Raju, J. Mandal, V. Bhateja (Eds.), Proceedings of the Second International Conference on Computer and Communication Technologies, Advances in Intelligent Systems and Computing, vol. 380, Springer, New Delhi, 2016.

[9] W. Yang, X. Wang, X. Song, Y. Yang, S. Patnaik, Design of Intelligent Transportation System Supported by New Generation Wireless Communication Technology, Int. J. Ambient Comput. Intell. 9 (1) (2018) 78–94. Web 3 February 2018, https://doi.org/10.4018/IJACI.2018010105.

[10] K. Belgharbi, M. Boufaida, Using event B to specify context awareness for service discovery in pervasive environments, Int. J. Ambient Comput. Intell. 8 (1) (2017) 1–22. Web 3 February 2018, https://doi.org/10.4018/IJACI.2017010101.

[11] S. Tyagi, S. Som, Q.P. Rana, Trust based Dynamic Multicast Group Routing Ensuring Reliability for Ubiquitous Environment in MANETs, Int. J. Ambient Comput. Intell. 8 (1) (2017) 70–97. Web 3 February 2018, https://doi.org/10.4018/IJACI.2017010104.

[12] M. Ausloos, M. Saeedian, T. Jamali, S. Vasheghani Farahanid, G.R. Jafari, Physica A Stat. Mech. Appl. (2017) 267–275.

[13] R. Albert, A.-L. Barabasi, Topology of evolving networks: local events and universality, Phys. Rev. Lett. 85 (2000) 5234–5237.

[14] L. Hedayatifar, F. Hassanibesheli, A.H. Shirazi, S. Vasheghani Farahani, G.R. Jafari, Pseudo paths towards minimum energy states in network dynamics, Physica A 483 (2017) 109–116.

[15] W.W. Zachary, An information flow model for conflict and fission in small groups, J. Anthropol. Res. 33 (1977) 452–473.

[16] M. Moore, An international application of Heider's balance theory, Eur. J. Soc. Psychol. 8 (1978) 401–405. M. Moore, Structural balance and international relations, Eur. J. Soc. Psycho. 9 (1979) 323–326.

[17] S.A. Marvel, J. Kleinberg, R.D. Kleinberg, S.H. Strogatz, Continuous time model of structural balance, Proc. Natl. Acad. Sci. U.S.A. 108 (2011) 1771–1776.

[18] K. Kuakowski, P. Gawroski, P. Gronek, The Heider balance—a continuous approach, Int. J. Modern Phys. C16 (2005) 707–716.

[19] J. Leskovec, D. Huttenlocher, J. Kleinberg, in: Predicting positive and negative links in online social networks, Proceedings of WWW'2010, ACM Press, New York, 2010.

[20] F. Hassanibesheli, L. Hedayatifar, P. Gawroski, M. Stojkow, D. Zuchowska Skiba, K. Kuakowski, Gain and loss of esteem, direct reciprocity and Heider balance, Physica A 468 (2017) 334–339.

[21] M. Szell, R. Lambiotte, S. Thurner, Multirelational organization of large scale social networks in an online world, Proc. Natl. Acad. Sci. U.S.A. 107 (2010) 13636.

[22] X. Zheng, D. Zeng, F.-Y. Wang, Social balance in signed networks, Inf. Syst. Front. (2014) 1–9.

[23] D. Cartwright, F. Harary, Structure balance: a generalization of Heider's theory, Psychol. Rev. 63 (1956) 277–293.

[24] P. Esmailian, S.E. Abtahi, M. Jalili, Mesoscopic analysis of online social networks: the role of negative ties, Phys. Rev. E 90 (2014).

[25] J. Kunegis, A. Lommatzsch, C. Bauckhage, in: The slashdot zoo: mining a social network with negative edges, Proceedings of the 18th International Conference on World Wide Web—WWW 2009, Madrid, Spain, 20–24 April; Association for Computing Machinery: New York, NY, USA, 2009, pp. 741–750.

[26] P. Doreian, Evolution of Human Signed Networks, Metodol. Zv. 1 (2004) 277–293.

[27] R.V. Guha, R. Kumar, P. Raghavan, A. Tomkins, in: Propagation of trust and distrust, Proceedings of the 13th International Conference on World Wide Web, New York, NY, USA, 17–20 May, 2004.

[28] S.A. Marvel, J. Kleinberg, S.H. Strogatz, The energy landscape of social balance, Phys. Rev. Lett. 103 (2009) 198701.

[29] T. Antal, P. Krapivsky, S. Redner, Social balance on networks: the dynamics of friendship and enmity, Physica D 224 (2006) 130–136.

[30] Z. Qian-Ming, L. Linyuan, W. Wen-Qiang, Z. Yu-Xiao, Z. Tao, Potential theory for directed networks, PLoS One 8 (2) (2013).

[31] A. Rijt, The micro-macro link for the theory of structural balance, J. Math. Sociol. 35 (2011) 94–113.

[32] A. Shirazi, A. Namaki, A.A. Roohi, G.R. Jafari, Transparency effect in the emergence of monopolies in social networks, J. Artif. Soc. Soc. Simul. 16 (1) (2013) 1–10.

[33] M.E.J. Newman, Finding community structure in networks using the eigenvectors of matrices, Phys. Rev. E 74 (2006).

[34] M.E.J. Newman, Modularity and community structure in networks, Proc. Natl. Acad. Sci. U.S.A. 103 (2006) 8577–8582.

[35] J. Kunegis, S. Schmidt, A. Lommatzsch, J. Lernery, E.W. De Luca, S. Albayrak, in: Spectral analysis of signed graphs for clustering, prediction and visualization, Siam Conference on Data Mining 2010, Society for Industrial and Applied Mathematics, Philadelphia, 2010, pp. 559–570.

[36] A. Faqeeh, K. Samani Aghababaei, Community detection based on the 'clumpiness' matrix in complex networks, Physica A 391 (7) (2012) 2463–2474.

[37] F. Krzakala, C. Moore, E. Mossel, J. Neeman, A. Sly, L. Zdeborová, P. Zhang, Spectral redemption in clustering sparse networks, Proc. Natl. Acad. Sci. U.S.A. 110 (52) (2013) 20935–20940.

[38] A. Capocci, V. Servedio, G. Caldarelli, F. Colaiori, Community detection in large networks, Lect. Notes Comput. Sci. 3243 (2004) 181–187.

[39] L. Donetti, M.A. Munoz, Detecting network communities: a new systematic and efficient algorithm, J. Stat. Mech. Theory Exp. (2004). 10012.

[40] F. Slanina, Z. Konopásek, Eigenvector localization as a tool to study small communities in online social networks, Adv. Comput. Syst. 13 (2010) 699.

[41] A. Namaki, R. Raei, G.R. Jafari, Comparing Tehran stock exchange as an emerging market with mature market by Random Matrix Approach, Int. J. Modern Phys. C 22 (4) (2011) 371–383.

[42] G. Jafari, A.H. Shirazi, A. Namaki, R. Raei, Coupled time series analysis: methods and applications, Comput. Sci. Eng. 13 (6) (2011) 84–89.

[43] A. Namaki, G.R. Jafari, R. Raei, Comparing the structure of an emerging market with a mature one under global perturbation, Physica A 390 (17) (2011) 3020–3025.

[44] E. Aronson, D. Linder, Gain and loss of esteem as determinants of interpersonal attractiveness, J. Exp. Soc. Psychol. 1 (1965) 156.

[45] E. Aronson, The Social Animal, W. H. Freeman and Co., NY, 1992.

[46] J. Tognoli, R. Keisner, Gain and loss of esteem as determinants of interpersonal attraction: a replication and extension, J. Pers. Soc. Psychol. 23 (1972) 201.

[47] J.W. Lawrence, C.S. Carver, M.F. Scheier, Velocity toward goal attainment in immediate experience as a determinant of affect, J. Appl. Soc. Psychol. 32 (2002) 788.

[48] A.T. Lehr, G. Geller, Differential effects of reciprocity and attitude-similarity across long-versus short-term mating context, J. Soc. Psychol. 146 (2006) 423.

[49] A. Filipowicz, S. Barsade, S. Melwani, Understanding emotional transitions: the interpersonal consequences of changing emotions in negotiations, J. Pers. Soc. Psychol. 101 (2011) 541.

[50] C. Reid, J.L. Davis, J.D. Green, The power of change: interpersonal attraction as a function of attitude similarity and attitude alignment, J. Soc. Psychol. 153 (2013) 700.

[51] T. Komatsu, H. Kaneko, T. Komeda, Investigating the effects of gain and loss of esteem, Lect. Notes Comput. Sci. 5744 (2009) 87.

[52] S.T. Allison, D. Eylon, J.K. Beggan, J. Bachelder, The demise of leadership: positivity and negativity biases in evaluation of dead leaders, Leadersh. Q. 20 (2009) 115.

[53] M.J. Krawczyk, M. del Castillo-Mussot, E. Hernandez-Ramirez, G.G. Naumis, K. Kułakowski, Heider balance, asymmetric ties, and gender segregation, Physica A 439 (2015) 66–74.

[54] P. Gawroński, K. Kułakowski, A numerical trip to social psychology: long-living states of cognitive dissonance, Lect. Notes Comput. Sci. 4490 (2007) 43.

[55] K.M. Carley, D. Krackhart, Cognitive inconsistencies and non-symmetric friendship, Soc. Network. 18 (1996) 1.

[56] H.S. Becker, Notes on the concept of commitment, Am. J. Sociol. 66 (1960) 32–40.

[57] S.M. Stanley, H.J. Markman, Assessing commitment in personal relationships, J. Marriage Fam. 54 (1992) 595–608.

[58] R. Clements, C.H. Swensen, Commitment to one's spouse as a predictor of marital quality among older couples, Curr. Psychol. 19 (2000) 110–119.

[59] M. Granovetter, The strength of weak ties, Am. J. Sociol. 78 (1973) 1360–1380.

[60] F. Hassanibesheli, L. Hedayatifar, H. Safdari, M. Ausloos, G.R. Jafari, Glassy states of aging social networks, Entropy 19 (2017) 246.

[61] J. Stehlé, A. Barrat, G. Bianconi, Dynamical and bursty interactions in social networks, Phys. Rev. E 81 (2010) 035101–035104.

[62] K. Zhao, J. Stehlé, G. Bianconi, A. Barrat, Social network dynamics of face-to-face interactions, Phys. Rev. E 83 (2011) 056109–056127.

[63] M. Karsai, K. Kaski, J. Kertész, Correlated Dynamics in Egocentric Communication Networks, PLoS One 7 (2012).

[64] D. Rybski, S. Buldyrev, S. Havlin, F. Liljeros, H. Makse, Communication activity in a social network: relation between long-term correlations and inter-event clustering, Sci. Rep. 2 (2012) 560. Nature Publishing Group: London.

[65] C. Vestergaard, M. Génois, A. Barrat, How memory generates heterogeneous dynamics in temporal networks, Phys. Rev. Lett. 90 (2014).

[66] M. Karsai, K. Kaski, A. Barabási, J. Kertész, Universal features of correlated bursty behavior, Sci. Rep. 2 (2012) 397. Nature Publishing Group: London.

[67] M. Karsai, N. Perra, A. Vespignani, Time varying networks and the weakness of strong ties, Sci. Rep. 4 (2014) 4001–4007. Nature Publishing Group: London.

[68] M. Saeedian, M. Khaliqi, N. Azimi-Tafreshi, G.R. Jafari, M. Ausloos, Memory effects on epidemic evolution: the susceptible-infected-recovered epidemic model, Phys. Rev. E 95 (2017).

[69] Z. Dezso, E. Almaas, A. Lukacs, B. Racz, I. Szakadat, A. Barabási, Dynamics of information access on the web, Phys. Rev. E 73 (2008) 066132–066137.

[70] E. Ebadi, M. Saeedian, M. Ausloos, G.R. Jafari, Effect of memory in non-Markovian Boolean networks illustrated with a case study: a cell cycling process, EPL 116 (2016) 30004.

[71] A. Lipowski, K. Gontarek, M. Ausloos, Statistical mechanics approach to a reinforcement learning model with memory, Physica A 388 (2009) 1849–1856.

[72] A. Szolnoki, M. Perc, G. Szabó, H.-U. Stark, Impact of aging on the evolution of cooperation in the spatial prisoner's dilemma game, Phys. Rev. E 80 (2009).

[73] H. Safdari, A.V. Chechkin, G.R. Jafari, R. Metzler, Aging scaled brownian motion, Phys. Rev. E 91 (2015).

[74] L.K. Gallos, D. Rybski, F. Liljeros, S. Havlin, H.A. Makse, How people interact in evolving online affiliation networks, Phys. Rev. X 2 (2012).

[75] V. Livina, S. Havlin, A. Bunde, Memory in the occurrence of earthquakes, Phys. Rev. Lett. 95 (2005).

[76] T. Kemuriyama, H. Ohta, Y. Sato, S. Maruyama, M. Tandai-Hiruma, A power-law distribution of inter-spike intervals in renal sympathetic nerve activity in salt-sensitive hypertension-induced chronic heart failure, Biosystems 101 (2010) 144–147.

[77] Z. Siwy, M. Ausloos, K. Ivanova, Correlation studies of open and closed states fluctuations in an ion channel: analysis of ion current through a large-conductance locust potassium channel, Phys. Rev. E 65 (2002).

[78] K. Kułakowski, Some recent attempts to simulate the Heider balance problem, Comput. Sci. Eng. 9 (2007) 80–85.

[79] K. Kułakowski, P. Gawronski, P. Gronek, The Heider balance-a continuous approach, Int. J. Mod. Phys. C 16 (2005) 707–716.

[80] C. Altafini, Dynamics of opinion forming in structurally balanced social networks, PLoS One 7 (2012).

[81] M. Saeedian, N. Azimi-Tafreshi, G.R. Jafari, J. Kertesz, Epidemic spreading on evolving signed networks, Phys. Rev. E 95 (2017).

[82] A. Barrat, M. Barthelemy, R. Pastor-Satorras, A. Vespignani, The architecture of complex weighted networks, Proc. Natl. Acad. Sci. U.S.A. 101 (2004) 3747–3752.

[83] S. Horvath, Weighted network analysis. applications in genomics and systems biology, Springer, Berlin/Heidelberg, 2011.

[84] M. Gligor, M. Ausloos, Clusters in weighted macroeconomic networks: the EU case. Introducing the overlapping index of GDP/capita fluctuation correlations, Eur. Phys. J. B 63 (2008) 533–539.

[85] I. Goychuk, Viscoelastic subdiffusion: from anomalous to normal, Phys. Rev. E 80 (2009).

[86] J.H. Jeon, R. Metzler, Fractional Brownian motion and motion governed by the fractional Langevin equation in confined geometries, Phys. Rev. E 81 (2010).

[87] B.J. West, M. Turalska, P. Grigolini, Fractional calculus ties the microscopic and macroscopic scales of complex network dynamics, New J. Phys. 17 (2015).

[88] H. Safdari, M.Z. Kamali, A.H. Shirazi, M. Khaliqi, G.R. Jafari, M. Ausloos, Fractional dynamics of network growth constrained by aging node interactions, PLoS One 11 (2016).

[89] M. Caputo, Linear Models of Dissipation whose Q is almost Frequency Independent-II, Geophys. J. R. Astron. Soc. 13 (1967) 529–539.

[90] A.A. Kilbas, H.M. Srivastava, J.J. Trujillo, Theory and Applications of Fractional Differential Equations, North-Holland Mathematics Studies, Elsevier Science, Amsterdam, The Netherlands, 2006.

[91] R. Garrappa, On linear stability of predictor-corrector algorithms for fractional differential equations, Int. J. Comput. Math. 87 (2010) 2281–2290.

[92] K. Diethelm, A.D. Freed, The FracPECE subroutine for the numerical solution of differential equations of fractional order, S. Heinzel, T. Plesser (Eds.), Forschung und Wissenschaftliches Rechnen, Gessellschaft für Wissenschaftliche Datenverarbeitung, Göttingen, Germany, 1998, pp. 57–71.

[93] C. Lubich, A stability analysis of convolution quadratures for Abel-Volterra integral equations, IMA J. Numer. Anal. 6 (1986) 87–101.

[94] V. Traag, P. Van Dooren, P. De Leenheer, Dynamical models explaining social balance and evolution of cooperation, PLoS One 8 (2013).

4

De-Anonymization Techniques for Social Networks

B.K. Tripathy

School of Computer Science and Engineering, VIT, Vellore, India

1 Introduction

A collection of nodes called actors get connected to each other through a set of connections to form a social network. The nodes may be individuals or business concerns or designated groups of individuals. The connections among the members of a social network are provided by some relations defined for the purpose and these connections bind the members. The study of social relationships beyond the study of the members makes the social networks interesting and popular among social analysts. Human beings are always interested to study the behavior of the individuals around them and inferring patterns, rules, and predicting futuristic events from the present scenario. Now that popular social networks are increasing in number and groups are formed among these social networks to keep track of the happenings around. A study of social networks can reveal the important aspects of social life. The basic purpose of forming social networks is to keep track of each other's activities and communicate information. Scientists involved in the research of communication technologies and behavioral sciences require the study of the general properties of social networks and also move on to the study of specific social networks. Instead of studying individuals, their study in a group or a part of a social network can reveal important relationships and the behavior of members as members of the communities. So, behavioral scientists focus more on the networks formed in the societies. The relationship among members may be single or multiple; it may vary from one group to another and so the study of relational information in social networks is crucial and critical in nature.

Social networks contain sensitive information of its members. The members would never like that their sensitive information be leaked in any form. So, before publishing a network for purposes like scientific study needs to be protected from the various attacks which can be made by the intruders. So, it is very much essential that care should be taken to protect the sensitive information of respondents before publishing them. Sometimes, the respondents are unaware of this disclosure to third parties due to lack of communication between the two parties involved, like in online networks [1]. This has necessitated

Social Network Analytics. https://doi.org/10.1016/B978-0-12-815458-8.00004-9

that the operators of online networks take care of privacy preservation of respondents in the form of both nodal information and the relationship between the nodes.

For business purposes and also for contracts with intermediate parties, the owners of the networks are compelled by the situation to inform the third parties about the information from the networks. Also, besides the intermediate parties, the publication of the networks helps the researchers to derive useful information through analysis of the data. Perhaps the most popular approach to achieve protection of respondents is to anonymize the networks before their publication. By anonymizing a network the privacy is protected as the information is mutilated and no fruitful conclusion about the respondents can be derived and connected to them.

1.1 Necessity of Publishing of Social Networks

There are several reasons as to why the owners of social networks would like to publish them although it is known to have the risk of sensitive information disclosure of the respondents. We mention below some of these situations/reasons for doing so.

1.1.1 Academic and Government Data Mining

At the national level, several networks are being used for fraud activities and relations which are common among participants. At the government level, several areas are under attention. These are related to social activities, diseases, geographical positions, human relationship, family welfare, sports, and financial activities. Human beings at different levels are associated with these areas. Government sections put these data on their sites, which are public. There is heavy amount of risk in these datasets for the release of information in these sites by the way privacy is not maintained. On the one hand, these data are very useful in scientific studies, but on the other hand malicious attacks on the information cannot be avoided. This necessitates the data being partially encoded or anonymized before their release. Also, academic institutions, whether government or private, have their own sites containing information about their students and teachers. Several trends in the education systems can be deduced by the study of such datasets in the form of rules for the prediction of futuristic events. Usually these datasets are not anonymized before their release. It is a fact that logging into these sites require authentication. But, several people at different levels can access these datasets, which creates security breaches. Moreover, the unique identifiers make it easy to derive information uniquely. So, some kind of anonymization in the form of removing identifiers and quasiidentifiers is very much necessary.

1.1.2 Advertising

Advertising has become an integral part of business, academics, government policies, cultural events, and many other spheres of society. In particular, the profit making concerns are bound to project their outcomes, achievements, and highlight them. As a consequence, it has become mandatory for them to disclose this information among their peers.

This may contain some sensitive information. Some of the social networks explicitly express in their agenda that they have to share some portions of the personalized information for the purpose of promotions without specifying the identity of the individuals [2].

1.1.3 Third-Party Applications

Third parties are neither directly involved with the source data nor they have any responsibility to maintain the secrecy. These parties do not take care of anonymizing the data before their release and, to be precise, this does not come under their privacy policy. It is different if they are to work on anonymized data provided by the direct parties involved. But, different third parties get different types of anonymized data. However, by aggregating these one can get some useful information. So, third parties with malicious intention have been able to get information about the members of the social networks involved even though they get anonymized information.

1.1.4 Aggregation

Information from more than one social network can be combined in a suitable manner or aggregated to derive privacy information and can hence pose threats than first-hand data released by the source. This information can be utilized by malicious parties to initiate several attacks on the respondents.

1.1.5 Other Data-Release Scenarios

The photographs taken in a group is likely to help the intruders to get the identity of a respondent from any other member in the photograph as the people in a photograph are very often likely to know each other. Thus, if a person is found in a group photograph can be traced and more often than not useful information can be obtained. So, although anonymization is mandatory on such photographs before release, it has little effect in protecting their identification.

1.2 Overview of Anonymization Techniques

The development of internet, cloud computing, and Internet of Things provides enough scope to adversaries to get electronic information about any member from a social network. The data collected by organizations can be handled in two different ways; either keeping it safe from nonmembers by not publishing the social network or by publishing it so that useful information can be deduced by scientific analysis. The first option makes the data useless partially as no scientific analysis can be performed on them. The second option has the risk of exposing sensitive information about respondents to the free access of adversaries. So, the two options are not healthy from the utility point of view and, as a consequence, some intermediate path is needed to be found out so that scientific study can be carried out and the sensitive information of respondents will remain intact. That is, even if an adversary gets some information from the published network, he/she will not be able to derive any fruitful information from them in the form of sensitive information of members. The process of social network anonymization helps in this direction. The real data is mutilated through some process so that the original data cannot be deciphered from the obtained information.

Sometimes an intruder uses his/her background knowledge about the members so that this knowledge can help him/her in possible identification of the respondents. As stated above, most of the social networks now days are through the electronic media and internet; privacy preservation has become an important component of published social networks. Sometimes the unique identifiers are removed and the quasiidentifiers are masked or randomized to achieve this.

Anonymizing social networks is to be such a way that it protects the privacy of individual users and simultaneously preserving the global network properties to study the network structure, dynamics, clustering patterns, etc.

2 De-Anonymization Techniques

De-anonymization is a process which when applied to an anonymized social network is likely to provide the original network as close as possible. It has two consequences. First, it may help the adversaries to get back the original networks so that a negative effect is attained, which is undesirable but unavoidable. Second, it will help the researchers who are developing anonymization algorithms to test the efficiency of their algorithms and make them more foolproof. We find that some of the researchers who have developed de-anonymization algorithms have claimed that their algorithms can de-anonymize any anonymized social network obtained as a result of any anonymization algorithm developed till that time.

Perhaps, the first algorithm for de-anonymization is found in Ref. [1]. It uses the following steps to complete the process:

- At first, the reason of data sharing in social networks and then state of the art is discussed. Also, this presentation includes a presentation on the risk in data sharing and back ground knowledge or supporting information, which can be used by the intruders to facilitate the process of de-anonymization.
- The relation between anonymization of nodes and privacy in social networks is discussed in a formal manner. The different forms of social network attacks the background knowledge of intruders and the resources they have in hand are used to differentiate attackers. Also, measures of the extent of privacy violations are introduced and analyzed.
- The main purpose was to put forth a reidentification algorithm which is not network specific and which does not have any assumptions other than the network structure for overlapping membership among different social networks. Large real networks in the form of Flickr and Twitter are used to explain the functionality of the proposed algorithm.

3 De-Anonymization Attacks

There are three types of attacks possible on an anonymized social network such as the following:

- Privacy breach
- Passive attack
- Active attack

3.1 Privacy Breach

Privacy breach deals with identifying nodes and learns the edge relations among them. Passive attack is to observe the released anonymized social network without interfering and is undetectable. Active attack creates some new nodes (e.g., new email accounts) and (patterned) edges among new nodes and to victim nodes. It is hard to detect.

3.2 Passive Attack

A network is studied carefully for loose points or points which can be captured under control easily. The information is gathered about a target node such that except for collecting the information no changes are made in their value or structure. Similar nodes form a group H in a network and an intruder can involve itself as a member in the community which is small and can be identified easily. The intruder can come to a secret understanding with the other $k-1$ nodes so that it becomes easier to know about other nodes which are in contact with the nodes in H. Of course, in order that such an attack can be fruitful, all the nodes in H should be aware of themselves and the connectivity inside H such that the members of H know the identity of the nodes outside their group.

3.3 Active Attack

In active attack, before releasing the anonymized network G of $n-k$ nodes an attacker does the following:

- selects a set of b-targeted users
- creates a subgraph H containing k nodes
- attaches H to the targeted nodes

Creating such a subgraph H is called structural steganography.
 After the anonymized network is released it performs:

- Find the subgraph H in the graph G
- Follow edges from H to locate b target nodes and their true location in G

Now, it is determined that all edges among these b nodes lead to the breach of privacy.
 Finding a subgraph H should have the following characteristics:

- Subgraph H must be uniquely and efficiently identifiable regardless of G
- No other subgraph $S \neq H$ in G such that S and H are isomorphic
- Subgraph H has no automorphism

3.3.1 Broad Category of Active Attacks

There are two types of active attacks proposed in Ref. [3]. These attacks are concerned with anonymizing social networks using privacy of edges. These attacks are conceived on the notion that the structure and size of the social network can be changed by the adversaries before the network is published. The set of nodes for which the intruder wants to violate their privacy is identified and by creating a few factious accounts it connects to all of the target nodes in such a manner that after the publication of the anonymized version, this structure can be easily identified. The intruder creates Sybil nodes (that is nodes which claim multiple identities in a social network), whose outgoing edges help reidentify nodes. The two categories of active attacks are as follows (Fig. 1):

- walk-based attack
- cut-based attack

In **walk-based attack**, the steps are:

- Generate subgraph $H = \{x_1, x_2, \ldots x_k\}$ with $k = \theta(\log n)$
- Link each targeted node w_i to distinct subset of nodes in H
- Create each edge within H with a probability of 0.5
- Number of compromised nodes $b = \theta((\log n)^2)$
  Construction of H can be carried out such that
- H = set of nodes X size $k = (2 + \delta) \log n$ $(\delta > 0)$
- W = set of targeted users size $b = O((\log n)^2)$
- External degree for node x_i is D_i, where $D_i \in [d_0, d_1]$ such that $d_0 \leq d_1 = O(\log n)$
- Each w_i connects to a set of nodes $N_i \subseteq X$.
- Set N_j must be of size at most $c = 3$ and are distinct across all nodes w_j.

Add arbitrary edges from H to $G - H$ to make it D_i for all x_i.
Add internal edges in H: edge $\{x_i, x_{i+1}\}$.
Add additional internal edges connecting $\{x_i, x_j\}$ with probability 0.5.

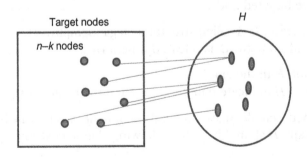

FIG. 1 Scenario

Therefore, each node x_i has total degrees of $D_i^{'}=D_i+\#$(internal edges).
In **cut-based attack**, the steps are:

Theoretical asymptotic lower bound for #new nodes: $\Omega(\sqrt{\log n})$.
Randomly generate subgraph $H=\{x_1,x_2,...x_k\}$ with $k=O(\sqrt{\log n})$.
Number of compromised nodes $b=\theta(\sqrt{\log n})$.

Construction of H can be carried out as follows:

For $W=\{w_1,w_2,...w_b\}$ is the set of targeted users,
Create $X=\{x_1,x_2,...x_k\}$ where $k=3b+3$ nodes.
Create links between each pair $\{x_i,x_j\}$ with probability $=0.5$.
Choose arbitrary b nodes $\{x_1,x_2,...x_b\}$.
Connect x_i to w_i.

A comparison between active and passive attack is shown in Table 1.

The applicability of active attack is limited to small-sized networks and cannot be applied to offline networks.

The intruder has control over the edges coming out of the nodes and has no control over other types of edges. In fact, the legal nodes are not likely to connect these Sybil nodes. So, it provides an indication to the network administrator about something fishy and hence he may anticipate about a Sybil attack [3].

The next limitation in these attacks is related to the link structure. The social networks which are online work on the principle that the connections between nodes should be both ways so that the information can be available. But, the connections from the added nodes to the existing nodes do not show up in the published network. If the size of active attacks increases, the number of Sybil nodes also increases in a huge way, which makes the process infeasible practically.

Again, the passive attacks were also considered in Ref. [3] so that a small group of nodes form an alliance among themselves so that the nodes around them (in a small neighborhood) can be identified by using the existing knowledge and structure of the nodes in the anonymized network. Again, the size of the network to which such attacks can be applied should be very small.

The algorithm proposed in Ref. [3] can be applied to larger sized networks and does not have the assumptions made above and requires a few Sybil nodes to be added.

Table 1   Comparison Between Active and Passive Attack

Passive Attack	Active attack
Attackers may not be able to identify themselves after seeing the released anonymized network	More effective. Work with high probability in any network
The victims are only those linked to the attackers	Can choose the victims
Harder to detect	Risk of being detected

The privacy protection techniques proposed so far are not that efficient as either they have some heavy assumptions like the intruders have restricted efficiency or the networks used for testing are small or synthetic ones which are different from the story when it comes to real social networks. One can take for instance the anonymization algorithm proposed in Ref. [4]. It does not take into consideration the background knowledge of the intruder. However, somewhat better architectural approaches are used in Refs. [5, 6], an idea which depends on a more sound architecture based on the server-side Facebook application.

For privacy, perhaps the most popular technique used is anonymity. In Ref. [7], the users represented by tokens drawn randomly are taken into consideration instead of the users themselves. Similarly, the approach in Ref. [2], unidentifiable graphs are generated from the information hold by the respondents and used in instead of them so that the information of social network will not be disclosed during the analysis process.

An idea where a group of p nodes are treated to be equivalent through an automated procedure such that a heavy requirement like the graph generated maps the nodes into one another is used in Ref. [5]. This heavy requirement is used in the case of very strong invaders. The concept of edge addition is used in Ref. [8] so that groups of p 1-neighborhoods are made to be similar through isomorphism to $p-1$ other 1-neighborhoods and are anonymized as a group. Here a liberal assumption is made that the attacker knows only the 1-neighborhood information of the nodes. The disadvantage in this case is that the process of addition of edges requires a high amount of nodes being used and it varies directly with the degrees of the nodes sharply.

Several conclusions are derived in Ref. [3]. We present them below.

It may be noted that k-anonymity criteria even when it is satisfied we cannot guarantee anonymity of the network as it is a syntactic property.

Another problem with these algorithms is that a lot of restrictions are imposed on the properties of the social network and also the knowledge of the attackers is supposed to be limited to a certain extent. This is a heavy restriction and in reality cannot be satisfied.

Moreover, the restriction that the information available with the intruders is to only 1-neighborhood is very strong and in most of real life situations it is much wider than this assumption.

The above observations encouraged the authors in [1] to develop an algorithm, which uses the background knowledge of the intruders to de-anonymize or reidentify the nodes after the anonymization is done by using any algorithm to this extent. This is a cyclic process as once some of the nodes are identified, more information gets available and this is added to the background knowledge of the adversaries to identify further nodes.

4 Two-Stage De-Anonymization Algorithm [1]

The proposed algorithm runs in two stages.

Stage 1: The attacker identifies a small number of "seed" nodes which are present both in the anonymous target graph and the attacker's auxiliary graph and maps them to each other.

Stage 2: It is a self-reinforcing process in which the seed mapping is extended to new nodes using only the topology of the network and the new mapping is fed back to the algorithm.

The eventual result is a large mapping between subgraphs of the auxiliary and target networks which reidentifies all mapped nodes in the later.

4.1 Seed Identification

A possible seed identification algorithm is described here. Another such algorithm is described in Ref. [3]. The basic assumption is that the attacker's individual auxiliary information consists of a clique of k nodes which are present both in the auxiliary and the target graphs. It is sufficient to know the degree of each of these nodes and the number of common neighbors for each pair of nodes.

Inputs:

1. The target graph
2. k seed nodes in the auxiliary graph
3. k node-degree values
4. $\binom{k}{2}$ pairs of common-neighbor counts
5. Error parameter ε

Procedure:

The algorithm searches the target graph for a unique k-clique with matching node degrees and common-neighbor counts. If found, the algorithm maps the nodes in the clique to the corresponding nodes in the auxiliary graph, otherwise failure is reported.

The above procedure seems to be a brute-force search and is exponential in k. However, in practice it does not create any problem due to the following:

1. If the degree is bounded by d, then the complexity is $O(n. d^{k-1})$.
2. The running time is heavily input dependent and the inputs with high running time turn out to produce a large number of matches.
3. Terminating the algorithm as soon as more than one match is found greatly decreases the running time.

4.2 Propagation

Input: Two graphs $G_1 = (V_1, E_1)$ and $G_2 = (V_2, E_2)$; a partial "seed" mapping μ_S between the two.

Output: A mapping μ.

Although probabilistic mappings may be thought of, finding a one-one mapping μ has been found to be simpler.

Procedure: The algorithm finds a new mapping using the topological structure of the network and the feedback from previously constructed mappings. It is robust to mild modifications of the topology such as those introduced by sanitization.

At each iteration the algorithm starts with the accumulated list of mapped pairs between V_1 and V_2. It picks an arbitrary unmapped node u in V_1 and computes a score for each unmapped node v in V_2, equal to the number of neighbors of u that have been mapped to neighbors of v. If the strength of the match is above a threshold, the mapping between u and v is added to the list and the next iteration starts.

4.3 Some Concepts

In this section, we introduce some concepts which are used in the development and implementation of the algorithm.

Eccentricity: It is a measure of the deviation of an item of a set from other nodes in it [1]. It is a heuristic and is given by the formula

$$\frac{\max(X) - \max_2(X)}{\sigma(X)}$$

The symbols used in the above formula self-indicative and standard notations used in the literature. We only note that $\max_2$ represents the second highest value in X.

In the algorithm, a threshold value is fixed such that a match is accepted or rejected depending on the eccentricity score being below or above this threshold value.

Edge Directionality: This is the sum of the two mapping scores; one is dependent on the incoming edges and the other one is based on the outgoing edges, which are computed by keeping in view that the algorithm deals with directed graphs. It is specific to a pair of vertices and is computed for each such pairs.

Node Degrees: Edge directionality is biased toward the high-degree nodes. In order to normalize this measure the node degree concept is introduced by dividing the edge directionality by the square root of its degree.

Revisiting nodes: Some nodes in the process of mapping are needed to be visited again as in the beginning the algorithm is supposed to make some errors and the number of mapped nodes is only a few. This increases as the algorithm progresses and settles down. So, the concept of revisiting nodes creeps into the system. It facilitates the mapping being computed as new by comparing to the mappings of earlier visited nodes.

Reverse Match: The algorithm is completely unconsequential about the semantics of the two graphs. It does not matter whether G_1 is the target graph and G_2 is the auxiliary graph or the other way it is true. Each time a node u maps to v, the mapping scores are computed with the input graphs switched. If v gets mapped back to u, the mapping is retained; otherwise it is rejected.

The complexity of the algorithm is $O(|E_1|d_2)$, where d_2 is abound on the degree of the nodes in V_2, if we ignore revisiting nodes and reverse matches. Assuming that a node is revisited only if the number of already mapped neighbors of the node has increased by at least 1, we get a bound of $O(|E_1|d_1.d_2)$, where d_1 is a bound on the degree of the nodes in V_1. Finally, taking reverse mapping into account the complexity becomes $O((|E_1| + |E_2|) d_1.d_2)$.

The de-anonymization algorithm developed in Ref. [1] is a significant step in the analysis of social networks and it opens the eye of the researchers who are working on developing anonymization algorithms by the way posing a challenge to them. The use of this algorithm may de-anonymize the high percentage of the nodes anonymized, which is illustrated by them through their demonstration where the graph of the microblogging services is taken for consideration. As pointed out, the success of these types of algorithms are dependent on the structure of the network and assuming that the nodes are completely anonymized. The process of reidentification is facilitated as all the anonymization algorithms leave some attributes of the respondents and the edges connecting them undisturbed.

5 Other De-Anonymization Techniques

The general process of de-anonymization uses a network alignment technique, which compares/maps the nodes of the anonymized network with a reference network and establishes a mapping from the first to the second one. In these approaches, external knowledge about the users are utilized. In Ref. [9] in the process of alignment of the networks additional attributes are not accessed. When, large overlapping between the two networks occur another network is replaced through the process of crawling of the network taken or it is replaced by another network with similar basis. The process of alignment is somewhat similar to the isomorphism of graphs problem which does not have a generic solution thus far. But, the processes proposed by the developers of de-anonymization techniques do not use stick to the development of a generic graph isomorphism algorithm. Rather they develop an alignment algorithm by using heuristics, which depend on the structural properties of the real-world networks such as heavy-tailed degree distributions and the presence of large cliques. Almost all of these procedures start with the common features in the two graphs and then gradually build upon it by the use of local properties of the graphs involved. It has been observed that these techniques require a large number of starting points and they are not robust to noise. Since there exist several small identical subgraphs in the full network local properties do not help much in the process of mapping.

It has been noted in Ref. [9] that using the divide and conquer paradigm the power of de-anonymization algorithms can be improved further. In this approach, partitioning of networks into communities is performed. The mapping is done in two phases; namely at the community level and the entire network level. Sometimes it is not possible to map the nodes explicitly. However, in these cases mapping can be done between the two networks using the community structure, which reduces the anonymity of users. This de-anonymization algorithm is more immunized to noise, it is highly scalable and has few initial values only. The division process is such that the societies are divided into communities and to achieve this community detection techniques are applied. As a result the main problem gets divided into subproblems and these problems can be solved by using the available alignment techniques recursively. First, this approach maps the community structure as a coarse-grained graph. Then nodes inside each community are mapped through network mapping techniques. This technique for boosting the communities helps as a catalyst to the algorithm [1] which uses microscopic mapping and substantially improves it. The degree of anonymity of the users gets reduced significantly by using this algorithm.

A common characteristic of many networks is community structure and so communities are important subunits of such systems. This characteristic is also termed differently as graph partitioning and has wide applications. Initially, graph partitioning was introduced to solve optimal allocation of processes in a distributed computing context [10]. Since then, it is being used for community detection in several areas [6, 11]. A community is referred as a group of nodes which are closely related to each other inside the community and are having lesser relationship with other communities. It is being pursued as a separate discipline of research extensively [12, 13].

The communities may overlap each other. However, in Ref. [9] partitioning of the network into communities are preferred. Also, for detecting communities the authors have selected to use the Infomap algorithm proposed in Ref. [14] as it is a very popular algorithm for determining partitioned communities of a network. The communities are not supposed to be meaningful social groups but as only smaller dense parts.

The degree of anonymity was first characterized by Chaum [15] as a measure of anonymity. In Refs. [11, 16] entropy was used to define the degree of anonymity achieved by the users of a system toward a particular attacker. The entropy $H(X)$ of the system is defined as

$$H(X) = -\sum_{i=1}^{N} p_i \log p_i$$

where N is the number of nodes in the network and p_i is the probability associated with node i.

The degree of anonymity $A(X)$ is defined as

$$A(X) = \frac{H(X)}{\log N}$$

$A(X)$ satisfies the property that $0 \leq A(X) \leq 1$.

This algorithm has four steps. These are:

- Community detection
- Community mapping
- Seed enrichment
- Global propagation

In the community detection step, Infomap algorithm is used to slice both the reference and the anonymized networks into smaller dense components. However, any other community detection algorithm can be used as well.

In the next step, mapping of communities obtained so far are carried out. The mapping is done using two strategies, using already known seeds and using the network communities. Once forming seeds at the community level is completed through mapping, the community blind propagation algorithm is used to the community graph to expand the set of mapped communities.

As a significant outcome of the community decomposition and mapping additional seeds are identified. This process of finding more seeds through community information is termed as "seed enrichment." After this the community-blind mapping algorithm is applied to each pair of matched communities using the enriched set of seeds.

The process of identifying seeds at the community level is based on two distance metrics defined over the degrees of the nodes (d) and the clustering coefficients (cc) $D_d(v_i, v_j)$ and $D_{cc}(v_i, v_j)$ defined below:

$$D_d(v_i, v_j) = \frac{|d(v_i) - d(v_j)|}{\max(d(v_i), d(v_j))}$$

and

$$D_{cc}(v_i, v_j) = \frac{|cc(v_i) - cc(v_j)|}{\max(cc(v_i), cc(v_j))}$$

$0 \leq D_{cc}(v_i, v_j) \leq 1$ and the value implies that the neighborhood is fully connected and the connectivity reduces as the values approach 0. For each pair of nodes inside the mapped communities, the values of the above two measures are obtained and then tested. The seeds are those nodes which have either the same degree or similarity is high for their clustering coefficients such that it is beyond a certain threshold value. The nodes inside the communities are used by applying the community-blind mapping algorithm locally on them. The inputs to this algorithm are two subgraphs taken from two different networks and the set of seeds in these communities. This algorithm has parallel properties.

Finally, the global propagation step community-blind algorithm is applied to the whole network using all the currently mapped nodes as seeds. This is an essential step as some of the communities might not have been mapped or not mapped correctly.

Using the fact that the anonymized social networks are vulnerable due to the non-analogous traces remaining from the user actions on them, a double-phase algorithm for de-anonymization was proposed in Ref. [17]. The proposed algorithm graph structure is used to identify the nodes from an anonymized graph structure, which they call as "seed-and-grow." Here, the many of the hidden assumptions in earlier works on the structure of the networks are traced and removed. In addition to this parameters without any basis are removed so that the accuracy and effectiveness are improved.

In Ref. [18] a very recent algorithm has been proposed. The algorithm has its base on the note that users have their own distinct social networks and the links used by them are having a higher probability than users who are not part of the networks. The browsing histories associated with these users are indicative of their identities. Models of behavior related to web browsing are parts of a user's identity and provide a maximum likelihood of their profile. The transactional data types are enriched by the above contribution and the noise components are not effective to these data. This algorithm generalizes a wide range of existing de-anonymization attacks.

There are two broad categories of de-anonymizability, namely perfect de-anonymizability and partial de-anonymizability of real world. Researchers can gauge the effectiveness of anonymization techniques through the technical networks which are in the general scenario use core information follow random models of distribution [17]. Some attacks for de-anonymization use this quantification as their theoretical model. So, in some sense the theoretical and practical methods used for de-anonymization can be tested through this quantification. So, evaluation of the extent of de-anonymizability of social networks can be evaluated by researchers using the quantified structural conditions.

6 Conclusions

In this chapter, the topic of de-anonymization of social networks is discussed. De-anonymization process has its advantages as well as disadvantages. As far as disadvantages are concerned, the hackers can use these techniques to get back the required information which is highly undesirable. As far as the advantage is concerned, after processing and analyzing an anonymized social network can be de-anonymized to translate the results obtained to the original network for predication. Also, we presented some problems for further research.

References

[1] A. Narayanan, V. Shmatikov, De-Anonymizing Social Networks, ar.Xiv:0903.3276v1[cs.CR] 19 Mar, 2009.

[2] K. Frikken, P. Golle, in: Private social network analysis: how to assemble pieces of a graph privately, WPES, 2006.

[3] L. Backstrom, C. Dwork, J. Kleinberg, in: Wherefore art thou R3579X? anonymized social networks, hidden patterns and structural steganography, WWW, 2007.

[4] E. Zheleva, L. Getoor, in: Preserving the privacy of sensitive relationships in graph data, PinKDD, 2007.

[5] M. Hay, G. Miklau, D. Jensen, P. Weis, S. Srivastava, Anonymizing social networks, Technical report 07-19, University of Massachusetts Amherst, 2007.

[6] W. Peng, F. Li, X. Zou, J. Wu, A two-stage de-anonymisation attack against anonymised social network, IEEE Trans. Comput. 63 (2) (2014) 290–303.

[7] A. Felt, D. Evans, in: Privacy protection for social networking APIs, W2SP, 2008.

[8] B. Zhou, J. Pei, in: Preserving privacy in social networks against neighborhood attacks, ICDE, 2008.

[9] S. Nilizadeh, S.A. Kapadia, Y.Y. Ahn, in: Community-enhanced de-anonymization of online social networks, CCS'14, Scottsadale, Arizona, USA, 2014.

[10] B.W. Kerninghan, S. Lin, An efficient heuristic procedure for partitioning graphs, Bell Syst. Tech. J. 49 (1) (1970) 291–307.

[11] A. Serjantov, G. Danezis, Towards an information theoretic metric for anonymity, Lecture Notes in Computer Science (including subseries Lecture Notes in Artificial Intelligence and Lecture Notes in Bioinformatics), vol. 2482, 2003, pp. 41–53.

[12] S. Fortunato, Community detection in graphs, Phys. Rep. 486 (3) (2010) 75–174.

[13] A. Pothen, Graph partitioning algorithms with applications to scientific computing, Parallel Numerical Algorithms, Springer, Dordrecht, 1997, pp. 323–368.

[14] K. Schlogel, G. Karypis, V. Kumar, Graph Partitioning for High Performance Scientific Simulations, Army High performance computing research centre, 2000.

[15] D. Chaum, The dining cryptographer's problem: unconditional sender and recipient untraceability, J. Cryptography 1910 (1988) 65–75.

[16] C. Diaz, S. Seys, J. Claessens, B. Preneel, Towards measuring anonymity, International Workshop on Privacy Enhancing Technologies (PET-2002), LNCS, vol. 2482, Springer, Berlin, Heidelberg, 2003, pp. 54–68.

[17] S. Ji, W. Li, N.Z. Gong, P. Mittal, R. Beyah, in: On your social network de-anonymisability: quantification and large scale evaluation with seed knowledge, NDSS'15, San Diego, CA, USA, 2015.

[18] J. Su, A. Shukla, S. Goel, A. Narayanan, De-Anonymising Web Browsing Data with Social Networks, ACM, ISBN TDB, 2017.

Further Reading

[19] R. Carthy, Will IRSeeK Have a Chilling Effect on IRC Chat? http://www.techcrunch.com/2007/11/30/will-irseek-have-a-chilling-effect-on-irc-chat/, 2007.

[20] Facebook, Facebook's Privacy Policy, http://www.new.facebook.com/policy.php, 2007.

[21] S. Guha, K. Tang, P. Francis, in: NOYB: privacy in online social networks, WOSN, 2008.

[22] M. Lucas, N. Borisov, in: Flybynight: mitigating the privacy risks of social networking, WPES, 2008.

5

An Analysis of Demographic and Behavior Trends Using Social Media: Facebook, Twitter, and Instagram

Amandeep Singh, Malka N. Halgamuge, Beulah Moses

School of Computing and Mathematics, Charles Sturt University, Melbourne, VIC, Australia

1 Introduction

Technology has become a very important part of everyone's life. Everyone from the age of 5 to 65 years is on social media every day with billions of users sending messages, sharing information, comments, and the like [1]. With the advancement in information technology, social networking sites such as Facebook, Twitter, Instagram, and LinkedIn are available for the users to interact with families, colleagues, and friends. As a result, social activities are shifting from real things to virtual machines [2]. Analyzing the behavior of individuals from social networking sites is a complex task because there are several methods used. By gathering information from different resources and then analyzing that information, the behavior of the users can be examined. In this research, we have collected different studies about assessing human behavior with the help of social media and compared them according to the different methods used by different authors [3].

To know the personal preference of the users on the social media is a very important task for businesses [4]. Companies can then target those interested customers who are active on the social media in related areas. By gathering information about user behavior pattern, the preferences of the individuals can be identified [5]. Different researchers have found various methods to collect information about human intentions. In this research, our main aim is to analyze how information is analyzed in social media and how this information is useful. This research is very useful as methods to detect human behavior that has been analyzed on different social media [6].

In this research, 30 research papers have been collected from different social media providers such as Facebook, Instagram, and Twitter. After analyzing the data given in these papers, the different methods used were examined. In particular, the behavior of users was analyzed from aspects such as likes, comment, and shares from Facebook, Instagram, and Twitter [7].

The first section provides the material and methods used by the 30 authors to predict the behavior of social media users. This section included data collection, data inclusion criteria, and data analysis [8]. The next section is the result section which provides the statistical analysis and the percentage of research completed on different social media. The result section includes a table which provides the research paper analysis according to the year along with pie chart figures, data collection, and behavior analysis methods and classifications based on different methods with line graphs [9]. The next section is a discussion on the given topic and the last section is the conclusion of this research work.

2 Material and Methods

Data were collected from different conference papers published in the IEEE. From these papers, different methods of analyzing the user behavior [10] was assessed. This report is based on a review of the published articles and analyzes the methods they have used. The data are given in a tabular form.

2.1 Data Collection

Data were collected from 30 various journal papers from the IEEE library regarding the analysis of the user behavior using social media from 2015 to 2017. The collected data were related to Facebook, Twitter, and Instagram in different countries [11]. The attributes that were used for data collection were: applications, methods used, description of the method, number of users, limitations, and results. This raw data is presented in Table 1 [32].

2.2 Data Inclusion Criteria

The different data attributes used to analyze the papers are given in Table 1. This included the following: author name, applications, methods used, detail of methods, number of users, limitations, and results. Data were gathered relating to different social networking sites [17]. In our analysis, the different methods that have been used by researchers to analyze the user's behavior are explored. In this research, three different social media datasets have been collected, which represents the methods and technologies used to understand the behavior of the users.

2.3 Analysis of Raw Data

The raw data presented in Table 1 specifies the attributes that were used to conduct this research. We pooled and analyzed 30 studies based on the impact of variables used in their studies. The descriptive details of the study based on the publication year were then analyzed to observe the behavior of the social media user from 2015 to 2017. A comparison of the methods they used to investigate the behavior of users was then done.

This research included papers from the last 3 years from 2015 to 2017. All papers used data from Facebook, Instagram, and Twitter.

Table 1 Behavior Analysis Using Social Media Data Extracted From 30 Scientific Research Papers During 2015–17

No.	Study	Social Media	Methods/Technologies Used	Description	Users	Limitations	Results
1.	Park et al. [9]	Instagram	Snowballing method Coding rules: binary coding Regression analysis	Quantitative method is used to analyze the relationship between sexual images and social engagement Number of likes were used Snowballing method was used to collect people's image data Binary coding rule was used to self-code the images collected Regression analysis was used to analysis the behavior of 200 users	200	Data does not show that who and why people get more interested in sexual images Causal relationship cannot use to prove the relationship between sexual images and number of likes	With number of likes degree of sexuality is known in the given images Results show that men and women get more like when they upload their selfies
2.	Farahani et al. [12]	Twitter	Regression and correlation methods were used Mean absolute percentage error (MAPE) and mean absolute error (MAE) Gaussian mixture model	Metrics were used to analyze the different behavior in different dimensions Data are collected and filtered on the basis of Iran election with maximum tweets Gaussian mixture model (GMM) was used to detect influential users	Top 20 users with 148,713 tweets	Correlation of other influence measures were not evaluated No prediction algorithm No weighted measure technique	Original Tweets (OTI) is very important Results shows that OTI and metrics play very crucial role Retweet impact has 3.9 MAE and 0.12 MAPE RT2 has 7.12 MPE and 0.0 MAPE RT3 has 4.5 MAE and 0.13 MAPE
3.	Castro et al. [13]	Twitter	Social network analysis techniques Machine learning Partition clustering	Methods were used to detect the political behavior of Venezuelan election	60,000	Political alignment of entire state was not determined Tweets were not	Average score of discriminative political features in both clusters were compared

Continued

Table 1 Behavior Analysis Using Social Media Data Extracted From 30 Scientific Research Papers During 2015–17—cont'd

No.	Study	Social Media	Methods/Technologies Used	Description	Users	Limitations	Results
			algorithm Text processing Term frequency-inverse document frequency (TF-IDF)	Clustering algorithm was used to analyze to citizen public speech Twitter communication pattern and linguistic dimension used For each tweet, unique identifier, publication date, geographical location, and tweet contents were used for analysis TF-IDF provides the score that gives how words are relevant to texts		analyzed in different time windows Different weighing alternatives to TF-IDF and geographical subdivision were not considered	Cluster state 1 represent opposition state and 0 represent government state TF-IDF represents 79.17% accuracy in election outcomes
4.	Mungen et al. [14]	Instagram	Fuse-motif analysis Mungan and Kaya's network motif Combination of Triad FG, motif-bases social position and quad closure methods	Motif-based analysis is based on the posts by the Instagram users Most influenced posts were used instead of most influenced person System calculates all language pairs Unique model was split in three different models such as creating graph, find most influenced people and influencing users only	20,000	Other factors related to Instagram are not considered such as images data, shared, and comments Models are complicated and hard to understand by the normal users	Result shows that four normal motifs have largest impact of 3.9 among others and with 22% frequency 1 norm-2 mid-1 pop motif has lowest impact of 1.2 with 2% frequency

5.	Wiradinata et al. [15]	Instagram	Path diagram model analysis Technology acceptance model (TAM)	TAM is used to know the factors for the acceptance of any system and data collection method used for sampling Path diagram model is used with statistical software AMOS 20 to know the behavior of consumers in small medium enterprise (SME) those using Instagram	200	Complex path analysis model as it uses normality testing, validity testing, reliability testing	Exogenous variables: technology-specific valuation (TSV), number of users (NOU), and perceived ease of use (PEOU) have influence (direct or indirect) on the endogenous variables Intervening variable perceived usefulness (PU) have influence on endogenous variable to behavioral influence (BI)
6.	Jiang et al. [11]	Twitter	CrossSpot algorithm Suspiciousness metric. Multimode Erdos–Renyi model KL-divergence principle Minimum Description Length (MDL) Principle	Fraud detection in twitter is main aim of this research Tensors was used to represents counts of events Suspicious metric is derived based on ERP model Five axioms were used to predict the behavior of different users	225	Metric based on more sophisticated model is not included	CrossSpot has more suspiciousness score than HOSVD in case of retweeting and hashing data
7.	Nasim et al. [16]	Facebook	Binary classification problem Simmel's theory Sociological theory "foci" behind friendship formation Facebook data was provided with Algopol project	Impact of additional interaction information were studied Binary classification problem was used for the link interface problem Third-party apps have access to the user profile and these can be used to	586 users and comments posted by 6400 users	Privacy is major concern Algorithm for news feed is not known Filtering is not done properly [16]	It has been observed that individuals who are friends with each others have similar interests Two evaluation metrics were used to judge the performance of classifier ROC and PR used to

Continued

Table 1 Behavior Analysis Using Social Media Data Extracted From 30 Scientific Research Papers During 2015–17—cont'd

No.	Study	Social Media	Methods/Technologies Used	Description	Users	Limitations	Results
			Tenfold cross validation method LR, linear discriminant analysis (LDA) and support vector machines (SVM)	access the information of users Theories suggest that interaction will take place among users who are connected			calculate different measures
8.	Jarvinen et al. [17]	Instagram	Partial least square (PLS) SmartPlus3 Software Path-weighing scheme	It is an extended version of UTAUT2 Model Out of 199 responses 187 respondents were used Given conceptual model was tested with SmartPlus3 software Hedonic motivation is important to derive consumer's intension to continue using SNS 86.6% users were used from Europe to analysis [17]	187	Generalizability is major limitation It is not sure that the sample shows the number of SNS users Data is not correct in terms of origin of users Results cannot be applied to global Instagram users	Variances explained in behavioral intension is 67% and use behavior is 46% which is higher compared to UTAUT2 model
9.	Geeta et al. [10]	Twitter	Demographic analysis	Data are collected from the tweets by users Opinions of different users have been analyzed and then sentiment analysis is performed and at the end demographic analysis is achieved to get the required data	30 million	Current location of users is not identified. So, it is not clear that user tweets from the real location or not	Result shows the opinions of users in five different countries United States has high percentage of tweets done in Oscar event, India has high percentage of tweets in T20 event, France user tweet more on Paris attack and Australian users tweets high on formula 1

No.		Platform	Technique	Description	Count	Limitations	Findings
10.	Dalton et al. [18]	Twitter	JavaFX application	JavaFX is the improvement in Maltego in which automation of entity is not possible. JavaFX automation uses text file and MySQL database as input and produce results	5000	Reliability of IP	Automation is possible in terms of more flexibility and speed
11.	Hosseinmardi et al. [6]	Instagram	Fivefold cross validation Logistic regression classifier with forward feature selection approach	Data are extracted from the initial posts. LRC was used to train a predictor. To analyze the behavior comment, images and followers on Instagram was used. Focus was on unigram and bigrams	25,000	Performance in classifier needs to be improved. Deep learning and neutral learning was not used. Less input features. Comments on previous shares was not used	This method achieves high performance in predicting behavior. 80% data used for training and 20% for testing. 0.68 recall and 0.50 precision was used to detect behavior
12.	Chinchilla et al. [19]	Instagram	Cross industry standard process for data mining (CRISP-DM). Clustering and association rules	CRISP-DM is designed for hierarchical process model. Data are collected from the 1435 records and after analyzing the data behavior of customers is evaluated	1435	Data mining models are limited to only Instagram and Facebook and other companies cannot use this data for behavior analysis	According to different clusters, attribute like has high number then others and TIPO_MODA is last in the numbers
13.	Dewan et al. [20]	Facebook pages	Supervised learning algorithms. Bag of words. Crowdsourcing technique: web of trust (WOT)	Like, comment and share are analyzed, and textual contents was collected from three sources: message, name, and link. Bag of words produced sparse vector and this vector used for classification	627 FB Pages and most recent 100 posts	Large group and events were not covered. Bag of words is based on limited history of 100 posts. Pages can change behavior over time	Results are based on the different classifier and it is concluded that Neural Network classifier of Trigram feature set has high rate of accuracy of 84.13%

Continued

Table 1 Behavior Analysis Using Social Media Data Extracted From 30 Scientific Research Papers During 2015–17—cont'd

No.	Study	Social Media	Methods/Technologies Used	Description	Users	Limitations	Results
14.	Toujani et al. [21]	Facebook	Fuzzy sentiment classification Fuzzy SVM I told you application to get old FB messages	Opinion mining was performed on the FB users Given system is consist of four phases: input (I), natural language processing (NLP), machine learning process (MLP), output (O) to produce the desired results Investigation is performed on the basis of coordination between machine learning and NLP	260	This system can only be used where users know Arabic and French/ English language No mobility-based machine learning	In basic SVM, 74% of precision and F-measure for positive opinion, whereas in Fuzzy SVM, 88.2%
15.	Lukito et al. [2]	Twitter	Analyze and comparison of three different statistical models Questionnaire based on big five personality inventory Java program was developed to answer the questions	Machine learning, lexicon based, grammatical rule approach models were used for analysis with comparison Data were collected from Facebook profile and then used twitter based on this data to predict the behavior	142 users with 2,00,000 tweets	Accuracy is low in term of IE, SN, and TF personality treats Variable accuracy	Based on the bar graph machine learning approach has high accuracy in IE personality factor, grammatical rule has high accuracy in SN factor, etc.

16.	Santos et al. [22]	Twitter	Visualization Different computational techniques Set of keywords was used for data collection	Data collected based on the tweets on World Cup 2014 which was held in 2014 in Brazil Visual system used to recognize patterns, spot trends and identify outliers Data and text mining and natural processing computational techniques were used After data pre-process, visualization was designed and handed over to journalists	851,292 tweets	Manual data process Emotions were not included This method has not included different versions Analyze data is complex process	Analysis was based on the focus group discussions on two major aspects such as journalism criteria and visualization techniques Graph A to Graph D was used to visualization
17.	Rabab'ah et al. [23]	Twitter	Twitter tweepy API tools was used for data collection NetworkX-METIS package was used to partition the retweet graph	Controversy level is identified with the help of tweets on social contents of Arabic language Data are collected from Twitter from September to October 2015 with hashtags on the trending topics Retweet graph was designed based on tweets and then retweet graph is portioned by removing noisy nodes Controversy measures RW, EC, and GMCK are applied	1.5 million tweets	This method is dependent on the structure of interaction between participants in the conversation only Retweet activity and retweet graph are only focus areas Other ways can be considered than these graphs	Controversy level was measures using random walk (RW) and embedded controversy (EC) Figures elaborate that in RW, most controversial topic is T6 with 0.822 value In GMCK, T6 is most controversial and in EC T6 is most controversial

Continued

Table 1 Behavior Analysis Using Social Media Data Extracted From 30 Scientific Research Papers During 2015–17—cont'd

No.	Study	Social Media	Methods/Technologies Used	Description	Users	Limitations	Results
18.	Lima et al. [24]	Twitter	Machine learning and text mining techniques Sentiment analysis Personality prediction David Keirsey classifications Myers Briggs type indicator test	Temperament predictor was designed to assess the individual behavior Message from twitter was captured using MBTI test 16 types of messages were monitored with Briggs and Myers words	29,200	Search for meta attributes is not available Collection of data for different classifier is a complex task [24]	Two hypotheses were tested named: single multiclass classifier and classification into binary problem Results show that there is best accuracy of 34.35% for NB Classifier Artisan and Guardian have high accuracy of an average of 87%
19.	Do et al. [5]	Twitter	Emotion analysis method Machine learning classifications State-of-the-art method Feature vector Classifier using support vector machine (SVM)	Middle East respiratory syndrome (MERS) case study was used for analysis Emotions expresses in twitter messages were exploited Public responses were analyzed using twitter messages Korean twitter messages were classified in seven categories which include neutral and Ekman's six basic emotions Messages were categorized in feature vector	5706 tweets	Complicated method Can only be used on twitter accounts Cannot apply on other social networking sites (SNS)	Figures show that 80% of the tweets is neutral and fear and anger dominates Trends of emotions over time were analyzed and shows that number of anger increase over time that result increase in public anger and fear and sadness decrease

#		Platform					
20.	Li et al. [25]	Twitter	Classic sentiment analysis Granular partitioning method Data mining algorithm Jtwitter.jar libraries getFriendTimeline() method. REST API Pearson product moment correlation coefficient	Relationship between twitter users with stock market was analyzed to know behavior Jtwitter.jar was used to get friends status on twitter REST API was used to know home timeline or own status Four types of data return formats were used such as XML, JSON, RSS, and Atom	30,000	Timeliness of data requirement is very high Low processing speed Time of data is not improved with the improvement in accuracy	Result show that 2807 happy modes users were on 11/12, sad modes were on 11/19, anger were on 11/17, fear on 11/16, disgust was on 11/20 and most surprised mode was on 11/19
21.	Rao et al. [26]	Twitter	SocialKB framework Closes world assumption (CWA) and open world assumption (OWA) Apache Spark's stream processing API and Twitter 4J Spark SQL to process collected tweets	SocialKB model was used for modeling and reasoning about twitter posts and to discover suspicious users User and nature of their post was analyzed SocialKB relies on KB to know behavior of users and their posts KB will have entities, relationships, facts and rules Tweets were collected using Apache Spark's API and Twitter 4J	20,000	Different attack models were not analyzed First-order formulas used in KB is the biggest barrier ScoialKB framework does not know that data is independently and identically distributed	Each tweet has over 100 attributes Predicate tweeted (userID, tweetID) has more than 27,000 counts Only 16. 6% of URLs output by SocialKB were incorrectly detected as malicious

Continued

Table 1 Behavior Analysis Using Social Media Data Extracted From 30 Scientific Research Papers During 2015–17—cont'd

No.	Study	Social Media	Methods/Technologies Used	Description	Users	Limitations	Results
22.	Modoni et al. [27]	Twitter	Psycholinguistic analysis REST API Index analyzer	Psycholinguistic analysis is done on the Twitter contents which are written in Italian language Main aim is to analyze index and automatic analysis of the Twitter social posts REST API used to get the twitter data Information is gathered on the basis of location and time zone Correlation between weather and health is performed	3000 posts per day	Lack of interoperability Linked data facility is not available to integrate data from different other social media platforms	Calculation is performed on the basis of temperature, humidity and depression Calculation of correlation between temperature and depression provides the result as −0.8, which indicates high negative correlation
23.	Maruf et al. [8]	Twitter	Textalytics Media Analysis API Sentiment analysis Linguistic-based analysis with LIWC tool Personality analysis	Category scores from tweets used to analysis the behavior of twitter users By combining information from different social media comprehensive virtual profile can build Response prediction, news feed prediction, advertisement research can be done with this method	105	Complex process Not suitable to detect individual behavior on different subjects	Results show that users with high conscientiousness interested in human rights, crime, law and justice, etc. Achievement, humans, perceptual process have high score in comments on political and social issues

No.	Author	Platform	Method	Process	Sample size	Limitations	Results
24.	Ghavami et al. [1]	Facebook	Classification algorithm and Pearson correlation coefficient formula were used for personality treat based on the user likes	Online questionnaire was designed 65 user's public posts were collected Comment-like-graph and post-like-graph was built Investigation on the correlation between each personality treat and 17 features from these two graphs	65	Small group of people participated in online survey and some did not show their trust to participate in the research	Correlation score table shows that N (Neuroticism) has weak correlation in CLI and CLP, whereas agreeableness and extroversion personality type have strong correlation
25.	Peng et al. [28]	Facebook	Jieba as a text segmentation tool for Chinese language Support vector machine (SVM) algorithm	Textual data was collected of FB posts of 222 users Feature extraction and feature selection were used for data processing Document matrix was designed SVM learning algorithm was used	222	Best accuracy is only 73.5% Experiment was conducted only on extraversion; not on other 4 factors	Table on average score of each personality shows that Openness to experience personality has high average score than others All user with more than 900 friends score high in extraversion personality factor
26.	Mihaltz et al. [3]	Facebook	TrendMiner Natural language processing (NLP) method	Collected data was processed using NLP tools such as segmentation, tokening with huntoken tool Sentiment analysis was performed to evaluate the behavior of users	14,000 public posts, 2 million comments, 1300 pages	Limited for Hungarian users only Limited users	Custom tool was evaluated for identification of psychological phenomena against human judgment
27.	Pang et al. [29]	Instagram	Demographic analysis Text analysis Image analysis Age detection process	Demographic was analyzed by photo with face detection and face analysis tools Tags associated with the pictures were analyzed Penetration is done by analyzing followers of the brand Drinking behavior is analyzed	600	Media data mining is not involved Fake information can be collected as some accounts are fake	Results shows that Heineken brand has high number of followers and 51.91% male above 18 drink this particular brand

Continued

Table 1 Behavior Analysis Using Social Media Data Extracted From 30 Scientific Research Papers During 2015–17—cont'd

No.	Study	Social Media	Methods/Technologies Used	Description	Users	Limitations	Results
28.	Bhagat et al. [4]	Twitter	Cut-based classification approach using messaged exchanged on social media	SetiStrength and Treebank analysis is evaluated and limitation in these methods are evaluated. New cut-based classification architectural approach is used to analysis the text documents with classification method	7 million	Graphical user interface (GUI) can be used for better understanding of users	Polarity, subjectively, and hierarchical polarity is used which shows that subjectively polarity analysis has more accuracy than other two
29.	Tsai et al. [30]	Facebook	Distributed data collection module. Social personal analysis using user operation complexity analysis. Personal preference analysis	Social personal analysis is designed using Facebook personal information. Data is collected on the basis of how many users like, share and join the pages on the Facebook. With the help of this data personal preference analysis is done	10,000	With the analysis of personal preference interest in the different innovative application services will be big issue of social analysis in the future. Not able to reach different application services areas in social analysis	The result show the data on the basis of different tests which shows: Page viewed by users, bounce rate, and Click rate. Table shows that Test_A has high PV, Test_B has high bounce rate, and Test_C has high click rate
30.	Ray et al. [31]	Facebook	Empirical analyze. Mathematical and empirical model. Inverse Gaussian distribution. Binomial distribution	Mathematical and empirical model used to analyze the behavior of Facebook users. Mathematical model will help to know the likeability of users from the point of view and with probability of viewing posts. IGD to know the viewing probability	1200	Effectiveness of mobile learning is not included. Software implementation is hard	Result shows that photos posted by users gets 39% more interaction than links, videos or any other text-based updates. Textual posts, liking and comments were used to analyze. 59% of users are those who are daily active and 96% are monthly users

3 Results

The aim of this research is to know the methods used by researchers to predict the behavior of social media users. In this research, data were collected based on the use of three different social networking sites such as Facebook, Instagram, and Twitter. A random user list was used to analyze the behavior. In our final analysis, we pooled the data, which showed a statistically significant difference in various parameters (published year, methods, results, and limitations) for different social media sites. The results section includes the percentage of research on the three social networking sites, research papers according to year with bar graph representations, data collection and behavior analysis methods and classification based on the different methods with line graph representations.

3.1 Statistical Analysis

We performed statistical analysis to organize the data and predict the trends based on the analysis. This showed the different social media sites used based on the data given in Table 1.

As shown in Fig. 1 and Table 2, 27% of data was based on Facebook users, 23% of data was based on Instagram users, and 50% of data was based on Twitter users. As such, it is clear that Twitter is used more than other two social media sites for the analysis of the behavior of users.

3.2 Research Papers According to Year

Table 3 represents the data based on the year published. This indicates that most of research was completed on Twitter in 2016 and there was no research done in 2017 on Facebook regarding the behavior of users.

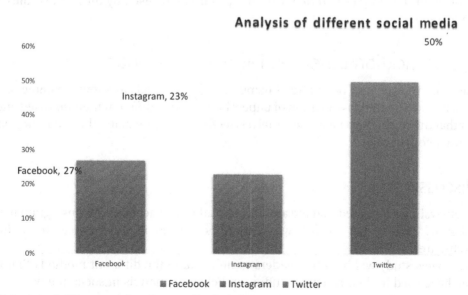

FIG. 1 Analysis of different social media to predict the behavior of users.

Table 2   Percentage of Number of Researches Completed in Three Different Social Media

Application	Number of Studies	Percentage
Facebook	8	27
Instagram	7	23
Twitter	15	50

Table 3   Number of Researches According to Year

Year	Social Media	Number of Studies
2015	Facebook	5
	Twitter	2
	Instagram	1
2016	Facebook	3
	Twitter	11
	Instagram	4
2017	Facebook	–
	Twitter	2
	Instagram	2

Fig. 2 shows that most of the research studies have been completed on Twitter in 2016. There was one research on the behavior analysis topic on Facebook in 2017.

3.3 Data Collection Method and Behavior Analysis Methods Used

Data collection techniques and behavior analysis methods used by different studies are shown in Table 4.

3.4 Classification Based on Different Methods

The behavior of users can be analyzed using different methods as shown in Table 5.

Fig. 3 is based on the classification of papers based on the different methods used and it is clear that the researchers have used analysis techniques more than others and they have rarely used coding rules.

4 Discussion

In this analysis, we observed that the amount of studies on Facebook and Instagram in the period from 2015 to 2017 was low, so there is a need of more research in these important areas.

This review study will help the readers to understand the different methods that the authors have used in their research studies on behavior analysis in social media.

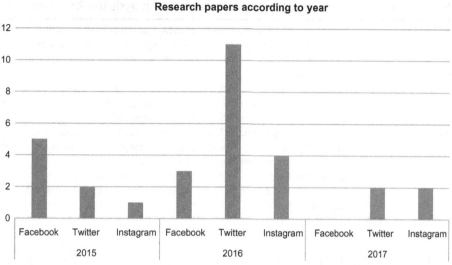

FIG. 2 Research papers according to 2015–17.

Table 4 Data Collection and Behavior Analysis Methods Used by Different Authors

Data Collection Techniques	Behavior Analysis Methods
Snowballing method, Gaussian mixture model (GMM), Quad closure methods, Binary classification problem, third-party apps, SmartPlus3 Software, Bag of words, Opinion mining, Questionnaire, Set of keywords, Twitter tweepy API, MBTI test	Regression analysis, quantitative method, correlation methods, machine learning, partition clustering algorithm, text processing, term frequency-inverse document frequency (TF-IDF), fuse-motif, CrossSpot algorithm, tenfold cross validation method, partial least square (PLS), JavaFX application, fivefold cross validation, cross industry standard process for data mining (CRISP-DM), supervised learning algorithms, fuzzy sentiment classification, NetworkX-METIS, Myers Briggs type indicator test, Jtwitter.jar libraries, REST API, index analyzer, LIWC tool, Jieba tool

An examination of the different methods of behavior analysis carried out with the help of social media is the main aim of this research. Thirty research studies were collected and analyzed to understand the personality of individuals who use social media such as Facebook, Twitter, and Instagram. Only three types of social network sites were included in this research. This analysis from the reported studies gives an overview of methods used to predict the personality of social media users.

As seen from Fig. 1, 50% of research was done on Twitter from 2015 to 2017, whereas as the other two social networking sites, Facebook and Instagram, only had 27% and 23%, respectively. Moreover, some studies [14, 21] proposed more than one method to analyze individuals' behavior.

Table 5   Classification Based on Different Methods to Analysis the Behavior of Users

Analysis techniques	Regression analysis, social network analysis, fuse-motif analysis, demographic analysis, fuzzy sentiment classification, sentiment analysis, classic sentiment analysis, psycholinguistic analysis, index analyzer, personality analysis, text/image analysis.
Coding rules	Binary coding
Models	Gaussian mixture model, path diagram model, technology acceptance model (TAM), multimode Erdos–Renyi model, machine learning, lexicon based, grammatical rule approach models, Mathematical, and empirical model
Algorithms	Machine learning, partition clustering algorithm, CrossSpot algorithm, supervised learning algorithms, feature vector, data mining algorithm, classification algorithm and Pearson correlation coefficient formula.
Principle	KL-divergence principle, minimum description length (MDL) principle.
API	Twitter tweepy API tools, REST API, Apache Spark's stream processing API, Textalytics media analysis API

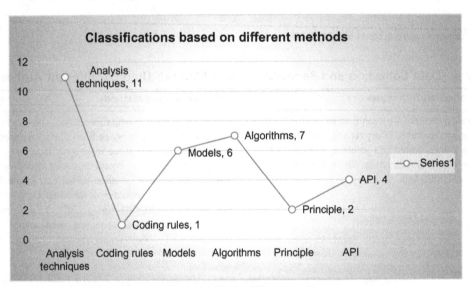

FIG. 3 Classification based on different methods used by 30 different studies.

A major issue in this area is the security and privacy of the information that the users put on the social media. However, some of the studies included in this review provided suggestions and methods to help secure the personal information of users. Many authors also discussed machine learning technique to observe the personality of social networking site users.

The results showed that most of the research completed in 2016 were on Twitter rather than Facebook and Instagram. In 2015, most research was done on Facebook and the least research was done on Instagram. On the other hand, in 2016 Twitter has the highest numbers of research papers and Facebook had the lowest numbers. In 2017, Twitter and Instagram had the highest number of research paper while Facebook had none at all.

Table 6 Demographic and Behaviour Trends From the Different Social Media

---

According to age: Age group between 45 and 55 use more Facebook than Twitter and Instagram. More than 79% of this age group use Facebook according to current trend

Use of smart phones: Another reason of using social media have been increased in the past year is smart phones. Smart phones have more visual interaction and people can access the social media easily. Advancement in the mobile phones play very important role in the increased users of social media

According to location: More people use the social media while they go out for dinner with family and friends. Other locations where people like to use social media is gym, cinema and home specially in lounge room area more than other rooms

According to time: More than 70% people use internet in the evening and 57% people use as a first thing in the morning. There is minimum use of social media during Breakfast, lunch, at work and commuting

Frequency of using social networking sites: More than 35% people use social media more than five times a day as compared to 20% people who never use social networking site in a day. There are only 3% people who use once a week

APPS: More than 68% use apps to access the social media and fewer people use websites to access the social media

---

Data collection and behavior analysis methods provided by authors were collected as raw data and analyzed. A classification based on the methods used by the authors for analysis was created.

Previous review studies did not include the limitations and number of users' attribute in their analysis. We have included these two attributes in Table 1 to make the research more specific and easy to understand for the readers [13].

The analysis of the papers indicated that Twitter has been the most used to predict the personality of social media users. Considering Table 1, there is a need for more variety in research methods on Instagram to understand the behavior of users.

A cut-based classification method was used to analyze the behavior of Twitter users by Bhagat et al. [4]. From the analysis done by these authors, they have concluded that cut-based classification method can be extended in the future to provide GUI for users for polarity classifications and subjectivity classifications. Real-time user messaging can also be analyzed in the future [18].

This review study is based on the analysis of behavior of individuals, who use social network in their daily life. This study benefits readers as it helps to identify the methods used by different researchers and the number of researchers that applied these methods. This review study provides a clear description of the methods, limitations, and results that have been used by previous researches in studies during 2015–17.

More than 37% people of the world use social media; however, the way social media users interact with each other vary greatly. There are demographic and behavioral trends from the Facebook, Twitter, and Instagram that are discussed in Table 6.

5 Conclusion

In this review paper, we have reviewed and analyzed data collected from 30 different published articles from 2015 to 2017 on the topic of behavior analysis using social media. It is found that there were 69 different methods used by the researchers to analyze their data. From these methods, the most common technique to analyze the behavior of individuals was analysis techniques. From this study, it is clear that there is need for more research to predict the personality and behavior of individuals on the Instagram. This study found that 50% of research was done on Twitter and 11 different analysis techniques were sued. While reviewing the research articles, it was clear that the researchers have used more than one method for data collection and behavior analysis. Table 1 has all the data analysis of the paper reviewed in the study. Furthermore, unlike past research papers, this chapter included the attributes of the number of users and the limitations of the work done. These studies mostly focused on Twitter with some research on Facebook and Instagram. In this research paper, we have attempted to fill the gap by including the number of users and limitation attributes. There are some challenges to find the solutions to the issues that have been discussed, but these require urgent attention. This study should be useful as a reference for researchers interested in the analysis of the behavior of social media users.

Author Contribution

A.S. and M.N.H. conceived the study idea and developed the analysis plan. A.S. analyzed the data and wrote the initial paper. M.N.H. helped in preparing the figures and tables, and in finalizing the manuscript. All authors read the manuscript.

References

[1] S.M. Ghavami, M. Asadpour, J. Hatami, M. Mahdavi, in: Facebook user's like behavior can reveal personality, International Conference on Information and Knowledge Technology, Tehran, Iran, 2015.

[2] L.C. Lukito, A. Erwin, J. Purnama, W. Danoekoesoemo, in: Social media user personality classification using computational linguistic, International Conference on Information Technology and Electrical Engineering (ICITEE), Tangerang, Indonesia, 2016.

[3] M. Miháltz, T. Váradi, in: TrendMiner: large-scale analysis of political attitudes in public facebook messages, IEEE International Conference on Congnitive Infocommunications, Budapest, Hungary, 2015.

[4] A.P. Bhagat, K.A. Dongre, P.A. Khodke, in: Cut-based classification for user behavioral analysis on social websites, Green Computing and Internet of Things (ICGCIoT), Noida, India, 2015.

[5] H.J. Do, C.-G. Lim, Y.K. Jin, H.-J. Choi, in: Analyzing emotions in twitter during a crisis: a case study of the 2015 Middle East respiratory syndrome outbreak in Korea, Big Data and Smart Computing (BigComp), Hong Kong, China, 2016.

[6] H. Hosseinmardi, R.I. Rafiq, Q. Lv, S. Mishra, in: Prediction of cyberbullying incidents in a media-based social network, International Conference on Advances in Social Networks Analysis and Mining (ASONAM), San Francisco, CA, USA, 2016.

[7] J. Kheokao, W. Siriwanij, in: Media use of nursing students in thailand, International Symposium on Emerging Trends and Technologies in Libraries and Information Services, Noida, India, 2015.

[8] A.H. Maruf, N. Meshkat, M.E. Ali, J. Mahmud, in: Human behaviour in different social medias: a case study of twitter and disqus, International Conference on Advances in Social Network Analysis and Mining, San Jose, CA, USA, 2015.

[9] H. Park, J. Lee, Do private and sexual pictures receive more likes on instagram? Research and Innovation in Information Systems (ICRIIS), Langkawi, Malaysia, 2017.

[10] G. Geeta, R. Niyogi, in: Demographic analysis of twitter users, Advances in Computing, Communications and Informatics (ICACCI), Jaipur, India, 2016.

[11] M. Jiang, A. Beutel, P. Cui, B. Hooi, Spotting suspicious behaviors in multimodal data: a general metric and algorithms, IEEE Trans. Knowl. Data Eng. 28 (8) (2016) 2187–2200.

[12] H.S. Farahani, A. Bagheri, E.H.K. Mirzaye Saraf, in: Characterizing behavior of topical authorities in twitter, International Conference on Innovative Mechanisms for Industry Applications, Tehran, Iran, 2017.

[13] R. Castro, L. Kuf'fo, C. Vaca, in: Back to #6D: predicting venezuelan states political election results through twitter, eDemocracy & eGovernment (ICEDEG), Quito, Ecuador, 2017.

[14] A.A. Mungen, M. Kaya, in: Quad motif-based influence analyse of posts in Instagram, Advanced Information and Communication Technologies (AICT), Lviv, Ukraine, 2017.

[15] T. Wiradinata, B. Iswandi, in: The analysis of instagram technology adoption as marketing tools by small medium enterprise, Information Technology, Computer, and Electrical Engineering (ICITACEE), Semarang, Indonesia, 2016.

[16] M. Nasim, R. Charbey, C. Prieur, U. Brandes, Investigating Link Inference in Partially Observable Networks: Friendship Ties and Interaction, Trans. Comput. Social Syst. 3 (3) (2016) 113–119.

[17] J. Järvinen, R. Ohtonen, H. Karjaluoto, in: Consumer acceptance and use of instagram, System Sciences (HICSS), 2016.

[18] B. Dalton, N. Aggarwal, in: Analyzing deviant behaviors on social media using cyber forensics-based methodologies, Communications and Network Security (CNS), Philadelphia, PA, USA, 2016.

[19] L.D.C.C. Chinchilla, K.A.R. Ferreira, in: Analysis of the behavior of customers in the social networks using data mining techniques, International Conference on Advances in Social Networks Analysis and Mining (ASONAM), San Francisco, CA, USA, 2016.

[20] P. Dewan, S. Bagroy, P. Kumaraguru, in: Hiding in plain sight: characterizing and detecting malicious facebook pages, IEEE/ACM International Conference on Advances in Social Networks Analysis and Mining (ASONAM), San Francisco, CA, USA, 2016.

[21] R. Toujani, J. Akaichi, in: Fuzzy Sentiment Classification in Social Network Facebook' Statuses Mining, International Conference on Sciences of Electronics, Technologies of Information and Telecommunications (SETIT), Hammamet, Tunisia, 2016.

[22] C.Q. Santos, R. Tietzmann, M. Trasel, S.M. Moraes, I.H. Manssour, M.S. Silveira, in: Can visualization techniques help journalists to deepen analysis of Twitter data? Exploring the "Germany 7 x 1 Brazil" case, Hawaii International Conference on System Sciences, Porto Alegre, Brazil, 2016.

[23] A. Rabab'ah, M. Al-Ayyoub, Y. Jararweh, M.N. Al-Kabi, in: Measuring the controversy level of arabic trending topics on twitter, International Conference on Information and Communication Systems (ICICS), Irbid, Jordan, 2016.

[24] A.C.E.S. Lima, L.N. de Castro, in: Predicting temperament from twitter data, International Congress on Advanced Applied Informatics, São Paulo, Brazil, 2016.

[25] Q. Li, B. Zhou, Q. Liu, in: Can twitter posts predict stock behavior, Cloud Computing and Big Data Analysis (ICCCBDA), Chengdu, China, 2016.

[26] P. Rao, A. Katib, C. Kamhoua, K. Kwiat, L. Njilla, in: Probabilistic inference on twitter data to discover suspicious users and malicious content, Computer and Information Technology (CIT), Nadi, Fiji, 2016.

[27] G.E. Modoni, D. Tosi, in: Correlation of weather and moods of the Italy residents through an analysis of their tweets, International Conference on Future Internet of Things and Cloud Workshop, Varese, Italy, 2016.

[28] K.-H. Peng, L.-H. Liou, C.-S. Chang, D.-S. Lee, in: Predicting personality traits of chinese users based on facebook wall posts, Wireless and Optical Communication Conference (WOCC), Taipei, Taiwan, 2015.

[29] R. Pang, A. Baretto, H. Kautz, J. Luo, in: Monitoring adolescent alcohol use via multimodal analysis in social multimedia, Big Data (Big Data), Santa Clara, CA, USA, 2015.

[30] C.-H. Tsai, H.-W. Liu, T. Ku, W.-F. Chien, in: Personal preferences analysis of user interaction based on social networks, Computing, Communication and Security (ICCCS), Pamplemousses, Mauritius, 2015.

[31] K.S. Ray, M. Saeed, S. Subrahmaniam, in: Empirical analysis of user behavior in social media, International Conference on Developments of E-Systems Engineering, Duai, United Arab Emirates, 2015.

[32] S. Kamal, N. Dey, A. Ashour, S. Ripon, E. Balas, M. Kaysar, FbMapping, an Automated System for Monitoring Facebook Data, 3 October, 2017.

Further Reading

[33] Statista 2014 Age Distribution of Active Social Media Users Worldwide as of 3rd Quarter 2014, by Platform https://www.statista.com.

6

Social Network Influence on Mode Choice and Carpooling During Special Events: The Case of Purdue Game Day

Pedro Henrique dos Reis Rezende*, Arif Mohaimin Sadri[†],
Satish V. Ukkusuri[‡]

*School of Engineering and Architecture, FUMEC University, Belo Horizonte, Brazil [†]Moss School of Construction, Infrastructure, and Sustainability, Florida International University, Miami, FL, United States [‡]Lyles School of Civil Engineering, Purdue University, West Lafayette, IN, United States

1 Introduction

Planned special events (PSE) are a major cause of concern for local transportation agencies because of the impacts on transportation system operations caused by increased travel demand and reduced capacity attributed to event staging [1]. The assembling of vehicles and people in a short period of time cause the transit authorities to often encounter significant challenges in controlling the induced traffic from different locations both before and after the event. These challenges include parking management, crowd management, pedestrian facility design, special facility for senior citizens and handicapped individuals, providing transit facility for captive riders, and so on. In addition, police enforcements often need to close several streets for security reasons, manage crowds who walk together to the location, and guide motorists to specific routes who are unfamiliar with the area. Individuals attending these events travel by various traffic modes, that is, walk, private car, and public transit.

Managing travel for special events, and facing its challenges, targets the following objectives: achieve predictability, ensure safety, maximize efficiency, and meet stakeholders' (both public and event patron) expectations [2]. Congestion that develops as a consequence of PSEs results in delays affecting both attendees and nonattendees of the events [1]. Overall benefits include reduced delay for both attendants and nonattendants and reduced overall traffic demand. System operation benefits include, among many others, attraction of new regular transit users and carpoolers and dissemination of lessons learned and solutions to technical problems. At a community level, benefits extend to an economical stage, with an increased knowledge of potential for investment and commercial activity in the community and also an increased potential to attract other special events. PSEs are known to generate a direct outside-of-event spending and secondary economic effects of the order of $164 billion annually, with college sports contributing up to $6.7 billion [1].

In recent times, the prevalence of social networks makes people travel in many different ways. Ride sharing is one such emerging options and people, having strong personal attachments, make joint trips with friends, neighbors, colleagues, and others for different activities. Individuals are more likely to share rides or carpool with friends as compared to conventional modes of travel such as driving one's own car, using transits, and so on. Such sharing is more prominent during special events when individuals make joint trips to a specific location on a given day and time from various parts of the city. As a result, accommodating for the travel demand and additional traffic generated during a special event is the key to its success. Although the importance of social network on social activities has been extensively studied and some models were developed to predict mode choice during special events, nothing has yet been presented which links social network, mode choice, and special events.

Since special events play a significant role on travel management plans and a relevant economic impact nationwide, it is important to understand how attendants choose a specific modal to reach the venue location. Efficient measures to control traffic and pedestrian flow can be developed based on the frequency distribution of mode choices. Hence, a behavioral model that can predict the mode choice during a given PSE is needed. The modal split forecast is an essential tool to help practitioners to develop more efficient management plans that would accommodate both current and future transit demand. In this matter, recognizing the explanatory factors that play into the selection of a mode is an essential part of the modal split forecast. As ridesharing is getting more popular and people are more likely to carpool with friends when attending such events, we believe that spectators' mode choice forecast should be made based not only on sociodemographic attributes, but it should also consider social network characteristics.

This research studies the role that social networks play in mode selection during a special event and how it fosters carpooling during high demand events such as game days. By collecting egocentric data network data, a multinomial logit model was developed to understand the mode choice of attendants during a college game day. Five different modes were considered in the survey: (a) own car, (b) walk, (c) carpool, (d) bus, and (e) others. The model contributes to mode choice research by determining the influential factors in selecting one of five mode choices, as a function of the social network characteristics such as homophily and heterogeneity indexes, network size, and network density. The findings of this study provide useful insights into the modal split during a special event that would help practitioners and campus policy developers to foster ride sharing and facilitate transit authorities to better plan for such occasions, facilitating access to the venue location, and improving the overall experience of attendants. The remainder of this paper is organized as follows. Section 2 provides a brief description on the dataset used in this study. Section 3 discusses the methodology used to develop the model in Section 4. Section 5 presents and discusses the estimation results. Finally, Section 6 summarizes the major findings and concludes the study.

2 Background and Related Work

Recent studies have explored the correlation between social network characteristics and social activities, showing that social activity patterns are likely to be inferred from an individual's social network [3–5]. The importance of people's social networks, information, and communication technology on the social travel demand has also been recognized as opposed to a purely sociodemographic approach, which would overlook important behavioral processes [4, 6]. Habib et al. [7] incorporated social dimension into an activity-based model showing the relevance of interpersonal interactions on the social-activity scheduling process. Using a zero-inflated Poisson model, Sadri et al. [8] discussed the relevance of personal network variables in the joint trip generation, revealing that recreational trips are more likely to occur the higher religion homophily and contact frequency between egos and alters are. The study has shown that individual's make more trips with alters of different income level and vehicle ownership status, linking the idea of network capital to ride sharing encouragement and potentially to mode choice [8].

Social network influence on travel behavior has been extensively studied in the literature [9, 10]. Pike [11] studied the role of social influence in travelers' (students) mode choice behavior using egocentric social networks approach. Maness et al. [12] proposed a generalized behavioral framework for choice models of social influence. The study also listed several behavioral and data concerns associated with such travel behavior. Maness and Cirillo [13] developed a latent class discrete choice model of an indirect informational conformity hypothesis to study social influence effects. Through a multinomial logit model, Cervero [14] listed three blocks of variables that influence mode travel: traditional travel time, cost, and demographic variables; attitudinal and lifestyle preference variables; and built-environment factors. The study suggested that drive-alone and group-ride automobile travel likelihood increased, when compared with transit, with vehicle ownership levels, the presence of a driver's license, and for female trip makers [14].

Some literatures have studied the importance of PSEs. PSEs include events at both permanent (i.e., arenas, stadiums, racetracks, fairgrounds, amphitheaters, convention centers, etc.) and temporary venues. Sporting events, concerts, festivals, and conventions and also less frequent public events such as parades, fireworks displays, bicycle races, sporting games, motorcycle rallies, seasonal festivals, and milestone celebrations illustrate the concept of a special event [15]. The term planned refers to the essence of such events because of their known locations, scheduled times of occurrence, and associated operating characteristics [2]. The Indianapolis 500 and Brickyard 400 are the two largest single-day sporting events in the world that are attended by >400,000 spectators [16]. On the other hand, universities and sports venues regularly host events that may attract >100,000 attendants [17].

A few studies are specific to the behavioral modeling of travel behavior for special events. For example, a multinomial logit model was developed based on travel characteristics (cost and time) and individual characteristics (car ownership) to predict the modal split during the sixth urban sports meeting held in Wuhan in 2007 [18]. Another multinomial logit model to forecast mode choice during a special event was developed by Yan et al., which used the socioeconomic situation and the attributes of transportation mode alternatives (travel time, access/egress time, fare, etc.) via a utility function [19]. Although the empirical literature was previously inconclusive about how social networks play a role into evacuation decision-making [20–23], recent studies have explored the notion of social influence in crisis communication such as evacuations [24, 25]. Some other relevant studies include methods dealing with large-scale datasets and their applications [26–34].

3 Data

This study focuses on personal network characteristics in order to determine the casual factors that influence the mode choice for an attendee on a college sports game day. The respondents were drawn from an undergraduate class at Purdue University. An email invitation, which included a link to the survey questionnaire on Qualtrics, was sent to the students. In all, 562 students completed the survey. The survey questionnaire asked five mode choices for students to choose from: car, walk, carpool, bus, and "other" option, which included any other modes not listed in the above (i.e., bicycle, taxi, etc.). This was done by asking the survey respondents the following question: "On a Purdue game day, how would you prefer to go to the Ross-Ade Stadium from the place you stay?" The use of a personal network research design (PNRD) elicited relevant information about the focal individual attributes (also known as ego), the ego's perceptions of the attributes of each alters (e.g., sex, race, income, etc.) and the shared relationship (e.g., duration, intensity, frequency, etc.) [24, 25, 35, 36]. However, unlike offline egocentric personal networks, many studies explored large-scale online social media communication networks [37–41].

Many structural characteristics can be used to investigate personal networks. Three different major dimensions exist for these characteristics, according to the level of analysis [42]: ego-alter tie attributes, alter-alter tie attributes, and network composition. Ego-alter tie characteristics are directly related to the amount of support, resource exchange and communication needed [43]. It was the basis to define the network size variable used in the model. Alter-alter ties allowed us to compute density across different networks. Density measurements show the extent of involvement of individuals in a network. A dense personal network is synonymy of closeness among alters and it is a way to easily access the resources of others [8]. Network composition was approached using both statistics of homophily and heterogeneity. Usually, the first step on a PNRD is to create a list of alters to which the ego has some kind of connection. Name generator questions serve this purpose. Name generator questions are by nature open ended and attention should be drawn to the fact that they might result in lengthy surveys causing order effects, fatigue, satisficing, nonredundancy, as well as interviewer effects [44–46]. In this survey, the authors used: "Looking back over the last 3 months, who are the people with whom you discussed matters important to you?" In order to derive respondents' travel-specific network relationships, they were asked to nominate exclusively nominate their friends in Indiana. The next step is to ask name interpreter questions. These questions reveal the egocentric nature of PNRD since the ego alone provides information about his and his alters attributes as well as ego-alter ties [35]. Two different measures of ego-alter tie attributes were computed: the duration of ties and the frequency of interaction. The averaged values of these two categorical variables were used as explanatory variables in the multinomial logit model developed. The personal network variables were analyzed and measured using *E*-NET [47].

4 Modeling Framework

To produce a reliable model, we split the dataset into two and created for each one of the subgroups a different choice set for the dependent variable, thus creating a different model for each subgroup. Ego networks were grouped based on vehicular ownership, a variable that was also introduced in the survey questionnaire. For those who responded positively to the question "Do you own a car or any other vehicle?" the five mode choices (car, walk, carpool, bus, and other) were considered, whereas the car mode was constrained for whoever responded negatively to the same question. After analyzing the frequency distribution of each mode, it was necessary to merge taxi and other, creating a more robust "other" option on both datasets due to the few number of observations on the taxi mode. The original dataset contained 548 observations on mode choice and after accounting for missing data on some of the explanatory variables, it reduced to a total of 504 observations altogether. Fig. 1 shows the frequency distribution of mode choices as well as the total number of observations computed for each model.

In this study, the mode choice decisions of car owners include five choices in order to reach the point of interest from different origins during a special event. These include:

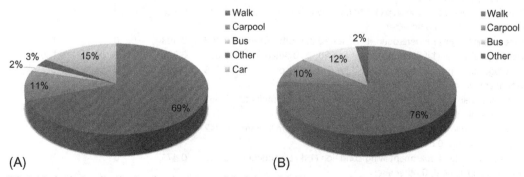

(A)   (B)

FIG. 1 Mode choice distribution for the two models. (A) Model 1(car owners) distribution and (B) Model 2 (non-car owners) distribution.

(a) car, (b) carpool, (c) walk, (d) bus, and (e) others. For individuals who do not own a car, the choice set reduces to four discrete choices excluding the car option. Discrete preferences like these can effectively be analyzed by using a logit-based modeling framework [48, 49]. Now, in order to explain the mode choice decisions, consider a function that defines the multinomial outcome of the mode choice preference for an individual i:

$$C_{m,i} = \beta_m V_{m,i} + \varepsilon_{m,i} \tag{1}$$

where

- $C_{m,i}$ is a function determining the mode choice category m in M ($m = 1, 2, 3, 4, 5$ for car owners and $m = 1, 2, 3, 4$ for non-car owners);
- $V_{m,i}$ is the vector of explanatory variables (see Table 1);
- β_i is the vector of estimable parameters and
- $\varepsilon_{m,i}$ is an error term.

Table 1 Descriptive Statistics of Explanatory Variables

Variable Description	Mean	Standard Deviation	Minimum	Maximum
Model 1 (car owners)				
Indicator variable for network size (1 if netsize ≥8, 0 otherwise)	0.587	0.493	0	1
Indicator variable for density (1 if density ≥7, 0 otherwise)	0.216	0.412	0	1
Indicator variable for average frequency of contact (1 if average frequency of contact ≥5.5, 0 otherwise)	0.465	0.500	0	1
Indicator variable of average duration of relationship (1 if average duration of relationship ≥2.8, 0 otherwise)	0.429	0.496	0	1
Homophily: sex (1 if homophily E-I of sex ≤ −0.2, 0 otherwise)	0.781	0.414	0	1
Homophily: age (1 if homophily E-I of age ranges from −0.5 to 0.5, 0 otherwise)	0.558	0.497	0	1
Homophily: race (1 if homophily E-I of race ≤ −0.2, 0 otherwise)	0.842	0.365	0	1
Homophily: marital status (1 if homophily E-I of marital status ranges from −0.6 to 0, 0 otherwise)	0.500	0.501	0	1
Homophily: income (1 if homophily E-I of income ranges from −0.3 to 0.2, 0 otherwise)	0.174	0.380	0	1
Homophily: vehicular ownership (1 if homophily E-I of vehicular ownership ≤ −0.1, 0 otherwise)	0.877	0.328	0	1
Heterogeneity: sex (1 if heterogeneity of sex ≥0.2, 0 otherwise)	0.797	0.403	0	1
Heterogeneity: age (1 if heterogeneity of age ≥0.75, 0 otherwise)	0.087	0.282	0	1
Heterogeneity: vehicular ownership (1 if heterogeneity of vehicular ownership ≥0.6, 0 otherwise)	0.235	0.425	0	1
Indicator variable of on-campus living condition (1 if respondent lives on campus, 0 otherwise)	0.655	0.476	0	1
Indicator variable of dorm living condition (1 if respondent lives in any Purdue dorm, 0 otherwise)	0.242	0.429	0	1
Indicator variable of apartment living condition (1 if respondent lives in an apartment, 0 otherwise)	0.342	0.475	0	1

Table 1 Descriptive Statistics of Explanatory Variables—cont'd

Variable Description	Mean	Standard Deviation	Minimum	Maximum
Indicator variable of number of people in the family (1 if number of people in the family ≥4, 0 otherwise)	0.735	0.442	0	1
Model 2 (non-car owners)				
Indicator variable for network size (1 if netsize ≥6, 0 otherwise)	0.655	0.476	0	1
Indicator variable for density (1 if density > 0.45, 0 otherwise)	0.488	0.501	0	1
Indicator variable for average frequency of contact (1 if average frequency of contact > 4.8, 0 otherwise)	0.803	0.399	0	1
Indicator variable of average duration of relationship (1 if average duration of relationship ≥2.8, 0 otherwise)	0.261	0.440	0	1
Homophily: sex (1 if homophily *E-I* of sex ≥0.8, 0 otherwise)	0.030	0.170	0	1
Homophily: age (1 if homophily *E-I* of age ranges from −0.3 to 0.1, 0 otherwise)	0.227	0.420	0	1
Homophily: race (1 if homophily *E-I* of race ranges from −0.9 to −0.3, 0 otherwise)	0.320	0.468	0	1
Homophily: income (1 if homophily *E-I* of income ≥0.8, 0 otherwise)	0.404	0.492	0	1
Homophily: vehicular ownership (1 if homophily *E-I* of vehicular ownership ranges from −0.5 to −0.2, 0 otherwise)	0.158	0.365	0	1
Heterogeneity: sex (1 if heterogeneity of sex ≥0.45, 0 otherwise)	0.271	0.446	0	1
Heterogeneity: age (Blau's index of heterogeneity)	0.393	0.262	0	0.84
Indicator variable of on-campus living condition (1 if respondent lives on campus, 0 otherwise)	0.803	0.399	0	1
Indicator variable of apartment living condition (1 if respondent lives in an apartment, 0 otherwise)	0.222	0.416	0	1
Indicator variable of dorm living condition (1 if respondent lives in any Purdue dorm, 0 otherwise)	0.498	0.501	0	1
Indicator variable of number of people in the family (1 if number of people in the family ≥5, 0 otherwise)	0.374	0.485	0	1

Now with the assumption that $\varepsilon_{m,i}$ is generalized extreme value distributed [50], the multinomial logit model results in the following equations [49]:

$$\Pr_m^i = \frac{\exp(\beta_m V_{m,i})}{\sum_M \exp(\beta_m V_{M,i})} \tag{2}$$

where $\Pr_m^i$ is the probability of the mode choice type m (among all the types M) for individual i.

The social network characteristics for the sociodemographic data, that is, homophily and heterogeneity were computed using the software *E-net*. Krackhardt and Stern's *E-I* statistic was used to measure similarities among an ego and his alters. The index is calculated by subtracting internal ties (i.e., from the same attribute category as the ego) from external ties (i.e., those that are from a different attribute category) and diving the subtraction by the network size. Ego's with an *E-I* score of −1 have ties exclusively to alters that belong to a same given attribute category as him, while an *E-I* score of +1 represents connection to alters that belong exclusively to other attribute categories. Blau's index was used to measure the diversity between alters. Given an attribute category, this index varies from 0 (all alters similar for that attribute) to 1 (meaning alters are more diverse for the given attribute). Fig. 2 shows examples of different networks found in the study, with some network characteristics computed.

5 Model Estimation Results

This section presents estimation results of multinomial logit models to predict the transportation mode chosen by attendees on a Purdue game day. To come up with the respective models, 504 decisions were analyzed inside a multinomial logit framework using Stata13 [51]. All of the explanatory variables used in the model are generic variables that are common among the alternatives. Goodness-of-fit measures are presented for the models, and the values of ρ and ρ^2 are reported. All being above 0.2 indicates good goodness of fit. Also the average marginal effects are presented for each explanatory variable in Tables 2 and 3, allowing for the evaluation of the change in probability given a unit change in the explanatory variable in the analysis, with all other variables equal to their means. A discussion on the final model parameters and on the findings is presented in the subsequent paragraphs:

5.1 Model 1 (Car Owners)

This first model was developed for respondents who reported that they owned a car or any other vehicle. The original choice set was maintained for the analysis, consisting of: car, carpool, bus, and other. Walk was set as the base outcome, so all the coefficients of other modes could be compared with it. The constants shown are defined for all modes in this model, and they indicate that, all else being equal, individuals are more likely to drive their own cars to the game.

5.1.1 Density, Network Size, and Ego-Alter Tie Attributes
Results presented on Table 2 show that the likelihood of using own car increases for network sizes greater than or equal to eight. This might be so because individuals who own a car might prefer to drive it instead of using any other mode, as shown by the constants values. The indicator variable of density was defined across car and carpool modes. Attendees with a network density greater or equal than seven are more likely to carpool than any other mode ($\beta = 1.355$). This result is expected in the sense that denser networks stimulate resource sharing [8]. On the other hand, individuals who either contact their alters more frequently or that have known their alters for a longer period of time are more likely to walk to the venue location. This result is understandable if we think the walk action as a group activity rather than a solo journey.

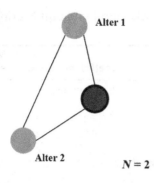

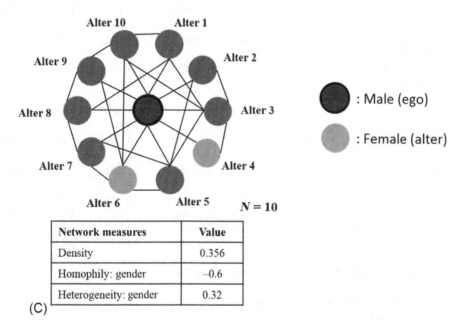

FIG. 2 Ego-network examples with different network characteristics. (A) Network size $N=2$, (B) Network size $N=5$, and (C) Network size $N=10$.

Table 2 Estimation Results of Model 1 (Car Owners) Multinomial Logit Model for Choice of Mode

Model 1 (Car Owners)	Coefficient	z-Stat	Marginal effect
Walk	(Base outcome)		
Car			
Constant	2.108	2.44	
Indicator variable for network size (1 if netsize $\geq$8, 0 otherwise)	0.993	2.35	0.096
Indicator variable for density (1 if density $\geq$0.7, 0 otherwise)	1.220	2.66	0.090
Indicator variable for average frequency of contact (1 if average frequency of contact $\geq$5.5, 0 otherwise)	−0.937	−2.18	−0.059
Homophily: sex (1 if homophily *E-I* of sex $\leq$ −0.2, 0 otherwise)	−0.433	−0.94	−0.023
Homophily: race (1 if homophily *E-I* of race $\leq$ −0.2, 0 otherwise)	−1.341	−2.79	−0.107
Homophily: income (1 if homophily *E-I* of income ranges from −0.3 to 0.2, 0 otherwise)	1.296	2.69	0.091
Homophily: vehicular ownership (1 if homophily *E-I* of vehicular ownership $\leq$ −0.1, 0 otherwise)	−1.440	−2.63	−0.168
Indicator variable of on-campus living condition (1 if respondent lives on campus, 0 otherwise)	−1.887	−4.03	−0.147
Indicator variable of dorm living condition (1 if respondent lives in any Purdue dorm, 0 otherwise)	−1.623	−1.94	−0.158
Indicator variable of apartment living condition (1 if respondent lives in an apartment, 0 otherwise)	0.603	1.39	0.035
Indicator variable of number of people in the family (1 if number of people in the family $\geq$4, 0 otherwise)	−1.089	−2.69	−0.106
Carpool			
Constant	−3.505	−2.13	
Indicator variable for density (1 if density $\geq$0.7, 0 otherwise)	1.355	2.35	0.073
Indicator variable for average frequency of contact (1 if average frequency of contact $\geq$5.5, 0 otherwise)	−1.484	−2.67	−0.088
Indicator variable of average duration of relationship (1 if average duration of relationship $\geq$2.8, 0 otherwise)	−1.931	−3.53	−0.141
Homophily: sex (1 if homophily *E-I* of sex $\leq$ −0.2, 0 otherwise)	−0.591	−1.14	−0.029
Homophily: age (1 if homophily *E-I* of age ranges from −0.5 to 0.5, 0 otherwise)	0.769	1.56	0.061
Homophily: race (1 if homophily *E-I* of race $\leq$ −0.2, 0 otherwise)	−1.083	−1.87	−0.050
Homophily: marital status (1 if homophily *E-I* of marital status ranges from −0.6 to 0, 0 otherwise)	1.193	2.39	0.087
Homophily: income (1 if homophily *E-I* of income ranges from −0.3 to 0.2, 0 otherwise)	1.413	2.7	0.072
Homophily: vehicular ownership (1 if homophily *E-I* of vehicular ownership $\leq$ −0.1, 0 otherwise)	1.339	1.44	0.128
Heterogeneity: sex (1 if heterogeneity of sex $\geq$0.2, 0 otherwise)	1.323	1.57	0.096
Heterogeneity: age (1 if heterogeneity of age $\geq$0.75, 0 otherwise)	1.936	3.12	0.141
Heterogeneity: vehicular ownership (1 if heterogeneity of vehicular ownership $\geq$0.6, 0 otherwise)	0.881	1.58	0.064
Indicator variable of on-campus living condition (1 if respondent lives on campus, 0 otherwise)	−1.221	−2.22	−0.044

Table 2 Estimation Results of Model 1 (Car Owners) Multinomial Logit Model for Choice of Mode—cont'd

Model 1 (Car Owners)	Coefficient	z-Stat	Marginal effect
Indicator variable of apartment living condition (1 if respondent lives in an apartment, 0 otherwise)	0.861	1.65	0.046
Bus			
Constant	−1.223	−2.3	
Homophily: age (1 if homophily *E-I* of age ranges from −0.5 to 0.5, 0 otherwise)	−2.501	−2.26	−0.053
Indicator variable of on-campus living condition (1 if respondent lives on campus, 0 otherwise)	−2.547	−2.92	−0.042
Other			
Constant	−2.967	−4.04	
Homophily: sex (1 if homophily *E-I* of sex ≤ -0.2, 0 otherwise)	−1.509	−2	−0.034
Homophily: income (1 if homophily E-I of income ranges from −0.3 to 0.2, 0 otherwise)	1.212	1.54	0.020
Indicator variable of apartment living condition (1 if respondent lives in an apartment, 0 otherwise)	1.185	1.6	0.024
Log-likelihood at zero, LL(0)	−295.5764		
Log-likelihood at convergence, LL(β)	−215.1506		
ρ^2	0.272		
Adjusted ρ^2	0.215		
Number of observations	306		

Table 3 Estimation Results of Model 2 (Non-Car Owners) Multinomial Logit Model for Choice of Mode

Model 2 (Non-Car Owners)	Coefficient	z-Stat	Marginal Effect
Walk	(Base outcome)		
Carpool			
Constant	−4.015	−3.08	
Indicator variable for density (1 if density >0.45, 0 otherwise)	1.141	1.88	0.074
Indicator variable for average frequency of contact (1 if average frequency of contact >4.8, 0 otherwise)	1.234	1.09	0.080
Homophily: sex (1 if homophily *E-I* of sex ≥ 0.8, 0 otherwise)	3.579	2.21	0.181
Homophily: age (1 if homophily *E-I* of age ranges from −0.3 to 0.1, 0 otherwise)	1.715	2.64	0.111
Homophily: race (1 if homophily *E-I* of race ranges from −0.9 to −0.3, 0 otherwise)	0.970	1.66	0.063
Indicator variable of on-campus living condition (1 if respondent lives on campus, 0 otherwise)	−1.254	−1.75	−0.060
Indicator variable of apartment living condition (1 if respondent lives in an apartment, 0 otherwise)	1.442	2.05	0.057

Continued

Table 3 Estimation Results of Model 2 (Non-Car Owners) Multinomial Logit Model for Choice of Mode—cont'd

Model 2 (Non-Car Owners)	Coefficient	z-Stat	Marginal Effect
Indicator variable of number of people in the family (1 if number of people in the family $\geq$5, 0 otherwise)	−1.275	−1.76	−0.082
Bus			
Constant	−2.859	−2.29	
Indicator variable for network size (1 if netsize $\geq$6, 0 otherwise)	−0.727	−1.25	−0.051
Indicator variable of average duration of relationship (1 if average duration of relationship $\geq$2.8, 0 otherwise)	−1.473	−1.49	−0.104
Homophily: sex (1 if homophily *E-I* of sex $\geq$0.8, 0 otherwise)	3.882	2.55	0.224
Homophily: income (1 if homophily E-I of income $\geq$0.8, 0 otherwise)	0.650	1.15	0.040
Homophily: vehicular ownership (1 if homophily E-I of vehicular ownership ranges from −0.5 to −0.2, 0 otherwise)	1.476	2.28	0.105
Heterogeneity: sex (1 if heterogeneity of sex $\geq$0.45, 0 otherwise)	1.289	2.28	0.091
Heterogeneity: age (Blau's index of heterogeneity)	−1.653	−1.53	−0.117
Indicator variable of on-campus living condition (1 if respondent lives on campus, 0 otherwise)	−1.848	−1.95	−0.117
Indicator variable of apartment living condition (1 if respondent lives in an apartment, 0 otherwise)	3.214	2.63	0.211
Indicator variable of dorm living condition (1 if respondent lives in any Purdue dorm, 0 otherwise)	2.505	2.12	0.177
Other			
Constant	−4.710	−4.58	
Homophily: sex (1 if homophily *E-I* of sex $\geq$0.8, 0 otherwise)	3.408	2.16	0.058
Homophily: income (1 if homophily E-I of income $\geq$0.8, 0 otherwise)	1.860	1.62	0.039
Log-likelihood at zero, LL(0)	−153.35972		
Log-likelihood at convergence, LL(β)	−107.11187		
ρ^2	0.302		
Adjusted ρ^2	0.204		
Number of observations	198		

5.1.2 Homophily Indexes

Both sex and race homophily show similar effects on carpool, when compared with the walk mode. The higher the homophily in those cases, the more likely the individuals are to walk to the game. This might be the case where the diversity of gender and race between an ego and his alters stimulates carpooling. The marginal effects of these two variables show that the carpool mode is more affected by a change in sex homophily (M.E=−0.029) than it is by a change in race homophily (−0.050). Individuals with intermediate values of age and income homophiles are more likely to carpool than any other mode. Again we see egos who have a network with different attributes than his own being more likely to carpool. Marital status homophily was defined only across the carpool. The range set on that variable reveals that values close to complete homophily or any value that approximates to heterophily might stimulate the individual to carpool.

Probably the most interesting result in terms of homophily is the one for vehicular ownership. Since in this model all respondents own a car, total homophily values mean exclusively connections to alters who also own car, and total heterophily means the exact opposite. The combined range and coefficients of that variable show that the more an ego who owns a car is connect to alters who also own a car, the more likely he is to carpool ($\beta = 1.339$), and the less likely he is to drive his own car alone ($\beta = -1.440$). The reason for that might lay on the fact that since more resource (i.e., car) is found in this type of network, individuals would be more willing to share it. Also, an ego who connects himself with other car owners would have more opportunities to carpool than others who connect themselves with non-car owners.

5.1.3 Heterogeneity Indexes

Heterogeneity variables were defined only for carpool, and all of them (sex, age, and vehicular ownership) show a positive association with this mode, indicated by the positive sign of the coefficients. The indicator variable for age heterogeneity is, in fact, the one with the greater impact on carpool. Its average marginal effect suggests that the probability of carpooling increases by 0.141. This is an indication that this mode is highly influenced by the diversification of one's network, and that individuals with a more diverse network are more likely to pursue resource sharing.

5.1.4 Location Variables

The indicator variables for on campus, dorm, and apartment behave as expected. Although far distances are not appropriately addressed in the survey questionnaire (meaning that overall proximity of all residences do not exceed 5 miles from the arena), the proximity to campus decreases the likelihood of adopting any other mode of transportation besides walk, while individuals living in apartments pursuit carpool more than any other mode.

5.2 Model 2 (Non-Car Owners)

This first model was developed for respondents who reported that they did not own a car or any other vehicle. The car mode was intuitively constrained in this case. Walk was set as the base outcome, so all the coefficients of other modes could be compared to it.

5.2.1 Density, Network Size, and Ego-Alter Tie Attributes

The results presented in Table 3 show that for individuals who did not own a car, the higher the density of personal network, the more likely they are to carpool as compared with any other mode of transportation taken into account ($\beta = 1.141$). Network size has an influence for bus mode in this model, with its likelihood decreasing for network sizes greater or equal to six, as compared with the other lower range. Indicator variable for frequency of contact shows a positive influence for carpool and indicator variable for average relationship duration decreases the likelihood of riding a bus.

5.2.2 Homophily Indexes

The *E-I* index of sex was a variable defined and categorized across all alternatives, and it indicates that the more heterophily of sex between egos and alters, the more likely individuals are to pursuit other modes other than walk. The coefficient result for age homophily indicates that individuals in the intermediate range are more likely to carpool. These two variable results would be another evidence that egos who seek connections to alters from different attribute categories than his would be more likely to carpool. Although this might seem counterintuitive (since we might think that the more like each other people in a network are the more they will do activities together), it has a plausible explanation. The diverse nature of the egos network might grant them access to a so likely diverse source of resources. Since these egos are used to make diverse connections, they might also be more likely to do activities that might involve the presence of people unknown to them. This result is consistent with the previous model. Homophily of race plays a positive influence on carpool ($\beta = 0.970$), showing that individuals who do not own a car are more likely to carpool with alters that pertain to the same race. Heterophily of income has a positive association with the likelihood of riding a bus in this model.

Once again vehicular ownership homophily is an interesting variable in the analysis. In this second model, total homophily means connections to alters who do not own a vehicle, whereas total heterophily represents exclusively connections to alters who do own a car. At the extent of values ranging from -0.5 to -0.2, individuals are more likely to ride a bus when compared with all other modes considered. This result seems logical, once egos connected to alters who do not own cars would be more willing to take a non-car-dependent mode such as a bus.

5.2.3 Heterogeneity Indexes and Location Variables

While heterogeneity of sex increases the likelihood of riding a bus ($\beta = 1.289$), heterogeneity of age decreases this same likelihood ($\beta = -1.653$). Variables showing living conditions behave as expected in this model. On campus residents are more likely to walk to the game, while dorm residents (which are part of the on campus share) are more likely to ride a bus. This might be so because dorm residents might be more used to ride buses, that is, to class on a daily basis. Apartments residents are more likely to ride a bus ($\beta = 3.214$), followed by carpool ($\beta = 1.442$).

6 Conclusions

While previous studies have explored mode choice during special events by taking into account utility functions and sociodemographic attributes, this study presents a network approach of social influence on modal splits during such events. The multinomial logit model incorporates explanatory variables related to social network characteristics, that is, homophily, heterogeneity, density, and network size. The model was developed based on a personal (egocentric) network research design approach that investigated which of the five different travel modes (car, walk, carpool, bus, and other) college students from

Purdue University take to reach the Ross-Ade-Stadium during a football game. Ego and alter attributes, as well as ego-alter and alter-alter tie attributes were the basis for the explanatory variables included in the model.

An analysis of the estimation results for both the models provides key insights with respect to the travel mode during a special event. Such insights include:

- Carpool mode revealed a strong positive correlation with network density, showing that dense networks are associated with more carpool travels.
- Homophily of age presented itself similarly across the models. Intermediate values, in both cases, are linked with higher likelihood of carpooling, meaning that egos who share connections with a diverse set of alters would be more likely to carpool than those who relate to more similar or totally different set of alters in terms of age.
- Homophily of sex and income in both models showed that an ego who seek connections to alters that are different than him would have a greater likelihood of carpooling.
- Individuals who own a car and who have a network composed mostly by alters who also own a car are more likely to carpool,
- Heterogeneity values in model 1, which included only car owner egos, showed that the more diverse the alters of an ego are in terms of gender, age, and vehicular ownership, the more likely the ego is to carpool.
- Bus is preferred by non-car owners (model 2).
- The closer the individuals are to the venue location, the less likely they are to take their own cars to reach the event.

The proposed model shows us that a dense and diverse network in terms of age and sex (both in terms of ego and alter attributes as well as for alter and alter attributes) would increase the likelihood of carpooling for an individual. With these findings, actions that promote the interaction of different individuals in a campus community could be encouraged. Bringing people together through college activities, international events such as food days and road trips, floor meetings, dorm game days, and so on, would be a way to reinforce the existing connections inside a network and promote the diversity and addition of new individuals to the network. Since proximity to the campus plays an influence on whether to use a car or not, a good way to foster ride sharing in this occasion would be to provide shuttle services serving high-density locations such as apartment complexes inside and outside campus during game days. The model developed would also help local transit agencies to better plan for such events, increasing the potential to promote such events, thus creating a path to generate income for locals, reduce congestion for both attendees and nonattendees, accommodate travel demand and parking needs and improve access to the venue location.

Although the model provides evidence of the effect of social network on mode choice during a special event, some limitations still remain. The effect of proximity to the venue location needs to be better addressed, since the survey was responded by Purdue college students who mostly reside in a radius no >5 miles to the arena. Intermodal travel was suppressed by the survey questionnaire design, that is, driving a car to a certain location and from there using a public transportation. Network composition for the egos interviewed could have led to more solid results if we knew to what extent people in the networks collected are used to interact with each other in terms of social activities on a daily basis, that is eating out, study, shopping, and so on. Again this would be better addressed with an inclusion in the survey questionnaire. In the face of the results and limitations of this study, the authors recognize the need for more research linking special events mode choice and social networks. We hope that the findings and propositions presented in this study are taken into account by campus city transportation agencies to foster carpool during high demand events. Joining such actions with the modal split forecast proposed by the two models in this study will help to improve the overall experience of attendants, reduce congestion, and also alleviate transit demand issues associated with special events.

References

[1] J. Skolnik, R. Chami, M. Walker, Planned Special Events–Economic Role and Congestion Effects, No. FHWA-HOP-08-022, 2008.

[2] W.M. Dunn Jr., Managing Travel for Planned Special Events Handbook: Executive Summary, No. FHWA-HOP-07-108, 2007.

[3] J.A. Carrasco, E.J. Miller, Socializing with people and not places: modelling social activities explicitly incorporation social networks, in: Computers in Urban Planning and Urban Management, 2005. London.

[4] J.-A. Carrasco, E.J. Miller, The social dimension in action: a multilevel, personal networks model of social activity frequency between individuals, Transp. Res. A Policy Pract. 43 (1) (2009) 90–104.

[5] J.A. Carrasco, B. Hogan, B. Wellman, E.J. Miller, Collecting social network data to study social activity-travel behavior: an egocentric approach, Environ. Plann. B Plann. Des. 35 (6) (2008) 961–980.

[6] P. Van den Berg, Social Activity-Travel Patters: The Role of Personal Networks and Communication Technology (PhD dissertation), Eindhoven University of Technology, Eindhoven, 2012.

[7] K. Habib, J. Carrasco, E. Miller, Social context of activity scheduling: discrete-continuous model of relationship between" with whom" and episode start time and duration, Transp. Res. Rec. J. Transp. Res. Board 2076 (2008) 81–87.

[8] A.M. Sadri, S. Lee, S.V. Ukkusuri, Modeling social network influence on joint trip frequency for regular activity travel decisions, Transp. Res. Rec. J. Transp. Res. Board 2495 (2015) 83–93.

[9] J. Kim, S. Rasouli, H.J.P. Timmermans, Social networks, social influence and activity-travel behaviour: a review of models and empirical evidence, Transp. Rev. (2017) 1–25.

[10] S. Pike, M. Lubell, Geography and social networks in transportation mode choice, J. Transp. Geogr. 57 (2016) 184–193.

[11] S. Pike, Endogeneity in Social Influence and Transportation Mode Choice Using Ego-Networks, No. 15-5879, 2015.

[12] M. Maness, C. Cirillo, E.R. Dugundji, Generalized behavioral framework for choice models of social influence: behavioral and data concerns in travel behavior, J. Transp. Geogr. 46 (2015) 137–150.

[13] M. Maness, C. Cirillo, An indirect latent informational conformity social influence choice model: formulation and case study, Transp. Res. B Methodol. 93 (2016) 75–101.

[14] R. Cervero, Built environments and mode choice: toward a normative framework, Transp. Res. Part D: Transp. Environ. 7 (4) (2002) 265–284.

[15] S.P. Latoski, W.M. Dunn Jr., B. Wagenblast, J. Randall, M.D. Walker, Managing Travel for Planned Special Events, No. FHWA-OP-04-010, 2003.

[16] J.S. Wasson, S.E. Young, J. Sturdevant, P.J. Tarnoff, J.M. Ernst, D.M. Bullock, Evaluation of Special Event Traffic Management: The Brickyard 400 Case Study, JTRP Other Publications and Reports, Paper 4, 2008. http://docs.lib.purdue.edu/jtrpdocs, https://doi.org/10.5703/1288284314673.

[17] M. Mekker, D.M. Bullock, S.M. Remias, H. Li, Leveraging Commercial Cloud Navigation and Maps for Special Event Route Management, Available at Purdue University Libraries, 2015. https://docs.lib.purdue.edu/roadschool/2015/posters/1/.

[18] L.-j. Xu, B. Wang, W.-b. Zhang, in: A disaggregate model of traffic mode split forecast for public events, Computational Intelligence and Software Engineering, 2009, CiSE 2009, International Conference on, IEEE, 2009, pp. 1–4.

[19] L.C. Yan, S.S. Yang, G.J. Fu, Travel demand model for Beijing 2008 olympic games, J. Transp. Eng. 136 (6) (2009) 537–544.

[20] A.M. Sadri, S.V. Ukkusuri, P. Murray-Tuite, H. Gladwin, How to evacuate: model for understanding the routing strategies during hurricane evacuation, J. Transp. Eng. 140 (1) (2013) 61–69.

[21] A.M. Sadri, S.V. Ukkusuri, P. Murray-Tuite, A random parameter ordered probit model to understand the mobilization time during hurricane evacuation, Transp. Res. Part C Emerg. Technol. 32 (2013) 21–30.

[22] A.M. Sadri, S.V. Ukkusuri, P. Murray-Tuite, H. Gladwin, Analysis of hurricane evacuee mode choice behavior, Transp. Res. Part C Emerg. Technol. 48 (2014) 37–46.

[23] A.M. Sadri, S.V. Ukkusuri, P. Murray-Tuite, H. Gladwin, Hurricane evacuation route choice of major bridges in Miami Beach, Florida, Transp. Res. Rec. J. Transp. Res. Board 2532 (2015) 164–173.

[24] A.M. Sadri, S.V. Ukkusuri, H. Gladwin, The role of social networks and information sources on hurricane evacuation decision making, Nat. Hazards Rev. 18 (3) (2017). 04017005.

[25] A.M. Sadri, S.V. Ukkusuri, H. Gladwin, Modeling joint evacuation decisions in social networks: the case of Hurricane Sandy, J. Choice Model. 25 (2017) 50–60.

[26] D. Acharjya, A. Anitha, A comparative study of statistical and rough computing models in predictive data analysis, Int. J. Ambient Comput. Intell. (IJACI) 8 (2) (2017) 32–51.

[27] M. Benadda, K. Bouamrane, G. Belalem, How to manage persons taken malaise at the steering wheel using HAaaS in a vehicular cloud computing environment, Int. J. Ambient Comput. Intell. (IJACI) 8 (2) (2017) 70–87.

[28] S. Kamal, N. Dey, A.S. Ashour, S. Ripon, V.E. Balas, M.S. Kaysar, FbMapping: an automated system for monitoring Facebook data, Neural Network World 27 (1) (2017) 27.

[29] S. Kamal, S.H. Ripon, N. Dey, A.S. Ashour, V. Santhi, A MapReduce approach to diminish imbalance parameters for big deoxyribonucleic acid dataset, Comput. Methods Prog. Biomed. 131 (2016) 191–206.

[30] M.S. Kamal, M.G. Sarowar, N. Dey, A.S. Ashour, S.H. Ripon, B.K. Panigrahi, J.M.R.S. Tavares, Self-organizing mapping based swarm intelligence for secondary and tertiary proteins classification, Int. J. Mach. Learn. Cybern. (2017) 1–24.

[31] M.S. Kamal, S. Parvin, A.S. Ashour, F. Shi, N. Dey, De-Bruijn graph with MapReduce framework towards metagenomic data classification, Int. J. Inf. Technol. 9 (1) (2017) 59–75.

[32] M.S. Kamal, S.F. Nimmy, M.I. Hossain, N. Dey, A.S. Ashour, V. Santhi, in: ExSep: an exon separation process using neural skyline filter, Electrical, Electronics, and Optimization Techniques (ICEEOT), International Conference on, IEEE, 2016, pp. 48–53.

[33] H. Matallah, G. Belalem, K. Bouamrane, Towards a new model of storage and access to data in big data and cloud computing, Int. J. Ambient Comput. Intell. (IJACI) 8 (4) (2017) 31–44.

[34] M. Yamin, A.A.A. Sen, Improving privacy and security of user data in location based services, Int. J. Ambient Comput. Intell. (IJACI) 9 (1) (2018) 19–42.

[35] D.S. Halgin, S.P. Borgatti, An introduction to personal network analysis and tie churn statistics using E-NET, Connections 32 (1) (2012) 37–48.

[36] A.M. Sadri, S.V. Ukkusuri, S. Lee, R. Clawson, D. Aldrich, M.S. Nelson, J. Seipel, D. Kelly, The role of social capital, personal networks, and emergency responders in post-disaster recovery and resilience: a study of rural communities in Indiana, Nat. Hazards (2018) 1–30.

[37] A.M. Sadri, S. Hasan, S.V. Ukkusuri, M. Cebrian, Understanding Information Spreading in Social Media During Hurricane Sandy: User Activity and Network Properties, arXiv preprint arXiv:1706. 03019, 2017.

[38] A.M. Sadri, S. Hasan, S.V. Ukkusuri, M. Cebrian, Crisis communication patterns in social media during Hurricane Sandy, Transp. Res. Rec. (2017). https://doi.org/10.1177/0361198118773896.

[39] A.M. Sadri, S. Hasan, S.V. Ukkusuri, J.E.S. Lopez, Analysis of social interaction network properties and growth on Twitter, Social Network Analysis and Mining 8 (1) (2018) 56.

[40] A.M. Sadri, S. Hasan, S.V. Ukkusuri, Joint Inference of User Community and Interest Patterns in Social Interaction Networks, arXiv preprint arXiv:1704.01706, 2017.

[41] S. Ukkusuri, X. Zhan, A. Sadri, Q. Ye, Use of social media data to explore crisis informatics: study of 2013 Oklahoma Tornado, Transp. Res. Rec. J. Transp. Res. Board 2459 (2014) 110–118.

[42] N. Park, S. Lee, J.H. Kim, Individuals' personal network characteristics and patterns of Facebook use: a social network approach, Comput. Hum. Behav. 28 (5) (2012) 1700–1707.

[43] C. Haythornthwaite, Social networks and internet connectivity effects, Inf. Commun. Soc. 8 (2) (2005) 125–147.

[44] P.V. Marsden, Interviewer effects in measuring network size using a single name generator, Soc. Networks 25 (1) (2003) 1–16.

[45] J.E. Pustejovsky, J.P. Spillane, Question-order effects in social network name generators, Soc. Networks 31 (4) (2009) 221–229.

[46] T. Van Tilburg, Interviewer effects in the measurement of personal network size: a nonexperimental study, Sociol. Methods Res. 26 (3) (1998) 300–328.

[47] S.P. Borgatti, E-NET Software for the Analysis of Ego-Network Data, Analytic Technologies, Needham, MA, 2006.

[48] K.E. Train, Discrete Choice Methods With Simulation, Cambridge University Press, 2009.

[49] S.P. Washington, M.G. Karlaftis, F. Mannering, Statistical and Econometric Methods for Transportation Data Analysis, CRC press, 2010.

[50] D. McFadden, Structural analysis of discrete data with econometric applications, in: Econometric Models of Probabilistic Choice, The MIT Press, Cambridge, MA, 1981, pp. 198–272.

[51] StataCorp, Stata Statistical Software: Release 13, StataCorp LP, College Station, TX, 2013.

Sentiment Analysis on a Set of Movie Reviews Using Deep Learning Techniques

Koyel Chakraborty*, Siddhartha Bhattacharyya†, Rajib Bag*,
Aboul Alla Hassanien‡

*Department of CSE, Supreme Knowledge Foundation Group of Institutions, Mankundu,
India †Department of CA, RCC Institute of Information Technology, Kolkata, India ‡Faculty of
Computers and Information Technology Department, Cairo University, Giza, Egypt

1 Introduction

Sentiment analysis is the area which deals with judgments, responses as well as feelings, which is generated from texts, being extensively used in fields like data mining, web mining, and social media analytics because sentiments are the most essential characteristics to judge the human behavior. This particular field is creating ripples in both research and industrial societies. Sentiments can be positive, negative, or neutral or it can contain an arithmetical score articulating the effectiveness of the sentiment. Sentiments can be expressed by calculating the judgment of people on a certain topic, approach, and sensation toward a unit [1], where a unit can be an occurrence, a theme, or even a character. Sentiment analysis and opinion mining are used interchangeably in several cases though there are occurrences where they hold minute dissimilarities among themselves [2]. Sentiment analysis works on discovering opinions, classify the attitude they convey, and ultimately categorize them division-wise. The reviews are first collected in the process, their sentiment recognized, features selected, sentiments classified, and finally sentiment polarization determined or calculated. Finding the appropriate dataset is a very important concern while dealing with sentiment analysis. Sentiment analysis can be functional for reviewing products for business, to ascertain the high and lows of stock markets [3, 4], to understand the mentality of people reading news [5], and also views expressed by people in political debates [6]. Sentiment analysis is done basically because not every review that is received gives a direct "good" or a "bad" notion. Though sentiment analysis is very much helpful, the enhancement of the analysis depends on the amount of training data that has been fed into the machine. Generally there are different ways of classifying sentiments, the Machine learning approach and the lexicon-based approach being famous. When the Machine Learning approach is considered, it can be further categorized

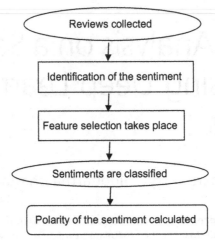

FIG. 1 Process of analyzing sentiments of reviews [1].

into supervised and unsupervised learning. While supervised learning can be defined as the process of learning from already known data to generate initially a model and further predict target class for the particular data, unsupervised learning can be defined as the process of learning from unlabeled to discriminate the provided input data. The process of sentiment analysis can be depicted through the following flowchart (Fig. 1):

Deep learning is considered to be a major part of Machine Learning which is mainly supported on methods and actions formalized to gain knowledge about multiple levels of feature depiction. Learning representations makes it easy to construct classifiers and predictors. The very latest applications that are being unearthed in the fields of deep learning are primarily in Automatic Speech Recognition, Image Recognition, Bioinformatics and also in Big Data Analytics [7], where features of Deep Learning were recognized which makes an impact on the analysis made in Big Data. Inclusion of Deep Learning procedures and availability of large datasets has made possible a great substantial evolution in the field of sentiment analysis. Deep learning has a huge advantage as it carries out involuntary trait selection hence saving time and manual labor as feature engineering is not required. Different deep learning architectures like convolution neural networks and recursive neural networks, deep convolution neural networks, long short-term memory neural networks and other types of networks have yielded good results and outperformed numerous characteristic manufacturing techniques. It is anticipated that overcoming the problem of accessibility of sufficient labeled data and integration of effective deep learning procedures with sentiment analysis shall create immense improvement in supervised as well as unsupervised learning.

This chapter is arranged in the following manner: Section 2 visits through the fundamentals of deep learning along with the process of training the neural networks, the curse of dimensionality and understanding the essence of deep learning with the related work done until now. Section 3 throws light upon sentiment analysis and its essentials. Section 4 emphasizes on the combinatorial advantages of sentiment analysis using deep learning, its effects in general and mentioning some of the related works. Section 5 describes the proposed methodology implemented in this chapter and Section 6 illustrates the dataset utilized. Reference section concludes the chapter citing the references used for this purpose.

2 Deep Learning

Deep learning can simply be defined as a learning using neural networks comprising numerous layers of nodes between the input and the output. All the succession of layers between the input and the output identifies features and does the required processing in a series of stages, very much similar to the human brain functioning process. Confusion may arise in the fact that as the existence of multilayer neural networks was evident for last 25 years why did deep learning all of a sudden create ruckus in the field of machine learning. The reason is that there always were present excellent algorithms for learning weights in networks with a solitary hidden stratum, but unfortunately, those were not sufficient enough to learn weights for networks with multiple hidden layers.

2.1 Learning Neural Networks

Let us examine how neural network weights are actually learned. For the logistic sigmoid function, say,

$$f(x) = \frac{1}{1 + e^{-x}}$$

which if being plotted in a graph would be as shown in Fig. 2.

Neural networks are poised of layers of computational components called neurons, with associations amid the neurons in dissimilar layers. These networks are designated to convert the data until it can classify an object as an output. Now, if the neural network

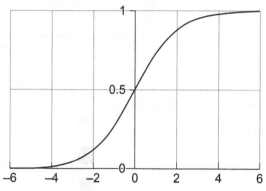

FIG. 2 Graph of the standard logistic sigmoid function [8].

is to be trained with the above function, sequences of calculations are to be performed where initially random weights are assigned to each of the connections to the nodes. The neuron then multiples an initial value by this weight and sums up the result of the other values which are approaching the same neuron. After this the calculated result is then attuned by the bias of the neuron, post which the result is normalized with an activation function as given earlier (Figs. 3 and 4).

The bias regulates the values of the neuron after all the correlations are processed. It is the duty of the activation function to make certain that the values supplied to the neurons are within a permissible range. This process is repeated multiple times to make the final prediction for classification.

Let us consider a small random data set to check how the weights are adjusted while neural networks are trained. The neural networks considered in the example are of multiple layers (Fig. 5).

The initial step in training this multilayered neural network is to assign random weights, after which the training set is presented to the model (Fig. 6).

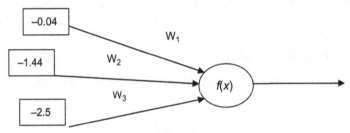

FIG. 3 Random weights assignment to the connections of a neuron.

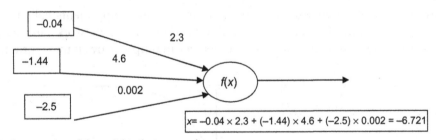

$$x = -0.04 \times 2.3 + (-1.44) \times 4.6 + (-2.5) \times 0.002 = -6.721$$

FIG. 4 Final summation of the weights that approach a neuron.

Data values	Expected result
1.3 3.7 2.9	0
3.8 3.7 3.9	1
5.4 8.8 3.7	1
4.9 0.6 0.8	0
etc ...	

FIG. 5 Example considering a dataset to train a network.

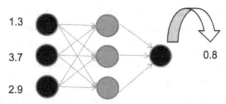

FIG. 6 Summing up the weights of the connections of the network.

Let us consider that after processing, the result yielded is 0.8. But the result that was expected was 0, hence giving rise to an error of 0.8 between the original expected value and the calculated value (Fig. 7).

Now, after comparing with the target output, the weights are adjusted based on the error (Fig. 8).

The identical course is frequented, thousands or perhaps millions of times, at all times considering arbitrary training instances and making necessary weight amendments.

It is to be kept in mind that numerous layers make logic, as it is our brains that function in a similar way. These multiple-layer network architectures must be competent of learning the accurate essential characteristics and "feature logic," and therefore simplify things perfectly (Fig. 9).

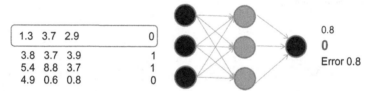

FIG. 7 Calculating the error after adding up all the weights.

FIG. 8 Adjusting the weights to reduce error.

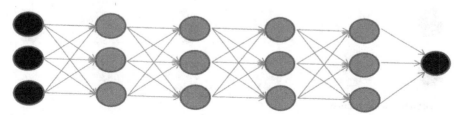

FIG. 9 Multiple-layered neural networks.

The existing weight-learning algorithms did not work on multilayer architectures, the barrier of which was broken by deep learning, where the method to train multiple-layered neural networks was by training each layer one by one sequentially. Every the nonoutput layer is trained to perform as an auto-encoder, being put on to learn the best features that are received from the preceding layers. The final layer is trained to predict the expected output on outputs based from the preceding layers. The hidden layers ultimately turns out to perform as excellent feature detectors. The transitional layers between the initial and the final layer are each trained to be auto-encoders which behave likewise (Figs. 10–12).

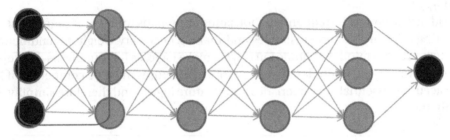

FIG. 10 The first layer being trained.

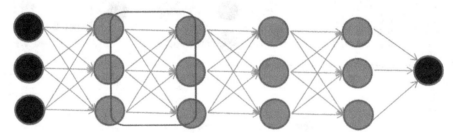

FIG. 11 Training the second layer.

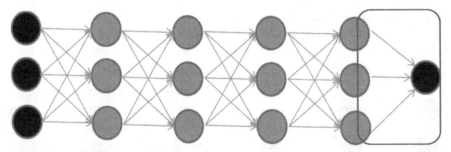

FIG. 12 The last layer being trained.

2.2 Curse of Dimensionality

Training neural networks are hard because the weights of these intermediate layers are highly interreliant. So in the case of a small tug in any of the connection, an effect is made not only on the neuron which is being pulled with, but the same propagates to all the neurons in the subsequent layers, hence affecting all the outputs. This is the reason why it is impossible to attain the finest set of weights by optimizing a single weight at a time, but to explore the complete space of the potential weight groupings concurrently. From here came the concept of applying random weights to connections and repeatedly evaluating the datasets to yield a near-optimum result.

But, how far can this random weight selection perform as in reality the proportion of a reasonably good set of weights is huge. If we are heading to apply a brute force random search approach, we need to clarify the estimate to acquire a superior set of weights. Let us consider an example, in a network where there are 750 input neurons, 20 neurons in a hidden layer, and 12 neurons in the output layer. Then the number of weights can be calculated as $750 \times 20 + 20 \times 12 = 15,240$ weights. This infers that there are 15,240 parameter dimensions to be considered, if there are biases then adding them to this number means we might have to make $10^{15,240}$ guesses, which turns out to be a humongous number.

This principle exhibited in the case of the example is termed as "the curse of dimensionality." However small the dimension we append to the search space, it leads to an exponential rise in the number of samples. So, methods were to be devised that would effectively compute these types of problems. One way to do so could be by the method of linear regression. Liner regression is the job of shaping "a line of best fit" within a set of data points, but there is also the existence of a far more reliable algorithm which provides much more flexibility to the neural networks than model functions.

The gradient descent method is one of the paradigm tools to optimize difficult functions iteratively contained in a problem. It can be acquired by figuring out the current state of the gradient and then take a step down the gradient so that the loss functions are minimized. The amount of modification in the parameters is guessed so that the error is reduced to the minimum, and this process is repeated until a satisfactory point is found.

2.3 Essence of Deep Learning

Deep learning essentially breaks an intricate job into straightforward, conceptual tasks at a hefty scale. For example, if we are to identify visually a square out of a set of quadrilaterals; let us plan on how to recognize the same from a set of shapes (Fig. 13).

The foremost task of our eyes will be to search for the figure where there are four equal lines associated. Then, might be the angles, the congruency of the sides as well as diagonals will be checked for. Hence, the complex job of picking out a square from a set of quadrilaterals is decomposed into small abstract tasks. Deep learning does this identical thing but at a generously proportioned scale. If the case of a creature recognizer machine learning problem is to be considered, where the system has to identify whether the provided image is that of a cow or a tiger, the most typical method of solving this would be to

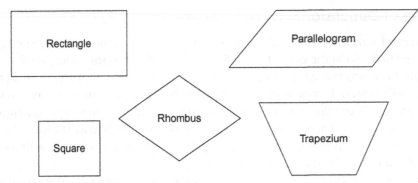

FIG. 13 Set of quadrilaterals.

define characteristics like whiskers or pointed ears being present on the images of the animal. Particularly, we identify the facial description and let the system make out which of the traits are most apt to categorize a particular animal. Deep learning makes the winning stroke in cases like these by automatically unearthing features which are important for classification. Deep learning would first spot the pertinent edges to identify a cow or a tiger, and taking the clue would build a hierarchy to search all possible combinations of shapes and edges that could be made, and based on the amalgamation of the series of identification of features, would then designate the feature responsible for making the final prediction.

One of the very important differences between machine learning and deep learning is their performance with data. Deep learning algorithms perform better with large amounts of data, as it is required to understand the features perfectly. On the other hand, traditional machine learning algorithms scale up to a level with the data provided, after which they act the same and remain at a constant level. Requirement of sophisticated machines is another aspect in which both machine learning and deep learning differ. While machine learning algorithms can work well on low-end machines, deep learning algorithms require a lot of intrinsic matrix multiplications for their functioning and hence are highly dependent on high-end machineries. Referring to learning or identifying of features, deep learning has taken a major leap from the traditional machine learning algorithms in a way that it works by learning features from the data, while machine learning algorithms consume most of the time and proficiency in identifying appropriate features and coding them accordingly. Hence, deep learning diminishes the chore of developing new trait detectors for each problem. Even while solving problems, machine learning algorithms break down the entire problem into varied segments, solve them, and amalgamate to yield the final result. Deep learning though would solve the same problem after completing the entire task at a go. For example, if an image was provided, where multiple objects were to be detected, the task is to identify the multiple objects present in the image along with its location. Machine learning approach of solving this problem would be to first detect and then recognize the image, whereas, if the image would be passed through a specific deep learning algorithm, the name and the location of the object together would come out as the result. Generally, it has been observed that deep learning algorithm takes longer to train as various parameters are associated with it, but takes less time to test data when compared on the basis of execution time of machine learning algorithms. When it comes to interpreting the results that have been yielded out of the deep learning and machine learning algorithms, the former outperforms the later, no doubt, but while traversing the actual reason behind the result cannot be tracked and hence failure in inferring the results is observed. But machine learning algorithms give the user precise reasons on their validation of giving a certain result and hence often secure its position in the industry.

2.4 Convolution Neural Networks

Convolution neural network model or CNN is one of the most popular models used for natural language processing. The most important advantage that this model carries is that it can mechanically detect significant characteristics by itself. CNN also proves to be proficient in calculations as well. They can be executed in any machine and bear the speciality of using special convolution and pooling operations. The term convolution represents the mathematical functionality of unification of two information sets. CNN maintains the nonlinearity feature as should be in an effective neural network. Pooling is used to reduce the dimensionality by dropping the amount of factors and hence shortening the time taken for execution. CNN is trained using backpropagation with gradient descent. There are two parts in the CNN model, namely, mining of features and categorizing them accordingly, and the convolution layers act as the major motivating force of the CNN model.

3 Sentiment Analysis

Sentiments can be referred to as feelings. Our approach, sensation, and judgment on a certain response or a certain event can be referred to as sentiments (Fig. 14). Sentiments cannot be quantified as particulars as they are personal imitations. In case of opinions, twofold theories are considered, like against/for, good/bad, etc. Semantic orientation and polarity are generally considered as sentiment analysis jargons. Sentiment analysis can be defined as the methods used to extort, recognize, or distinguish the sentiment substance of a manuscript. Opinions can be excavated as well as hauled out in sentiment analysis.

One of the chief widespread interests of civilization has been in unrestricted judgment. It is a fashion to take onboard the crowd analysis on the recognition or refutation on a condition, produce, or a measure. Sentiment analysis, a task of natural language processing, automatically discovers features communicated by any type of text [9]. With the current outburst of budding social media trends, opinions are continually being congregated and are also pursued by individuals for their own interests through the social networks, blogs, and tweets. Companies exploit these opinions to survey and appraise customer gratification, partiality, and merchandize reviews.

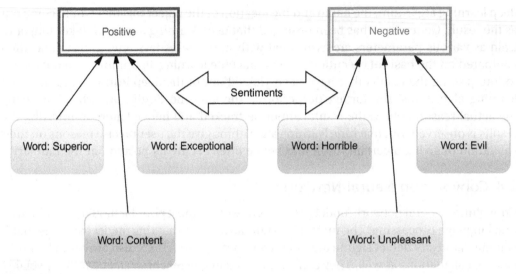

FIG. 14 Sentiments.

Sentiments may pour in through questions like whether the manufactured goods review was optimistic or pessimistic, whether a customer email is contented or disappointed, how is the mass reacting to a newly released advertisement campaign or how has the attitude of the bloggers' changed since the release of a statement by some celebrity. Other than this, information can be unearthed; judgment-related queries can be responded to; and summarization against several perspectives can be accomplished through sentiment analysis. Social and ethical woks such as ascertaining content appropriate for kids based on remarks, detection of partiality in news broadcast resources, and classifying unsuitable substance can be made out with sentiment analysis. From the point of view of a businessman, he/she may apply sentiment analysis to track the question as to why clients are not being fascinated in their product and hence can clear out the ambiguities or the misconceptions prevailing against that particular product or brand. Keeping in mind that it is nearly impossible to find the number of people who have opted for another company for the same product, it is advisable to explore for web-based judgments and reviews of the clients who by now have bought and used the product. On the basis of these, subsequent and necessary changes can be incorporated into the product to increase sales. Not only that sentiment analysis have been used in collecting opinions or sentiments against products, it also has a diversified use of being implemented in political opinions, law, sociology, and psychology. With the wavering political scenario that is faced nowadays, assessment of the outlook of the supporters, debate on the policies of the parties is of concern, which can be handled with the help of sentiment analysis. Considering sociology, thought proliferation throughout clusters is a significant conception, as opinions to facts are pertinent to the acceptance of novel ideas and analyzing response can give a notion of this procedure [10]. Overall, considering the fact that human beings are prejudiced creatures, being able to cooperate with people after exploring their sentiments has many rewards for information systems.

3.1 Challenges Faced While Analyzing Sentiments

If the challenges of sentiment analysis are to be well thought of, the foremost thing that is to be kept in mind is the fact that human beings favor giving multifaceted judgments, where the lexical substance can itself be deceiving. Dealing with cynicism, mockery, and repercussions is a big issue in the field of sentiment analysis. While dealing with the opinions, variations in matter or reversals within the wordings is also to be considered. The categorization factor is also of importance in terms of analyzing, for example, we can grade the consumers or the text itself, or the sentences along with paragraphs, or the preset adjective expressions, or even single words or a single comment. Short phrases, for example, can serve as building blocks of sentiment analysis. Phrases like "highest prices" and "lowest quality" brings out the actual essence of the sentiment present in a text, so a method should be devised before advancing toward sorting. If we consider that there is some connection between equal polarity words and reviews, a set of keywords might be favorable enough to identify polarity. Other than human-generated keyword lists, there is existence of information-driven methods as well which yield better lists than those of humans, but unigram means can give up to 80% accuracy while listing keywords. One of the popular ways to address sentiments is by analyzing smileys or emoticons in tweets or texts (Fig. 15).

Smileys have the advantage that they have very short texts associated with them, hence the overhead is low and sentiments can be expressed very precisely with these emoticons. Sentiment research-related datasets are very much domain sensitive and at the same time it is complicated to accumulate or construct them. Pang and Lee provides reviewed movie datasets, scaled sentiment datasets as well as subjectivity datasets [11]. If datasets for sentiment analysis is to be created, both self-annotated and hand-annotated data have to be used. While the former has built in labeling by the creator, the latter has annotated data autonomous of the creator resulting in the process to be more laborious and varies on

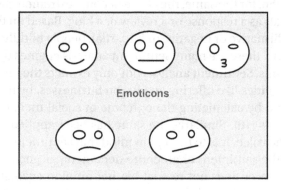

FIG. 15 Emojis or smileys.

reliability. It has been observed that to extract the sentiment of a phrase, the best possible technique is to assign a real number measure and categorize as affirmative or negative sentiment of that phrase. From here rose the concept of polarity, which is a dual value, either representing positive or negative sentiment of the phrase, in which Pos and Neg categories are used to categorize the relevant words [12]. Another way of extracting sentiments from words is by using the Wordnet, where similar meaning words are grouped in synsets, and the relationship between words were found out. Even, polarity identification was combined with WordNet [13], where a set of similar adjectives of identified orientation is started with. To find out the proximity of unknown adjectives, synonymy or antonymy is used to group them. Labeling is done based on the familiarity to positive or negative words. Ultimately, latest labeled words are added to the set. Then to uncover the polarity of a sentence, judgment-based sentences which contain the predefined set of adjectives are extorted. At the end, the sentences are evaluated based on the number of positive or negative word counts. This experiment reveals high accuracy results, and it is done quickly, with no training data being necessary.

4 Related Works

As mentioned earlier an effective machine learning algorithm accounts its credit due to superior feature learning capability. Depiction of data or features should be such that it assists extraction of information to build proper predictors [14]. Deep learning surfaced to surmount the dilemma of gradient descent so that training architectures were possible by gripping data with immense nonlinear hierarchical mannerism layers. Deep networks can be visualized as an assemblage to ascertain characteristics using a number of stages of irregular procedures where the order of attribute production at the highest stage starts from the subordinate stage [15]. Deep learning should bestow its accomplishment for having subsequent massive quantity of training data, authoritative computational infrastructure, and progress in academia.

Sentiment analysis is performing one of the most important roles in almost all social media. It has been a general trend that people depend on opinion given by people for the smallest of decisions. So, for the same, they have become extremely dependent on opinion specified by individuals as a response or a review or a blog. Based on the mass assumption of a situation, be it affirmative or negative or impartial, people blindly follow them. Adding to this present scenario, there are many sentiment analysis engines that are used for opinion collection intentions. Sentiment analysis not only extracts the intention of the text but has far more functionalities like offering an idea on businesses, by providing instant feedback on materials, and by calculating the outcome of social media marketing strategies applied on the products [16]. Similarly, the same has been applied to many fields which directly engross public voice. It is to be kept in mind that sentiment analysis does not only deal with extracting the sentiment of an entire document, as generally for example, in a movie review, the reviewer does not restrict his/her opinion against only one particular facet of the movie. Instead, it might vary from the script, to the acting, to the direction, to the sound, to the feel, or even the vibe. Hence, an effective review would be that which considers maximum possible features. It is not that only positive or negative review should be considered, but that it stretches far into neutral or sarcastic sentiments as well. Analyzing the sentiment on the coarse level is necessary so that each sentiment connects to the feature which it supports. Analysis is based on the flavor of the expression being positive, negative, or neutral [17], or on the foundation of stances, that is, pros and cons [18], or by identifying the target, that is, whether it is a product or a measure [13], or it might be the owner of an opinion [19]. Analysis is also done on effects [20] or by determining the feature of the target that people like or dislike [21]. Depending on the application, it is to be remembered that more refinements can be done on the analyzing criteria. Document level, sentence level, entity, and access levels are the general classifications of sentiment analysis techniques [22].

Of late, deep learning algorithms are showing excellent performance in normal language processing applications counting sentiment analysis through several datasets [23]. These models can easily detect complicated features by themselves. Considering the single components of neural networks might appear to be straightforward, hoarding nonlinear components consecutively can fabricate models which will be competent to become skilled in exceedingly complicated judgment margins. The attribute mining is hence allotted to neural networks [24]. So, it becomes suitable for these models to plot words with the same semantic and syntactic properties so that it is suggestive of accepting the implication of the terms. Recursive neural networks can efficiently value the construction of the sentences [25], which puts together deep learning models as an ideal fit for a mission like that of reaction study or sentiment analysis. Studies clearly suggest that sentiment analysis is playing a major role in verdict making. An April 2013 analysis depicts that around 90% of decisions taken for various commodities have been influenced by online reviews [26]. So polarity, [17], attitude [18], identification [13], whether being a possessor of an opinion [19], or effects [20] can easily be utilized to analyze the sentiment of a text or document. Three sentiment analysis types have been branded, namely, document level, sentence level, and entity and aspect level as cited in Ref. [22].

Natural language processing is profoundly associated with sentiment analysis. To keep intact the association of the client, it becomes essential for the company to accurately be aware of the judgment expressed by the client [27,28]. Similarly, by analyzing the product review the prospect of the manufactured goods can be estimated or predicted. This same thing is applied for observations available in social media, for a picture, promotion, or a movie. Studies as mentioned in Ref. [29], clearly illustrate the brunt of tweets on susceptible grounds like market prediction. Sentiment analysis also plays a significant position in stock markets. Hybridization of genetic algorithms and support vector machines has been implemented to achieve efficiency in these cases.

Research of sentiments in the field of blogging is emerging very quickly. With the abundance of internet facilities pumped up by the advancement in technology, there has been a rapid rise in the number of bloggers which leads to a humongous amount of unformatted, massive, and inaccurate text formats. To overcome all such discrepancies, sentiment analysis is used. Multidimensional feature mining is considered to be the most vital component of sentiment analysis. Words in sentiment analysis are categorized by virtue of semantic orientation. Semantic orientation provides excellent help in accumulating reviews, and always refers to the strength of the words in addition to predict the sentiment of a text. Semantic orientation involves adjectives, phrases, words, texts, adverbs, verbs, and noun.

5 The Proposed Methodology

This chapter has been implemented using Mikolov et al.'s word2vec model and doc2vec model. The word2vec model was introduced to discover dispersed representations in neural networks. It works on the theory that adjacent words are likely to have analogous meanings. There are two main forms of training methods available, Continuous Bag-of-Words (CBOW) and Skip-Gram model. While CBOW uses a bag of words to predict the target word, Skip-Gram does the opposite by using a particular word to predict its neighbors (Figs. 16 and 17). After this, similar types of words can be clustered within a huge corpus of words.

The CBOW model checks within a set of relevant words provided, that what should be the near similar meaning word that is likely to be present at the same place. Skip-Gram model, on the other hand, checks that based on a word provided, what should be the other relevant words that should appear in its immediacy. The former model works well on syntactic representations, while the latter performs better for semantic representations. Both the models overcame the disadvantage of the bi-gram model of including both the preceding and subsequent words.

Similarly, there are two models in Doc2Vec, the Distributed Bag-of-Words model and the Distributed Memory model (Figs. 18 and 19). The Distributed Bag-of-Words model

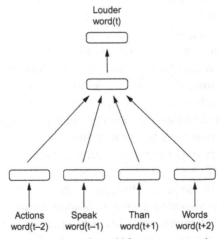

FIG. 16 *CBOW architecture* where target words are foretold from source words.

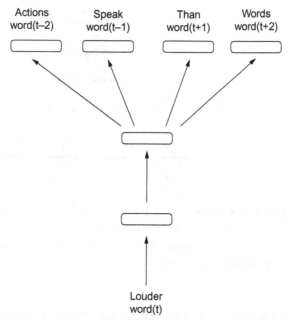

FIG. 17 *Skip gram architecture* which guesses the context words from source target words.

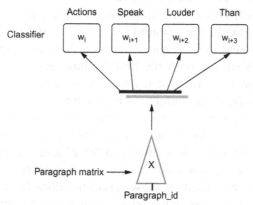

FIG. 18 Distributed Bag-of-Words architecture.

trains faster and disregards the order of the words; it predicts a random group of words in a paragraph based on the provided paragraph vector. In the Distributed Memory model, the paragraph is treated as an extra word, which is then averaged with the local relevant word vectors and predictions are made, that is, it predicts a word based on the provided words and a paragraph vector. This method however incurs additional calculation and complication.

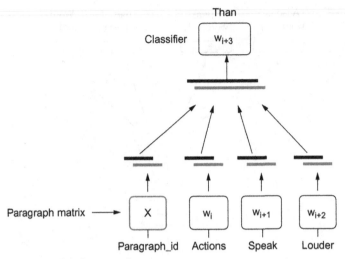

FIG. 19 Distributed Memory Model of paragraph vectors.

The entire method portrayed in this chapter has been executed in python language. Unlabeled training data set has been occupied as the input, on which data cleaning and text processing were done. This preprocessing concerned elimination of all HTML tags and punctuations by "Beautiful Soup" Python Library, replacing figures and acquaintances by tags and finally eliminating stopwords. Stopwords are frequently used words that have been programmed to be uncared for, as they might redundantly take up space in the database and also eat the preprocessing time. Natural Language Toolkit in Python has a list of stopwords stored in 16 dissimilar languages. After this, the unprocessed reviews are transformed to a string of words. The reviews are then collected, cleaned, and parsed. Eventually the chief characteristics are mined.

Word2Vec takes as input words and its prime work is to stir up vectors from those words. These are required to bring out similar words, where it shows that the words "man" and "woman" are more or less similar to "king" and "queen," further establishing the relationship that "man is to woman what king is to queen." This method is hailed as word embedding. Doc2Vec enhances these representations by demonstrating complete sentences as well as documents. For execution of the program, gensim, numpy, and sklearn have been used. The classifier used for the best performance is the Logistic Regression Classifier. While Word2Vec translates a word to a vector, Doc2Vec does that and also combines every word of a sentence together into a vector. The model is then built and trained accordingly. As training the model requires time, it is saved and can be loaded into for further use. The model is then checked for results as when we analyze sentiments, the results ought to be checked. Next for classifying the sentiments, the vectors are used to train a classifier. The classifier is trained using the training data and the accuracy is obtained. For example, "doesnt_match" function can be used to find out the odd word out from a group of words:

> *>>> model.doesnt_match("man woman child kitchen".split())*
> *'kitchen'*

Hence, the word kitchen is understood to be the odd one out of the other words in the group. The "most_similar" function helps us achieve all the words under a cluster:

> *>>> model.most_similar("man")*
> *[(u'woman', 0.6056041121482849), (u'guy', 0.4935004413127899), (u'boy',*
> *0.48933547735214233), (u'men', 0.4632953703403473), (u'person',*
> *0.45742249488830566), (u'lady', 0.4487500488758087), (u'himself',*
> *0.4288588762283325), (u'girl', 0.4166809320449829), (u'his', 0.3853422999382019),*
> *(u'he', 0.38293731212615967)]>>> model.most_similar("man")[(u'woman',*
> *0.6056041121482849), (u'guy', 0.4935004413127899), (u'boy', 0.48933547735214233),*
> *(u'men', 0.4632953703403473), (u'person', 0.45742249488830566), (u'lady',*
> *0.4487500488758087), (u'himself', 0.4288588762283325), (u'girl', 0.4166809320449829),*
> *(u'his', 0.3853422999382019), (u'he', 0.38293731212615967)]*

The process described above is illustrated in the form of a flowchart (see Fig. 20):

5.1 Movie Reviews Used

This work has been executed using a labeled dataset that encompasses 50,000 IMDB reviews of movies, predominantly chosen to analyze sentiments. A maximum of 30 reviews are allowed. The dataset has an equal number of positive and negative reviews. Separate datasets have been used as there is no guarantee that the model performs the same in both known and unknown data. Sentiments have been articulated in the binary format, that is,

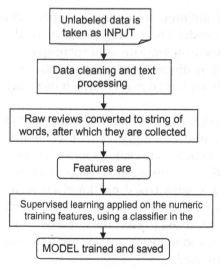

FIG. 20 The proposed methodology represented in a flowchart.

the value 0 is assigned as a sentiment score if the IMDB rating is less than 5, and 1 if the IMDB rating is greater than or equal to 7. The utmost number of reviews for each movie is not more than 30. It has been checked that there is no presence of any of the same movies in the 25,000 review labeled training set and in the 25,000 review test set. Other than this, 50,000 IMDB reviews have also been made available which are not rated with any labels.

5.1.1 File Descriptions
1. **labeledTrainData**—This is a tab-delimited file which contains the labeled training set. There is a header row along with 25,000 rows comprising an id, sentiment and text for an individual review.
2. **testData**—This tab-delimited file contains the test set, whose sentiment is to be predicted. There is a header row along with 25,000 rows having an id and test for an individual review.
3. **unlabeledTrainData**—This is an additional training set which are not labeled. The file is tab-delimited containing a header row along with 50,000 rows of an id associated with a text for each review.

5.1.2 Data Fields
id depicting the exclusive ID of each review.
sentiment demonstrating the review sentiment; 1 signifies a positive review and 0 a negative one.
review is to designate the text of the review.

6 Results and Discussion

In all, 300-dimensional space, 40 minimum words and 10 words in context have been used as features to train the Word2vec model. These categories of vector demonstrations call for a lot of advantages. It makes it easy to increase the concept of space, and distance between words can be found out as well as discovery of semantic alike words as illustrated in Table 1. "Gensim" [30] Python library has been used, which takes as input a bulky dataset for training.

Clustering has been done using K-means algorithm using built in "cython" [31] package. K-means is a sort of unsupervised learning, which is used for data without fixed class. The main aim of this clustering method is to search for clusters within the data, and the number of cluster being denoted by K. This method works in a repetitive manner to allot each data point to any of the K groups based on the given features. Data points are grouped based on the similarity of characteristics. The results include the centroids of the clusters, which can be further utilized to label the latest data along with labels which signify the data points allocated to a sole cluster. To yield accurate classification, the Logistic Regression Classifier has been used.

While utilizing Doc2Vec to explore the reviews, it is first trained on the unlabeled reviews. Then the process followed in the Word2Vec has been followed using DBOW

Table 1   Semantic Words Analogous to "Man" as Resulted in Word2Vec Model

Words	Number of Trees	Measures
Woman	50	0.6236
Guy		0.5179
Men		0.5253
Person		0.5180
Lady		0.5848
Woman	200	0.6345
Guy		0.5110
Men		0.5101
Person		0.5074
Lady		0.5988
Woman	500	0.6374
Guy		0.5236
Men		0.5213
Person		0.5102
Lady		0.5960

and DM vectors by joining them. Ultimately, the classifier is used over the review vectors. This work verifying the different techniques of deep learning being implemented for sentiment analysis shows minor improvements in the classification as the Bag-of-Words model results in 0.81 classification accuracy; Word2Vec gives 0.83; and Doc2Vec provides 0.91 classification accuracy. The Doc2Vec model clearly outperforms the other two existing models on the IMDB movie reviews.

7 Discussions and Conclusion

All the above-mentioned methods behave diversely and required dissimilar implementation time for training. But there lies similarity in the fact that all of them maps text material into vectors to further classify them. Semantic analysis is more to be exposed, so that more necessary information is dug up. Achieving more accuracy by implementing state-of-the-art techniques are to be tested and aimed for. Punctuations, varied symbols, and emotions reflecting smileys should be taken into account for further enhancement of the accuracies. Also, different types of classifiers must be applied on the data sets to augment the classification.

This chapter shows the execution of a deep learning technique on Word2vec and the Doc2vec model. Other than these, assorted classifiers can be used other than the one already stated above and can be judged if the optimum classifier could be found out for these types of purposes. It ought to be declared that tactical use of other clustering algorithms like DBScan, Fuzzy-C-Means, etc. can be used on this on hand model. Methods remain to be investigated regarding Sarcasm Detection and Question Identification is to be enhanced. Last but not the least lot of testing can be implied in the trait choice procedure which can be expected to bring in loads of fresh scope to deep learning approaches in sentiment analysis. The authors are currently engaged in this direction.

References

[1] W. Medhat, A. Hassan, H. Korashy, Sentiment analysis algorithms and applications: A survey, Ain Shams Eng. J. 5 (2014) 1093–1113.

[2] T. Mikalai, P. Themis, Survey on mining subjective data on the web, Data Min. Knowl. Discov. 24 (2012) 478–514.

[3] L.-C. Yu, J.-L. Wu, C. Pei-Chann, C. Hsuan-Shou, Using a contextual entropy model to expand emotion words and their intensity for the sentiment classification of stock market news, Knowl.-Based Syst. 41 (2013) 89–97.

[4] M. Hagenau, M. Liebmann, D. Neumann, Automated news reading: stock price prediction based on financial news using context-capturing features, Decis. Support Syst. 55 (2013) 685–697.

[5] T. Xu, P. Qinke, C. Yinzhao, Identifying the semantic orientation of terms using S-HAL for sentiment analysis, Knowl.-Based Syst. 35 (2012) 279–289.

[6] M. Isa, V. Piek, A lexicon model for deep sentiment analysis and opinion mining applications, Decis. Support Syst. 53 (2012) 680–688.

[7] N.F. Hordri, A. Samar, S.S. Yuhaniz, S.M. Shamsuddin, A systematic literature review on features of deep learning in big data analytics, Int. J. Adv. Soft Comput. Appl. 2074-8523, 9 (1) (2017).

[8] https://en.wikipedia.org/wiki/File:Logistic-curve.svg (Retrieved 20 December 2017).

[9] B. Liu, Sentiment analysis and opinion mining, Synth. Lect. Hum. Lang. Tech. 5 (2012) 1–167.

[10] A. Kale, et al., Modeling trust and influence in the blogosphere using link polarity, in: Proceedings of the International Conference on Weblogs and Social Media (ICWSM 2007), March 2007.

[11] http://www.cs.cornell.edu/People/pabo/movie-review-data/.

[12] V. Hatzivassiloglou, K.R. McKeown, Predicting the semantic orientation of adjectives, in: Proceedings of the 35th Annual Meeting of the ACL and the 8th Conference of the European Chapter of the ACL, ACL, New Brunswick, NJ, 1997, pp. 174–181.

[13] M. Hu, B. Liu, in: Mining and summarizing customer reviews, Paper Presented at the Proceedings of the Tenth ACM SIGKDD International Conference on Knowledge Discovery and Data Mining, 2004.

[14] Y. Bengioy, A. Courville, P. Vincenty, Representation learning: a review and new perspectives, IEEE Trans. Pattern Anal. Mach. Intell. 35 (8) (2014) 1798–1828.

[15] Y. Bengio, Learning deep architectures for AI, in: Foundations and Trends in Machine Learning, vol. 2 (1), Now Publishers Inc., Hanover, MA, 2009, pp. 1–127.

[16] B. Pang, et al., Opinion mining and sentiment analysis, in: Foundations and Trends in Information Retrieval, Now Publishers Inc., Hanover, MA, 2008.

[17] P. Turney, in: Thumbs up or thumbs down? Semantic orientation applied to unsupervised classification of reviews, Paper Presented at the Proceedings of the 40th Annual Meeting of the Association for Computational Linguistics, Philadelphia, PA, 2002.

[18] S. Somasundaran, J. Wiebe, in: Recognizing stances in ideological on-line debates, Proceedings of the Human Language Technologies: The 2010 Annual Conference of the North American Chapter of the Association for Computational Linguistics. 2010 Workshop on Computational Approaches to Analysis and Generation of Emotion in Text, 2010.

[19] S.-M. Kim, E. Hovy, in: Extracting opinions, opinion holders, and topics expressed in online news media text, Paper Presented at the Proceedings of the Workshop on Sentiment and Subjectivity in Text, 2006.

[20] L. Deng, J. Wiebe, in: Sentiment propagation via implicature constraints, Proceedings of the 14th Conference of the European Chapter of the Association for Computational Linguistics, 2014.

[21] Y. Jo, A.H. Oh, in: Aspect and sentiment unification model for online review analysis, Proceedings of the Fourth ACM International Conference on Web Search and Data Mining, 2011.

[22] B. Liu, Sentiment analysis and opinion mining, Syn. Lect. Human Lang. Tech. (2012).

[23] R. Collobert, J. Weston, L. Bottou, M. Karlen, K. Kavukcuoglu, P. Kuksa, Natural language processing (almost) from scratch, J. Mach. Learn. Res. 12 (2011) 2493–2537.

[24] T. Mikolov, et al., Distributed representations of words and phrases and their compositionality, Adv. Neural Inf. Proces. Syst. 26 (2013) 3111–3119.

[25] R. Socher, et al., in: Parsing natural scenes and natural language with recursive neural networks, Proceedings of the 28th International Conference on Machine Learning, 2011.

[26] P. Ling, C. Geng, Z. Menghou, L. Chunya, What Do Seller Manipulations of Online Product Reviews Mean to Consumers? (HKIBS Working Paper Series 070-1314), Hong Kong Institute of Business Studies, Lingnan University, Hong Kong, 2014.

[27] R. Varghese, M. Jayashree, A survey on sentiment analysis and opinion mining, Int. J. Res. Eng. Technol. (2319-1163).

[28] B.B. Nair, V.P. Mohandas, N.R. Sakthivel, A genetic algorithm optimized decision tree-SVM based stock market trend prediction system, Int. J. Comput. Sci. Eng. 2 (9) (2010) 2981–2988.

[29] https://ireneli.eu/2016/07/27/nlp-05-from-word2vec-to-doc2vec-a-simple-example-with-gensim/.

[30] Gensim, Topic Modeling for humans, https://radimrehurek.com/gensim/.

[31] Cython C-Extensions for Python, http://cython.org.

8

Sentiment Analysis for Airlines Services Based on Twitter Dataset

Prayag Tiwari[*], Pranay Yadav[†], Sachin Kumar[‡], Brojo Kishore Mishra[§],
Gia Nhu Nguyen[¶], Sarada Prasad Gochhayat[*], Jagendra Singh[‖],
Mukesh Prasad[#]

*Department of Information Engineering, University of Padua, Padua, Italy †Research and
Development Department, Ultra-Light Technology (ULT), Bhopal, India ‡College of IBS,
National University of Science and Technology MISiS, Moscow, Russia §C.V. Raman College of
Engineering, Department of IT, Bhubaneswar, India ¶Duy Tan University, Da Nang, Vietnam
‖Associate Professor, Inderprastha Engineering College, Ghaziabad, India #Centre for
Artificial Intelligence, School of Software, FEIT, University of Technology Sydney,
Sydney, NSW, Australia

1 Introduction

Air transport is one of the fastest modes of public transport which connects international boundaries. Air transport allows people from different countries to cross international boundaries and travel other countries for personal, business, medical, and tourism purposes. Although, air transport provides the fastest means by saving the time of journey, another aspect of air transport is the facilities and comfort level of the passengers.

There are lots of air transport companies such as Air India, Indigo airlines, Aeroflot, etc. Nowadays, there is a competitive environment among the airline industries. Every company is providing a variety of facilities to attract the passengers. The only motive is to improve their profit. Few years back, it was difficult to identify the needs and desires of passengers. But with the advancement of social media like Facebook, Twitter, etc., passengers are sharing their views on different types of airline facilities during their travel on social media platforms. This sharing of information plays a huge role to increase the competitiveness among the airline industries. It also provides a chance to improve their services and facilities for the travelers worldwide.

But the fact is how to analyze the need and important requirements of travelers just with the information they shared on social media. The millions of travelers traveling in the airlines and sharing their views on social media generate a huge amount of data. In this study, we use a dataset of different tweets. Tweet is a name given to the information sharing on Twitter platform. Twitter is the one of the most preferable information sharing platforms for all travelers. Wherever a traveler goes, whatever he does, he just tweets his view about his activity and experiences on Twitter.

Social Network Analytics. https://doi.org/10.1016/B978-0-12-815458-8.00008-6

Sentiment is another name for the view and opinion that is held or expressed. The sentiment may represent a feeling of joy, happiness, sadness, or sometimes anger. And this is what travelers' tweets about on Twitter. Every journey on airlines can bring either pleasure or discomfort during travel for any passenger. If the traveler is not happy with the services, his tweet represents a sentiment of discomfort. If he is fully satisfied with the services, he will show a feeling of happiness in his tweet. The British airways further took it seriously and resolved the issues of the respective traveler.

Therefore, tweets do not only allow the airlines to sort out the problems of individual passengers but also help them to improve their services. The one or two people are just exceptions. The important thing to be concerned is the opinion of majority of travelers. To understand the psychology and opinion of the majority of travelers from all around the world, we must look into everyone's view, which is a rather impossible job. As millions of people are traveling daily from one place to another and tweeting about their journey experience, it creates a huge database of tweets. Therefore, it is important to use a technique which has the power to analyze such a huge data of tweets.

Here the machine learning role comes into existence. Machine learning is a set of techniques such as classification, clustering, association rule mining, and anomaly detection. These techniques are very much powerful and have been widely used in different applications. In this chapter, we are using machine learning techniques for sentiment analysis of airline tweets data. The rest of the part is organized as follows: Section 2 introduces the literature survey which consists of different important related work and their achievements. Section 3 covers the concept and architecture and Section 4 covers an overview of the techniques being used in this work. In Section 5, we discuss about the experiments and their results which is followed by the conclusion in last section [1–20].

2 Literature Survey

Nowadays, Companies are trying harder than before to bring the customers close to them to improve customer satisfaction as well as to improve the revenue, productivity, and innovation, by using real-time communications, such as instant messaging, connecting through microblogging sites. Customers use these means of communication to express their views and opinions. Hence, in the era of connected world, these views and opinions are very important as users can share their opinion on available plethora of microblogging sites, which would have a direct impact on the brand values of the companies. The author Kusen et al. have shown that the direct correlation between the winner of 2016 Austrian presidential elections and his popularity and influence on Twitter than his opponent [21].

Tiwari et al. utilized supervised machine learning methods such as support vector machine (SVM), maximum entropy (ME), naive Bayes (NB) to classify movie review dataset (Rotten Tomatoes movie dataset) because these methodologies gave better accuracy and n-gram approach was utilized. It was found that accuracy of classifiers start decreasing when increasing the value of "n." It was found that for $n = 1, 2, 3$ accuracy was increasing but it starts decreasing when $n > 4$ [22].

Nowadays social media is considered the backbone of a democratic country. Most of the democratic countries use social media for representation of their own views, thinking, and sentiments. Twitter is one the most important platforms to share one's own views in front of the whole world. That is why most of the industries use twitter-based sentiment analyses to find the quality of any products, not only the quality of a product but also check the quality of services and hospitality. For the improvement of performance in the aviation industry, sentiment analysis plays a vital role. In the last decade, there are different organizations that focus on sentiment analysis of client reviews and comments on the social media. In this, the survey part discusses the different sentiment analysis method used in the 5 years. These methods provide help to understand the different sentiment analysis processes. In 2012, Gräbner et al. in this research work, the researcher proposed a lexicon-based way to deal with client audits in the tourism sector. Specialists have thought about on opinion examination. This anticipated a dictionary-based way to deal with order customer audits inside the business space. The proposed model provided a high precision and recall and demonstrated a good progress in the customer audit inside the business space. Especially, the three target variables are used (i.e., good, neutral, and bad) which is very common to describe the target variables, from the obtained results, positive and negative sentiment have high precision. At long last, the examination underpins the meaning of future investigation styles and improvement objectives to upgrade the execution of customer classifiers upheld conclusion esteems. In extra detail, such upgrades are portrayed beneath: first, the examples taken from the corpus affirm the standard of the vocabulary. The examination of arrangement comes about and furthermore the extent of the vocabularies demonstrate that expanding the example estimate influences the specific vocabulary utilized for customer surveys. This can be substantiated by the undeniable reality that customer surveys are somewhat short archives [23].

Continuing this work in 2013, Yiming Zhao [23a] presented test sentiment analysis in social networks. In this analysis the authors focus on the Chinese microblog data analysis. There are three different optimizations applied in the dataset, the first one is the data structure optimization, second is query strategy optimization, and the final is the parallel optimization performed [24].

There are many enhancements required in this work like the autolearning process. For the improvement of this work Adeborna et al., in 2014, proposed an improvement in the previous work that is the sentiment topic recognition (STR) method for airline query rating. The structure of this present work consists of different stages: the first step is data preparation—in this step create a database of social sites that is based on the collection of the related web comments discussing a particular subject (e.g., AirTran) from the tweets. After that apply lexicon includes around 6800 seed adjectives with best-known orientation of 2006 positive and 4783 negative words. Within the next step, apply Naïve Bayes algorithmic program for our sentiment analysis. Finally every sentiment extracted by the approach has some underlying topic(s) and provides an overall information and scope of the various client sentiments [25].

As progress in research works, further improvement in this field of research work by Yun Wan et al., in 2015 which compares the different classification techniques of sentiment analysis on the basis of Precision Recall F-measure Lexicon-based methods. The methods are Naïve Bayesian, Bayesian Network, SVM, C45, Decision Tree, and Random Forest Ensemble. These past work looks at numerous totally changed antiquated order ways and chooses the chief right individual characterization philosophy to execute sentiment grouping. For the aircraft administrations area, the sentiment classification accuracy is sufficiently high to actualize customer fulfillment examination. This approach is appropriate for the aircraft partnerships to examine the twitter data concerning their administrations [26].

After this Zhang et al. presents a framework for estimating client satisfaction. This vital work demonstrates the framework via taking the case of six American airlines. The analysis of the result obtained by framework will offer nice valuable insight for firms to enhance their services and to facilitate or deepen the macromanagement of the key-note of the longer-term development. This is also an alert for all firms to enhance their service quality, so will be additional competitive within the market. And moreover this sort of a small counseled system may facilitate customers notice a decent compromise in terms of varied aspects reckoning on the customers' demands and create appropriate selection that is an additional cost-benefit and may create them to feel additionally satisfied [24].

Further enhancement of this work by Pandey et al. presents twitter sentiment examination by hybrid cuckoo search method. During this analysis article, a unique hybrid clustering technique has been acquainted which inquire about the sentiments of tweets exploitation K-means clustering method. The result of the examination has been contrasted and ICS, GCS, PSO, DE, SVM, and NB. From the experimental and related results, the performance of the current model has been improved. Be that as it may, the arranged system demonstrates higher precision when contrasted with existing routes, change in exactness keeps on being wanted. Hence, more work can grasp to investigate the probabilities of precision change by presenting some component decision strategy and applying very surprising variations of change ways [27].

3 Concept and Architecture of Sentiment Analysis

In this section, we describe the proposed concept and architecture of sentiment analysis and the components which are designed in Fig. 1.

Opinion mining or sentiment analysis approach to the utilization of text analysis, natural language processing, biometric and computational linguistic to retrieve, identify, and quantify hidden information comprehensively.

First from the dataset, which was in the raw format, several features are selected which were informative and extracted informative features. We divided the extracted features into two subsets (data frame and document term matrix) that we could make cloud of

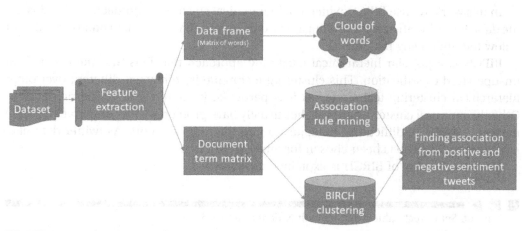

FIG. 1 The proposed sentiment analysis architecture.

words which could provide better visualization of words from the data frame; and we could apply association rule mining and clustering on the document term matrix to get association of words.

3.1 Description of Dataset

This dataset we used for our evaluation is about US Airlines and the passenger tweets. There were several features available like tweets id, airline sentiment, negative reason, airline, airline sentiment gold, negative reason gold, re-tweet count, tweet location, tweet time zone, etc. but we selected some features and especially the text features where passenger tweets were available. There are some features like airline sentiments (positive, negative), airlines, negative reasons which were useful for further analysis.

4 Proposed Methodologies

This section explains about the machine learning techniques used to analyze the twitter data set. In this study, BIRCH clustering and Association rule mining are used for the analysis of data. Both the techniques have been defined as follows:

4.1 BIRCH Clustering (Balanced Iterative Reducing and Clustering Using Hierarchies)

Clustering mechanism is used to group a set of similar objects based on their attributes and proximity in the vector space. All clustering algorithms generally fall under one of the following approaches: (1) partitioning approach, such as K-means; (2) hierarchical approach, such as BIRCH, ROCK and (3) density-based approach, such as DBSCAN.

In this work, we use BIRCH which is a hierarchical clustering approach; and it clusters the data points by efficiently handling noisy data points, that is, the data points that do not follow the underlying pattern.

BIRCH is a popular hierarchical clustering approach that falls into the category of unsupervised classification. This clustering technique is somewhat different over other hierarchical clustering techniques as it is particularly useful for large metric datasets. Other hierarchical clustering approaches usually have problems with comparatively large datasets, which are difficult to be adjusted into the main memory. As twitter dataset is large in size BIRCH has been chosen for analysis in this study.

The functionality of BIRCH is explained as follows:

■ ■ ■ ▬▬▬▬▬▬▬▬▬▬▬▬▬▬▬▬▬▬▬▬▬▬▬▬▬

Input: Set of real-valued vectors with N data points.
Output: Clusters data points.
Procedure: The BIRCH algorithms work in four phases:

1. Phase 1 creates a CF (clustering feature) tree from a set of data points. This tree is a height-balanced tree
2. In Phase 2, the algorithm traverse all the leaf node entries in the initial CF tree and then rebuilds a new CF tree which is the optimized version of the initial CF tree
3. In Phase 3, AGNES (agglomerative hierarchical clustering algorithm) is applied to the subclusters, which are represented by respective CF vectors
4. The result of phase 3 is a set of clusters which captures the major distribution pattern in the dataset. However, some minor and localized inaccuracies may exist.
5. Phase 4 is an optional step which can be used to remove some outliers and minor localized inaccuracies. It can be used as a refinement for phase 3 results. The output of phase 3 will be the refined version of phase 3 clusters.

▬▬▬▬▬▬▬▬▬▬▬▬▬▬▬▬▬▬▬▬▬▬▬ ■ ■ ■

4.2 Association Rule Mining

After the clustering is done, association rule learning is applied to find interesting relations between the clustered elements. Association rule mining is a machine learning approach based on finding the association between variables in large datasets. In association rule mining, minimum support threshold is first applied to find the frequent elements; and then a minimum confidence constraint is used on the frequent elements to formulate the rules [28].

The associativity of two attributes of crashes is dictated by the recurrence of their event together in the informational collection. A run $X \rightarrow Y$ demonstrates that if X happens then Y will likewise happen.

Given a dataset D of n exchanges where every exchange $T \in D$. Let $I = \{I1, I2, \dots In\}$ is an arrangement of things. A thing set X will happen in T if and just if $X \subseteq T$. $X \rightarrow Y$ is and affiliation manage, given that $X \subset I$, $Y \subset I$ and $X \cap Y = \emptyset$.

Agrawal and Srikant proposed a calculation known as a priori calculation to discover the affiliation rules from substantial datasets. The pseudocode for customary affiliation administer digging calculation for incessant item set era is as per the following:

AK = {recurrence item set of K size}
BK= {Candidate item set of K size}
C1= {recurrence 1 item set}
While (AK-1 ≠ Φ) then
      BK+1=candidate produced from AK
    For every transaction t ε D do
        Augment the counts of candidate in BK+1 that also hold in t
    AK+1= candidates in BK+1 with the lowest aid
    K=K+1;
  Return UKAK

4.2.1 Interestingness Computation

An association rule is considered as a solid control if it fulfills the base limit criteria, that is, support and confidence. A base bolster S of a control $X \rightarrow Y$ shows that in $x\%$ of all exchanges X and Y together happens and it can be figured utilizing Eq. (1); though a certainty c of a decide shows that in $c\%$ of all exchange when A happens then B additionally happens and it can be ascertained utilizing Eq. (2). Lift is another intriguing quality measure of manage, which can be computed utilizing Eq. (3). An esteem more noteworthy than 1 for the lift measures depicts that the presence of A and B together is more than expected though an esteem lower than 1 demonstrates invert of the idea. So a control is considered as solid on the off chance that it has an esteem more noteworthy than 1 for the lift parameter.

Furthermore, an association rule is created from the successive item sets and solid principles in light of Interestingness computation are taken for the examination:

$$\text{Support} = P(X \cap Y) \tag{1}$$

$$\text{Confidence} = P(X|\ Y) = \frac{P(X \cap Y)}{P(X)} \tag{2}$$

$$\text{Lift} = \frac{P(X \cap Y)}{P(X)P(Y)} \tag{3}$$

5 Result and Discussion

Several feature extraction techniques have been used like removing stop words, transform to lower case, remove punctuations, and remove white spaces. During the data preprocessing step, all tweets had tag like starting from @ and the airline name which was demonstrating the airlines and the message for that airline. To further work with this text data, this tag is not relevant that could provide some better result so we removed this tag from the text. We further split tweets into two data frames on the basis of their negative and positive sentiments.

5.1 Word Frequency Consideration and Cloud of Words Formation for Every Sentiments

There are several words which come quite often in the tweets and those do not seem informative and they are removed from the tweets to get more enhanced results. Matrix of words are generated after analyzing text which return data frame containing tweets, word and word count. There were availability of several stop words, punctuations so they were removed and transformed to lower case as well as matrix was kept 97% sparse.

There are 24 words which are repeated in positive sentiments with some certain contingency. It was amalgamated from the count of words over all the positive-based tweets. It can be seen from Fig. 2 that thanks comes 1061 times, flight comes 371, and so on.

There are 39 words which are repeated in negative sentiments with some certain contingency, but here mentioned which has more count. It amalgamated the count of words over all the negative-based tweets. As it can be seen from Fig. 3 flight comes 2900 times, service 740 times, and so on.

Cloud of word has been mentioned in Fig. 4 to visualize those positive and negative tweets more properly.

Word cloud gives a decent visual portrayal of the word recurrence for each kind of opinion in which the left ones are positive and the right ones are negative. The span of the word relates to its recurrence across all tweets. We can have a thought of what the passengers are discussing. For instance, for negative opinion, passengers appear to gripe about delay of flight, cancellation of flights, service seems bad for that flight, hours holding up, etc. Be that as it may, for positive opinion, passengers are thankful and they discuss extraordinary administration/flight.

Thanks	Flight	Great	Just	Service	Love	Get	Will
1061	371	233	179	159	133	114	114
Customer	Much	Guys	Good	Best	Awesome	Got	Time
113	109	109	107	105	99	99	94
Now	Today	Help	Airline	Amazing	Jetblue	Back	
88	82	82	80	77	77	71	

FIG. 2 Positive tweets and their count.

Flight	Get	Cancelled	Now	Service	Hours	Can	Just
2900	982	920	821	740	644	624	614
Help	Hold	Customer	Time	Plane	Delayed	Cant	Still
610	607	604	583	515	493	481	479
Amp	Call	Flightled	Hour	One	Will	Flights	Bag
472	448	442	435	433	432	418	408
Gate	Dont	Late	Need	Back	Phone	Waiting	Please
407	404	377	372	369	360	337	323
Thanks	United	Got	Airline	Like	Trying	Ive	
309	308	296	290	290	288	284	

FIG. 3 Negative tweets and their count.

FIG. 4 Word cloud of positive and negative opinion.

5.2 Determining the Association Between Words

Here the document term matrix has been generated containing tweets, word, and word count instead of data frame after analyzing text corpora. There were availability of several stop words, punctuations so there were removed and transformed to lower case as well as matrix was kept 97% sparse. Here the discovered words that are more related with these mentioned words at a correlation of 60% and its threshold value.

For positive opinion tweets, it can be seen from Fig. 5 that flight is more related with great, recommending that passengers had great experience in the flight. Amazing is related to the word customer, which is thus related to the service, showing that passengers encountered an amazing service for customers in numerous open doors. Also, without

```
$Flight
Great
 0.13

$Awesome
Guys
0.07

$Amazing
Customer      Best
     0.08     0.06

$Service
Customer      Great      Today      Best
     0.67      0.16       0.08      0.06
```

FIG. 5 Association of positive words.

```
$Flight
Cancelled       Late Flightled   Delayed
     0.36       0.25       0.23      0.16

$Customer
Service
   0.65

$Gate
Waiting  Plane
   0.09   0.08

$Phone
Cant Help
0.09 0.07
```

FIG. 6 Associations of negative words.

having really perused any tweet, with this investigation we get a thought of what individuals are saying in regard to the airlines.

As it can be seen from Fig. 6 about the negative tweets, the presence of the word flight relates with the word canceled, delayed, flight led, and late, demonstrating that people are grumbling about the flight delay. Customer is related to service, which is normal, as customer service was an intermittent issue in negative tweets. Curiously, the word gate is related with the plane and waiting, which most likely implies that passengers were left waiting at the entryway for quite a while before flight. So from this investigation, and without having perused any tweet, we comprehend what individuals are by and large grumbling about.

5.3 Cluster Analysis of Words and Their Association

BIRCH clustering has been implemented to identify the association between several words. In Fig. 7, the words which are linked with the smaller arm have more association. AIK, BIK selection criteria have been used which satisfies for the number of cluster is 5.

From the dendrogram in Fig. 7, it can be seen that some words with shorter arm like customer and service, today and help, amazing, back, etc. are more informative and provide some more understanding of association.

From this dendrogram in Fig. 8, it can be seen that it is not so informative because it provided almost the same result as during determining the association between several words. Association of words like canceled flight, customer service, etc. show passenger tweets regarding their complaint about airlines.

6 Conclusion and Future Work

In this study, dataset was analyzed by using association rule mining and BIRCH clustering. When determining the association between several words by using the association rule we

Positive opinion

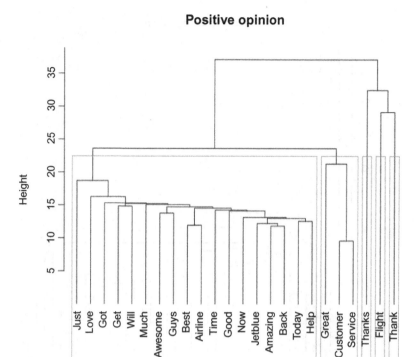

FIG. 7 Positive opinion with size *k*=5.

understood for positive opinions that flight is more related with great, recommending that passengers had great experience in the flight. Amazing is related to the word customer, which is thus related to the service, showing that passengers encountered an amazing service for customers in numerous open doors. Also, without having really perused any tweet, with this investigation we get a thought of what individuals are saying in regard to the airlines. It is also seen for negative opinions that the presence of the word flight relates with the word canceled, delayed, flight led, and late, demonstrating that people are grumbling about the flight delay. Customer is related to service, which is normal, as customer service was an intermittent issue in negative tweets. Curiously, the word gate is related with the plane and waiting, which most likely implies that passengers were left waiting at the entryway for quite a while before the flight. So from this investigation, and without having perused any tweet, we comprehend that individuals are by and large grumbling about. When BIRCH clustering was used to understand the association of words it was almost the same result about negative opinion but gave a better understanding about positive opinion. From these opinions of passengers, it will be easier for airlines to understand about negative and positive opinion of people and can be figured out to enhance airline services in the near future. This analysis can be useful to authors who would like to mine more hidden information from dataset in the near future.

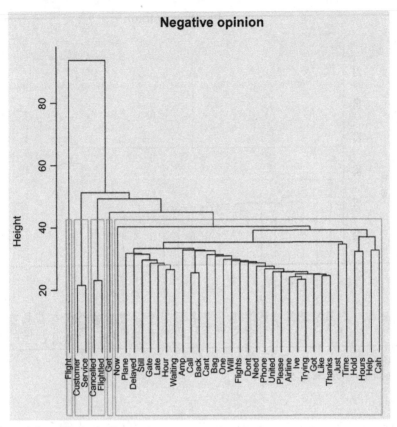

FIG. 8 Negative opinion with size $k=5$.

References

[1] P. Tiwari, H. Dao, G.N. Nguyen, Performance evaluation of lazy, decision tree classifier and multilayer perceptron on traffic accident analysis, Informatica 41 (1) (2017) 39.

[2] P. Tiwari, S. Kumar, D. Kalitin, in: Road-user specific analysis of traffic accident using data mining techniques, *International Conference on Computational Intelligence, Communications, and Business Analytics*, Springer, Singapore, 2017, pp. 398–410.

[3] P. Tiwari, Comparative analysis of big data, Int. J. Comput. Appl. 140 (7) (2016).

[4] S. Kumar, P. Tiwari, K.V. Denis, Augmenting classifiers performance through clustering: a comparative study on road accident data, Int. J. Inf. Retr. Res. 8 (1) (2018) 57–68.

[5] K. Sachin, V.B. Shemwal, P. Tiwari, K. Denis, A conjoint analysis of road accident data using K-modes clustering and bayesian networks, Ann. Comput. Sci. Inf. Syst. 10 (2017) 53–56.

[6] P. Tiwari, A.C. Mishra, A.K. Jha, Case study as a method for scope definition, Arab. J. Bus. Manag. Rev. S1 (002) (2016).

[7] P. Tiwari, in: Advanced ETL (AETL) by integration of PERL and scripting method, Inventive Computation Technologies (ICICT), International Conference on, vol. 3, IEEE, 2016, pp. 1–5.

[8] P. Tiwari, in: Improvement of ETL through integration of query cache and scripting method, *Data Science and Engineering (ICDSE), 2016 International Conference on*, IEEE, 2016, pp. 1–5.

[9] P. Tiwari, S. Kumar, A.C. Mishra, V. Kumar, B. Terfa, in: Improved performance of data warehouse, *Inventive Communication and Computational Technologies (ICICCT), 2017 International Conference on*, IEEE, 2017, pp. 94–104.

[10] J. Singh, M. Prasad, Y.W. Daraghmi, P. Tiwari, P. Yadav, N. Bharill, M. Pratama, A. Saxena, in: Fuzzy logic hybrid model with semantic filtering approach for pseudo relevance feedback-based query expansion, *IEEE Symposium Series on Computational Intelligence (SSCI) on*, 2017, pp. 1–7.

[11] V. Kumar, D. Kalitin, P. Tiwari, Unsupervised learning dimensionality reduction algorithm PCA for face recognition, in: International Conference on Computing, Communication and Automation (ICCCA), IEEE, 2017.

[12] N. Dey, S. Samanta, X.S. Yang, A. Das, S.S. Chaudhuri, Optimisation of scaling factors in electrocardiogram signal watermarking using cuckoo search, Int. J. Bio-Inspir. Com. 5 (5) (2013) 315–326.

[13] S. Samanta, S.S. Ahmed, M.A.M.M. Salem, S.S. Nath, N. Dey, S.S. Chowdhury, in: Haralick features based automated glaucoma classification using back propagation neural network, *Proceedings of the 3rd International Conference on Frontiers of Intelligent Computing: Theory and Applications (FICTA) 2014*, Springer, Cham, 2015, pp. 351–358.

[14] S. Hore, S. Chatterjee, V. Santhi, N. Dey, A.S. Ashour, V.E. Balas, F. Shi, Indian sign language recognition using optimized neural networks, in: Information Technology and Intelligent Transportation Systems, Springer, Cham, 2017, pp. 553–563.

[15] A.S. Ashour, S. Samanta, N. Dey, N. Kausar, W.B. Abdessalemkaraa, A.E. Hassanien, Computed tomography image enhancement using cuckoo search: a log transform based approach, J. Signal Inform. Process. 6 (03) (2015) 244.

[16] N. Kausar, S. Palaniappan, B.B. Samir, A. Abdullah, N. Dey, Systematic analysis of applied data mining based optimization algorithms in clinical attribute extraction and classification for diagnosis of cardiac patients, in: Applications of Intelligent Optimization in Biology and Medicine, Springer, Cham, 2016, pp. 217–231.

[17] W.B.A. Karaa, N. Dey, Mining Multimedia Documents, CRC Press, 2017.

[18] W.B.A. Karaa, A.S. Ashour, D.B. Sassi, P. Roy, N. Kausar, N. Dey, MEDLINE text mining: an enhancement genetic algorithm based approach for document clustering, in: Applications of Intelligent Optimization in Biology and Medicine, Springer, Cham, 2016, pp. 267–287.

[19] W. Ben Abdessalem Karaa, Z. Ben Azzouz, A. Singh, N. Dey, A.S. Ashour, H. Ben Ghazala, Automatic builder of class diagram (ABCD): an application of UML generation from functional requirements, Software Pract. Ex. 46 (11) (2016) 1443–1458.

[20] M.S. Kamal, S. Parvin, A.S. Ashour, F. Shi, N. Dey, De-Bruijn graph with MapReduce framework towards metagenomic data classification, Int. J. Inf. Technol. 9 (1) (2017) 59–75.

[21] E. Kušen, M. Strembeck, An Analysis of the Twitter Discussion on the 2016 Austrian Presidential Elections, (2017).arXiv preprint arXiv:1707.09939.

[22] P. Tiwari, B.K. Mishra, S. Kumar, V. Kumar, Implementation of n-gram methodology for rotten tomatoes review dataset sentiment analysis, Int. J. Knowl. Discov. Bioinformatics 7 (1) (2017) 30–41.

[23] D. Gräbner, M. Zanker, G. Fliedl, M. Fuchs, Classification of Customer Reviews Based on Sentiment Analysis, Springer, Helsingborg, Sweden, 2012, pp. 460–470.

[23a] Y. Zhao, K. Niu, Z. He, J. Lin, X. Wang, Text sentiment analysis algorithm optimization and platform development in social network, in: Sixth International Symposium on Computational Intelligence and Design (ISCID), 2013, vol. 1, IEEE, 2013, pp. 410–413.

[24] L. Zhang, Y. Sun, T. Luo, in: A framework for evaluating customer satisfaction, Software, Knowledge, Information Management & Applications (SKIMA), 2016 10th International Conference on, IEEE, 2016, pp. 448–453.

[25] E. Adeborna, K. Siau, in: An approach to sentiment analysis-the case of airline quality rating, PACIS, 2014, p. 363.

[26] Y. Wan, Q. Gao, in: An ensemble sentiment classification system of twitter data for airline services analysis, Data Mining Workshop (ICDMW), 2015 IEEE International Conference on, IEEE, 2015, pp. 1318–1325.

[27] A.C. Pandey, D.S. Rajpoot, M. Saraswat, Twitter sentiment analysis using hybrid cuckoo search method, Inform. Process. Manag. 53 (4) (2017) 764–779.

[28] R. Agrawal, T. Imieliński, A. Swami, in: Mining association rules between sets of items in large databases, ACM Sigmod Record, vol. 22, no. 2, ACM, 1993, pp. 207–216.

Further Reading

[29] http://business.time.com/2013/09/03/man-spends-more-than-1000-to-call-out-british-airways-on-twitter/. at 1115 hours.

[30] http://www.thegenxtimes.com/trends/man-tweets-indigo-about-misplaced-luggage-glad-to-hear-that-replies-indigo/. at 1124 hours.

9

Multilateral Interactions and Isolation in Middlemen-Driven Network Games

Loyimee Gogoi*,†, Surajit Borkotokey*, Diganta Mukherjee†

*Department of Mathematics, Dibrugarh University, Dibrugarh, India †Sampling and Official Statistics Unit, Indian Statistical Institute (ISI), Kolkata, India

1 Introduction

Importance and strategic position of middlemen in many relationships cannot be emphasized enough. For example, consider the situations of (i) international trade between manufacturing and consuming countries taking place through a third country, trader, (ii) labor market negotiations between workers and management through the labor union, (iii) political lobbying for parliamentary agenda by corporate houses, expedited through specialist agencies, and (iv) use of common server networks by telephone companies and so on. In the scientific literature the middlemen are often described as facilitator or market maker but it is not always that the middlemen are depicted in a positive light. Sometimes we may also have a situation where middlemen create concentration of (bargaining) power and hold the relationship between the other two parties to ransom. In such situations, the middlemen may be extracting too large a share of the value created by himself/herself. Real life examples of such situations have been historically seen during the OPEC oil crisis (1973) or the Opium wars (1839–60).

Issues of channel control by middlemen have been part of the marketing literature for many years (see Bucklin [1]). This literature talks about open distribution where absence of collusion causes an increasing number of middlemen to cut prices, lowering the gross margin. As a result, middlemen interest in the brand declines. On the other hand, a limited distribution by limiting the number of middlemen in a trading area may not improve matters. The award of an exclusive distributorship transfers the market power inherent in a manufacturer's brand to the middleman. Historically three different roles of middlemen: trader, distributor, and provider are identified. The changing business conditions and roles of other agents in the market network is the key to the change of the role of the middleman and him/her business, see Gadde and Snehota [2]. Another pertinent area where middlemen play a key role is in the analysis of supply chain management. Here the middlemen can influence the entire flow of goods and services along with the process of

Social Network Analytics. https://doi.org/10.1016/B978-0-12-815458-8.00009-8

inventory and thus increases the utility of the players in the chain. A possible intermediary activity of the middlemen in the supply chain management is to make some predictive analysis of the market trend, weather conditions, logistics, and inventory management and provide these information to the stack holders, see Christopher [3].

Informed by the above-mentioned literature, in this chapter, we introduce the notion of middlemen in Network games from the perspective of channel control. Kalai et al. [4] introduced the notion of a middleman under cooperative situations and compared the core allocations to the middlemen, Rubinstein and Wolinsky [5] discussed this concept in further detail. In industrial organization this concept has been used by Yavas [6] for a search problem and Johri and Leach [7] for modeling a heterogeneous goods market. Recently Arya et al. [8] also applied the middleman concept to analyzing supply chains. Here we look at the notion of a middleman in Network games from a different point of view. We consider that each middleman engages in some intermediary activities in a network. This intermediary activity will result in value augmentation. But whether all parties benefit from this or not will critically depend on the network architecture. We develop an allocation rule for this class of games that accounts for the intermediary activities.

The remaining portion of the chapter proceeds as follows. In Section 2 we mention the prerequisites of Network games. In Section 3 we characterize our allocation rule using some standard cooperative game theoretic axioms in the line of the Position value for Network games due to van den Nouweland and Slikker [9]. We call this value the network middlemen efficient (NME) value. Then we show that the NME value is satisfied only for a small set of networks. To address other types of networks, in Section 4, we provide an alternative allocation rule to the NME value replacing the axiom of efficiency by multilateral interactions due to Borkotokey et al. [10] and call this value the network middlemen multilateral interaction (NMMI) value. This solution concept does not guarantee that the concerned parties will all get positive payoffs. To ensure that, we actually need the players to have links with other (nonmiddleman) players. This feature we characterize as our nonisolated property (NIP). We go on to show that NIP indeed guarantees that all parties benefit strictly from the presence of a middleman. Using international trade data and internet server traffic data, we create two numerical illustrations to highlight and substantiate our theoretical findings in Section 5. Section 6 concludes the chapter.

2 Preliminaries

This section presents the definitions and results necessary for our model formation. To a large extent this section builds on Jackson and Wolinsky [11], Jackson [12], and Borkotokey et al. [10].

Let $N = \{1, 2, ..., n\}$ be the player set. Subsets of N are called coalitions. Let us denote the size of each coalition S, T, etc., by the corresponding small letters s, t, etc. Also, we avoid braces for singletons for simplicity and use $S \setminus i$, $S \cup i$, etc., instead of $S \setminus \{i\}$, $S \cup \{i\}$, etc.

A network g comprises of a finite set of elements called nodes corresponding to players and a finite set of pairs of nodes called links, which correspond to bilateral connections among players. Thus g is a list of unordered pairs of players $\{i, j\}$, where $\{i, j\} \in g$ identifies a link in the network g. To make notations simple, we write ij to represent the link $\{i, j\}$.

The degree of a player in a network is the number of links it has in the network. Let g^N be the set of all possible links formed by the nodes of N. We call g^N the complete network with n nodes. Denote by $G^N = \{g | g \subseteq g^N\}$ the set of all possible networks on N. A path in a network is a sequence of nodes such that from each of its nodes there is a link to the next node in the sequence.

Let $N(g)$ denote the set of players having at least a link in g that is, $N(g) = \{i \mid \exists j \text{ such that } ij \in g\}$. Let $n(g) = \#N(g)$. For $g \in G^N$, let $l(g)$ be the total number of links in g and denote by $L_i(g)$ the set of links of player i. Thus $L_i(g) = \{ij \mid \exists j : ij \in g\}$. Let $l_i(g) = \#L_i(g)$. Thus we have $l(g) = \frac{1}{2}\sum_i l_i(g)$.

Given any $S \subseteq N$, let g^S denote the complete network formed by the players in S. Let $g|_S$ be the subnetwork of g formed by the players in S. Formally we have $g|_S = \{ij \mid ij \in g \text{ and } i \in S, j \in S\}$.

For any $g_1, g_2 \in G^N$, denote by $g_1 + g_2$ the network obtained through adding networks g_1 and g_2 and by $g_1 \setminus g_2$ the network obtained from g_1 by subtracting its subnetwork g_2.

Definition 1 (Jackson and Wolinsky [11]). A value function is a function $v: G^N \to \mathbb{R}$ such that $v(\varnothing) = 0$, where $\varnothing$ represents the empty network, that is, network without links.

The set of all possible value functions is denoted by V. The value function specifies the total worth generated by a given network structure. It may involve both costs and benefits whenever this information is available.

Definition 2 (Jackson and Wolinsky [11]). A *Network game* is a pair, (N, v), consisting of a set of players and a value function. If N is fixed and no confusion arises about this, we denote the Network game by only v. Consider the class V_g of all Network games defined on all subnetworks of a network g.

Definition 3 (Jackson and Wolinsky [11]). A Network game v is *monotonic* if for g, $g' \in G^N$ with $g' \subseteq g$, we have $v(g') \leq v(g)$.

Definition 4 (Borkotokey et al. [10]). Given a network $g \in G^N$, each of the following special value functions is a *basis* for V.

$$\hat{v}_g(g') = \begin{cases} 1 & \text{if } g \subseteq g' \\ 0 & \text{otherwise} \end{cases} \tag{1}$$

$$v_g^*(g') = \begin{cases} 1 & \text{if } g \underset{\neq}{\subset} g' \\ 0 & \text{otherwise} \end{cases} \tag{2}$$

and

$$\tilde{v}_g(g') = \begin{cases} 1 & \text{if } g = g' \\ 0 & \text{otherwise} \end{cases} \tag{3}$$

Thus every $v \in V$ can be written as a unique linear combination of value functions $\hat{v}_g$ or v_g^* or $\tilde{v}_g$, that is, $v = \sum_{g \subseteq g^N} a_g \hat{v}_g$ or $v = \sum_{g \subseteq g^N} b_g v_g^*$ or $v = \sum_{g \subseteq g^N} c_g \tilde{v}_g$, where a_g, b_g, $c_g \in \mathbb{R}$ are coefficients of v and a_g's are called *unanimity coefficients*.

Note that the notion of a basis in V plays a significant role in axiomatizing the solution concepts. Since each value function is a linear combination of its basis vectors, the corresponding characterization of a solution in terms of the basis vectors would essentially ensure the same for the original game.

Definition 5 (Jackson and Wolinsky [11]). An *allocation rule* is a function $Y : G^N \times V \to \mathbb{R}^n$ such that $Y_i(g, v)$ represents the payoff to player i with respect to v and g.

Definition 6 (Jackson [12]). An allocation rule Y is *link-based* if there exists $\Psi : G^N \times V \to \mathbb{R}^{\frac{n(n-1)}{2}}$ such that

$$\sum_{ij \in g^N} \Psi_{ij}(g, v) = v(g) \tag{4}$$

$$\text{and } Y_i(g, v) = \sum_{i \neq j} \frac{\Psi_{ij}(g, v)}{2} \tag{5}$$

Definition 7 (Borkotokey et al. [10]). Let v be a value function with unanimity coefficients $(a_{g'})_{g' \subseteq g}$ and network g be given. Then the *network position value* $Y^{NPV}(g, v)$ is defined by,

$$Y_i^{NPV}(g, v) = \sum_{g' \subseteq g} \frac{a_{g'} \, l_i(g')}{2 \, l(g')} \quad \forall i \in N \tag{6}$$

It follows that for every link l of g, if Φ_l^{Sh} denotes the Shapley value of the restriction $v|_g$ of the value function v to the subsets of g considering the links as players, then we have,

$$\Phi_l^{Sh}(g, v|_g) = \sum_{g' \subseteq g: \, l \subseteq g'} \frac{a_{g'}}{l(g')} \tag{7}$$

Combining Eqs. (6), (7), we obtain

$$Y_i^{NPV}(g, v) = \sum_{l \in L_i(g)} \frac{1}{2} \Phi_l^{Sh}(g, v|_g), \quad \forall i \in N \tag{8}$$

The network position value $Y^{NPV} : G^N \times V \to \mathbb{R}^n$ is formally given by

$$Y_i^{NPV}(g, v) = \sum_{\substack{i \neq j, \\ ij \in g}} \left(\sum_{g' \subset N \setminus ij} \frac{1}{2}(v(g' + ij) - v(g')) \right) \frac{l(g')! \, (l(g) - l(g') - 1)!}{l(g)!} \tag{9}$$

Let us call the network position value by position value in short.

Definition 8 (Borkotokey et al. [10]). An allocation rule Y is said to satisfy the axiom of *linearity (Lin)* if for Network games v, w and $a, b \in \mathbb{R}$,

$$Y_i(g, av + bw) = aY_i(g, v) + bY_i(g, w), \quad \forall i \in N \tag{10}$$

Definition 9 (Borkotokey et al. [10]). Let π be a permutation on N. For each $v \in V_g$, we define the game $\pi v \in V_{\pi g}$ by, $\pi v(\pi g') = v(g')$, $\forall g' \subseteq g$. An allocation rule Y is said to satisfy the axiom of *anonymity* (AN) if for all $v \in V_g$ and permutations π on N,

$$Y_i(g, v) = Y_{\pi i}(\pi g, \pi v), \quad \forall i \in N \tag{11}$$

The axiom *AN* suggests that the payoff to each player does not depend on him/her identity.

Definition 10 (Borkotokey et al. [10]). An allocation rule Y is said to satisfy the axiom of *monotonicity* (Mon) if for every monotonic value function v, $Y_i(g, v) \geq 0$ for every $i \in N$.

Definition 11 (Borkotokey et al. [10]). An allocation rule Y satisfies the axiom of *efficiency* (Eff) for $v \in V_g$ if

$$\sum_{i \in N} Y_i(g, v) = v(g) \tag{12}$$

Definition 12 (Borkotokey et al. [10]). Let $v \in V_g$ be a game on the network g. Fix a player i, $g_i \subseteq L_i(g)$. The *reduced game* with respect to g_i is a game denoted by $v_{[g_i]}^{g \backslash g_i + [g_i]}$ defined on the network $g \backslash g_i + [g_i]$ of $l(g)l(g_i) + 1$ links, where $[g_i]$ indicates a single hypothetical link such that as if i is connected to the network $g \backslash g_i$ only through this link. We call the new network $g \backslash g_i + [g_i]$ the reduced network of g for g_i. The reduced game is defined as for every $g' \subset g \backslash g_i$,

$$
\begin{aligned}
v_{[g_i]}^{g \backslash g_i + [g_i]}(g') &= v(g') \\
v_{[g_i]}^{g \backslash g_i + [g_i]}(g' + [g_i]) &= v(g' + g_i)
\end{aligned}
\tag{13}
$$

Following Borkotokey et al. [10], the value $l(g_i) \in \{1, ..., n\}$ denotes the level of interactions of player i with other players through him/her links in g_i. Thus if for example, $l(g_i) = 1$, player i is connected to the network through only one link and so him/her level of interaction in this case is 1.

Definition 13 (Borkotokey et al. [10]). An allocation rule Y is said to admit the Position value for the game v at each level of interactions if for each $i \in N$, it can be expressed as,

$$Y_i(g, v) = \sum_{\varnothing \neq g_i \subseteq L_i(g)} Y_i\left(g \backslash g_i + [g_i], v_{[g_i]}^{g \backslash g_i + [g_i]}\right) \tag{14}$$

where for each $\varnothing \neq g_i \subseteq L_i(g)$,

$$Y_i\left(g \backslash g_i + [g_i], v_{[g_i]}^{g \backslash g_i + [g_i]}\right) = Y_i^{NPV}\left(g \backslash g_i + [g_i], v_{[g_i]}^{g \backslash g_i + [g_i]}\right) \tag{15}$$

Definition 14 (Borkotokey et al. [10]). An allocation rule Y is said to satisfy the axiom of *multilateral interactions* (MI) if it admits the Position value for any Network game v at each level of interaction.

3 Network Game With Middlemen

In the following we define a Network game with middlemen. Recall that in Network games a middleman involves in some intermediary activities. Therefore, each subnetwork can generate extra value. Thus we have the following.

Definition 15 Let $g \in G^N$ be fixed. A Network game $v \in V_g$ is said to be a *Network game with middlemen* if there is $M \subset N$ and a set of real numbers $\{\eta_{g'} > 1 \mid \varnothing \neq g' \subseteq g\}$ satisfying the following conditions.

$$
\left.
\begin{array}{l}
\text{(i)For each } i \in M, \ v(g' + g_i) = \eta_{g' + g_i} v(g'), \ \forall \ \varnothing \neq g_i \subseteq L_i(g), g' \subseteq g\backslash g_i \\
\text{(ii) } v(g' + g_i) > v(g' + g_j), \ \forall \ g' \subseteq g\backslash(g_i + g_j), \text{ where } i \in M, j \in N\backslash M \text{ and} \\
\qquad\qquad g_i \subseteq L_i(g), \ g_j \subseteq L_j(g) \\
\text{(iii) } v(g') = 0, \ \forall \ g' \subseteq g|_M
\end{array}
\right\} \tag{16}
$$

In Eq. (16), although the players in M (i.e., the middlemen) and subnetworks of $g|_M$ (i.e., the links among the middlemen) do not generate any worth; however, they can increase the worth by linking with $g \setminus g|_M$. This increment of the worth is more in comparison to the worth increased by adding any subnetwork from $g \setminus g|_M$. In particular, this would imply that links with a middleman will fetch more worth that links without a middleman. Let $V\mathcal{M}g$ be the class of all Network games with middlemen and the player set N defined on g. If i satisfies Eq. (16), we say that player $i \in M$ engages in some intermediary activities for $v \in V\mathcal{M}g$. We call each player in M a middleman and the remaining players in $N \setminus M$ beneficiaries and the set $\eta^{NG} := \{\eta_{g'} > 1 \mid \varnothing \neq g' \subseteq g\}$ a scheme of intermediary activities (SIA) in v of players in M.

To develop an allocation rule for the class $V\mathcal{M}g$, we adopt the approach of Borkotokey et al. [10] for the characterization of our value. Thus our first axiom is *Lin*. This, however, applies to the larger class V_g of Network games defined on a fixed network g.

Lemma 1 *Let* Y *(g, v) satisfy* Lin *for a given network* g *and* v $\in$ V$_g$. *Then for every* v $\in$ V$_g$ *and* i $\in$ N, *there exists a family of real constants* $\{\alpha^i_{g'}(g)\}_{\varnothing \neq g' \subseteq g}$ *such that* $Y_i(g,v) = \sum_{\varnothing \neq g' \subseteq g} \alpha^i_{g'}(g) v(g')$.

Proof. Suppose Y (g, v) satisfy *Lin* for a given network g and $v \in V_g$.

Since the collection $\{\tilde{v}_{g'} \in V_g : g' \subseteq g\}$ given by Eq. (3) is a standard basis for V_g, thus we have $v = \sum_{\varnothing \neq g' \subseteq g} v(g')\tilde{v}_{g'}$. It follows that

$$
Y_i(g,v) = \sum_{\varnothing \neq g' \subseteq g} \alpha^i_{g'}(g) v(g') \tag{17}
$$

where $\alpha^i_{g'}(g) := Y_i(g, \tilde{v}_{g'})$.

For the remaining axioms to follow, we consider the class $V\mathcal{M}g$. Our next axiom is the axiom of middlemen (MA). In this axiom we consider that each middleman gets a portion from $v(g)$, which is determined by the players in the game through consensus. Later we will show that the factor so obtained can generate a parametric family of our proposed allocation rule. Thus we have the following axiom.

The axiom of middleman (MA) : If i is a middleman for $v \in V\mathcal{M}g$, then $Y_i(g, v) = \xi_i v(g)$ for an exogenously determined $\xi_i \in (0, 1)$.

Let us call the quantity $\xi_i v(g)$ the intermediary fee to middleman i. Let $\boldsymbol{\xi} = (\xi_1, ..., \xi_n) \in [0, 1)^n$ with $\xi_i = 0, \forall i \in N \setminus M$. We call $\boldsymbol{\xi}$ the intermediary factor or IF in short. The next lemma follows.

Lemma 2 *Let* $Y(g,v)$ *satisfy* Lin *and* MA, *then given an IF* ξ *for every* $v \in V\mathcal{M}g$ *and* $i \in N \setminus M$ *there exist real constants* $\{\delta^i_{g'+g_i}(g)\}_{g_i \subseteq L_i(g),\ g' \subseteq g\setminus g_i}$ *such that*

$$Y_i(g,v) = \begin{cases} \displaystyle\sum_{\varnothing \neq g_i \subseteq L_i(g)}\ \sum_{g' \subseteq g\setminus g_i} \delta^i_{g'+g_i}(g)\left[v(g'+g_i) - \eta_{g'+g_i}v(g')\right], & \text{if } i \in N\setminus M \\ \xi_i v(g), & \text{if } i \in M \end{cases} \tag{18}$$

Proof. By Lemma 1, under *Lin*, for each $i \in N$ there exist real constants $\{\alpha^i_{g'}(g)\}_{\varnothing \neq g' \subseteq g}$ such that

$$Y_i(g,v) = \sum_{\varnothing \neq g' \subseteq g} \alpha^i_{g'}(g)v(g') \tag{19}$$

For $v \in V\mathcal{M}g$, after rearranging the coefficients, we obtain

$$Y_i(g,v) = \sum_{g' \subseteq g\setminus L_i(g)} \left(\sum_{\varnothing \neq g_i \subseteq L_i(g)} \alpha^i_{g'+g_i}(g)v(g'+g_i) + \alpha^i_{g'}(g)v(g') \right) \tag{20}$$

Eq. (20) can be rewritten as

$$Y_i(g,v) = \sum_{\varnothing \neq g_i \subseteq L_i(g)}\ \sum_{g' \subseteq g\setminus g_i} \left[\beta^i_{g'+g_i}(g)v(g'+g_i) + \beta^i_{g'}(g)v(g') \right] \tag{21}$$

under the following substitution[1]

$$\alpha^i_{g'+g_i}(g) = \left(\sum_{k=1}^{l(g_i)} C_k^{l(g_i)} + \sum_{k=1}^{l_i(g)-l(g_i)} C_k^{l_i(g)-l(g_i)} \right)\beta^i_{g'+g_i}(g)$$
$$= (2^{l(g_i)} + 2^{l_i(g)-l(g_i)} - 2)\beta^i_{g'+g_i}(g)$$

Assume that i is a middleman for $v \in V\mathcal{M}g$, we have

$$Y_i(g,v) = \sum_{\varnothing \neq g_i \subseteq L_i(g)}\ \sum_{g' \subseteq g\setminus g_i} \left[\beta^i_{g'+g_i}(g)\eta_{g'+g_i} + \beta^i_{g'}(g) \right]v(g') \tag{22}$$

Note that Eq. (22) holds for any $v \in V\mathcal{M}g$ such that i is a middleman for v, in particular for all games in $V\mathcal{M}g$ satisfying for a given $\varnothing \neq g_i \subseteq L_i(g)$ and $\varnothing \neq g' \subseteq g\setminus g_i$,

$$\left. \begin{array}{l} v(g_1 + g_i) = \eta_{g_1+g_i}v(g_1) \\ v(g_1) = \tilde{v}_{g'}(g_1) \end{array} \right\} \quad \forall\, g_1 \subseteq g\setminus g_i \tag{23}$$

For the given IF ξ using *MA*, we have

$$Y_i(g,v) = \xi_i v(g)$$
$$\Rightarrow \sum_{\varnothing \neq g_i \subseteq L_i(g)}\ \sum_{g' \subseteq g\setminus g_i} \left[\beta^i_{g'+g_i}(g)\eta_{g'+g_i} + \beta^i_{g'}(g) \right]v(g') = \xi_i v(g)$$

---

[1]For example, let $N = \{1, 2, 3, 4\}$ and $g = \{12, 13, 23, 24\}$, then $\alpha^1_g(g) = 3\beta^1_g(g)$, $\alpha^1_{\{12,13,23\}}(g) = 3\beta^1_{\{12,13,23\}}(g)$, $\alpha^1_{\{12,13\}}(g) = 3\beta^1_{\{12,13\}}(g)$, $\alpha^1_{\{12\}}(g) = 2\beta^1_{\{12\}}(g)$, $\alpha^1_{\{23\}}(g) = 3\beta^1_{\{23\}}(g)$, etc.

$$\Rightarrow \beta_g^i(g)\eta_g + \beta_{g\backslash L_i(g)}^i(g) = \xi_i \eta_g$$

$$\Rightarrow \beta_g^i(g) = \xi_i - \frac{\beta_{g\backslash L_i(g)}^i(g)}{\eta_g}$$

and $\beta_{g'+g_i}^i(g)\eta_{g'+g_i} = -\beta_{g'}^i(g),\ \forall g_i \subset L_i(g),\ g' \subseteq g\backslash g_i$

Set $\gamma_{g'+g_i}^i(g) := \beta_{g'+g_i}^i(g)\eta_{g'+g_i} = -\beta_{g'}^i(g),\ \forall g_i \subset L_i(g),\ g' \subseteq g\backslash g_i$ in Eq. (21). Thus we obtain for every $i \in N$,

$$Y_i(g,v) = \xi_i v(g) - \frac{\beta_{g\backslash L_i(g)}^i(g)}{\eta_g}v(g) + \beta_{g\backslash L_i(g)}^i(g)v(g\backslash L_i(g))$$

$$+ \sum_{\varnothing \neq g_i \subset L_i(g)} \sum_{g' \subseteq g\backslash g_i} \gamma_{g'+g_i}^i(g)\left(\frac{v(g'+g_i)}{\eta_{g'+g_i}} - v(g')\right)$$

Again set $\qquad \delta_{g\backslash L_i(g)}^i(g) = -\frac{\beta_{g\backslash L_i(g)}^i(g)}{\eta_g}$

and $\qquad \delta_{g'+g_i}^i(g) = \frac{\gamma_{g'+g_i}^i(g)}{\eta_{g'+g_i}},\ \forall\ g_i \subset L_i(g), g' \subseteq g\backslash g_i$

We obtain

$$Y_i(g,v) = \xi_i v(g) + \sum_{\varnothing \neq g_i \subseteq L_i(g)} \sum_{g' \subseteq g\backslash g_i} \delta_{g'+g_i}^i(g)\left[v(g'+g_i) - \eta_{g'+g_i}v(g')\right]$$

Thus we obtain our desired result as follows.

$$Y_i(g,v) = \begin{cases} \sum_{\varnothing \neq g_i \subseteq L_i(g)} \sum_{g' \subseteq g\backslash g_i} \delta_{g'+g_i}^i(g)\left[v(g'+g_i) - \eta_{g'+g_i}v(g')\right], & \text{if } i \in N\backslash M \\ \xi_i v(g), & \text{if } i \in M \end{cases} \tag{24}$$

It is evident from Eq. (24) that the allocation rule $Y(g,v)$ evolves so far depends on the choice of ξ, which is exogenously determined. This further implies that we get a parametric family of allocation rules determined by IF ξ Thus to highlight this fact and with an abuse of notations, from now onward we denote our allocation rule by the symbol $Y(g,v,\xi)$.

Recall that *Mon* suggests each player to receive nonnegative payoff in a monotonic game. Lemma 3 uses *Mon* to ensure the nonnegativity of the coefficients in the expression given by Eq. (24).

Lemma 3 *If* $Y(g,v,\xi)$ *satisfies* Lin, MA, *and* Mon *then every* $v \in V\mathcal{M}g$ *and* $i \in N\backslash M$ *there exist nonnegative real constants* $\{\delta_{g'+g_i}^i(g)\}_{g_i \subseteq L_i(g),\ g' \subseteq g\backslash g_i}$ *such that*

$$Y_i(g,v,\xi) = \begin{cases} \sum_{\varnothing \neq g_i \subseteq L_i(g)} \sum_{g' \subseteq g\backslash g_i} \delta_{g'+g_i}^i(g)\left[v(g'+g_i) - \eta_{g'+g_i}v(g')\right], & \text{if } i \in N\backslash M \\ \xi_i v(g), & \text{if } i \in M \end{cases} \tag{25}$$

Proof For $\eta \in (1,\infty)$ and $g' \subseteq g$, define the game $u_{g'}^\eta$ as follows.

$$u_{g'}^\eta(g_1) = \begin{cases} \eta & \text{if } g' \subsetneqq g_1 \\ 0 & \text{otherwise} \end{cases} \tag{26}$$

Observe that $u''_{g'} \in V\mathcal{M}g$ and is monotonic. Therefore, $Y_i(g, u''_{g'}, \boldsymbol{\xi}) = \eta \delta^i_{g'+g_i}(g) \geq 0$ and the result follows immediately.

The next axiom, namely *AN* implies that the coefficients $\delta^i_{g'+g_i}(g)$, for all $i \in N \setminus M$ and $g_i \subseteq L_i(g)$, $g' \subseteq g \setminus g_i$ will depend only on its number of links and the SIA $\{\eta_{g'} : g' \subseteq g\}$ depends on the size of g', $\forall g' \subseteq g$.

Lemma 4 *If* Y *(g, v, ξ) satisfies* Lin, MA, Mon, *and* AN, *then for every* $v \in V\mathcal{M}g$ *and* $i \in N \setminus M$ *there exist real constants* $\delta_{l(g')+l(g_i)}(g)$ *where* $l(g_i) = 1, 2, ..., l_i(g)$, $g_i \subseteq L_i(g)$ *and* $l(g') = 0, ..., l(g) - l(g_i)$, $g' \subseteq g \setminus g_i$ *such that*

$$
Y_i(g, v, \boldsymbol{\xi}) = \begin{cases} \displaystyle\sum_{\varnothing \neq g_i \subseteq L_i(g)} \sum_{g' \subseteq g \setminus g_i} \delta_{l(g')+l(g_i)}(g) \left[v(g'+g_i) - \eta_{l(g')+l(g_i)} v(g') \right], & \text{if } i \in N \setminus M \\ \xi_i v(g), & \text{if } i \in M \end{cases}
\tag{27}
$$

Proof. For any $i \in N \setminus M$, let g'_i, $g''_i \subseteq L_i(g)$ and $g' \subseteq g \setminus g'_i$, and $g'' \subseteq g \setminus g''_i$ such that $l(g' + g'_i) = l(g'' + g''_i)$.

Let π be a permutation on N such that $\pi i = i$ and $\pi g' = g''$, $\pi g'_i = g''_i$.

For $\eta \in (1, \infty)$ and $g' \subseteq g$, define the game $\tilde{v}^{\eta}_{g'}$ as follows.

$$
\tilde{v}^{\eta}_{g'}(g_1) = \begin{cases} \eta & \text{if } g' = g_1 \\ 0 & \text{otherwise} \end{cases}
\tag{28}
$$

By *AN*, we have

$$
Y_i(g, v_{g'+g'_i}, \boldsymbol{\xi}) = Y_i(\pi g, \pi v_{g''+g''_i}, \boldsymbol{\xi})
\tag{29}
$$

Using $\pi v_{g'+g'_i} = v_{g''+g''_i}$, we have from Eq. (25),

$$
\delta^i_{g'+g_i}(g) = \delta^i_{g''+g''_i}(\pi g)
\tag{30}
$$

Next take $i, j \in N \setminus M$ such that $i \neq j$ and $\pi i = j$ and $\pi g_i = g_j$, for all $g_i \in L_i(g)$ and $g_j \in L_j(g)$: $l(g_i) = l(g_j)$ while leaving every $g' \subseteq g \setminus (g_i + g_j)$ unchanged.

It follows from *AN*,

$$
\delta^i_{g'+g_i}(g) = \delta^j_{g'+g_j}(\pi g) \; \forall g' \subseteq g \setminus (g_i + g_j)
\tag{31}
$$

This implies that there exist constants $\{ \delta_{l(g')+l(g_i)}(g) : l(g_i) = 1, 2, ..., l_i(g), l(g') = 0, ..., l(g \setminus g_i) \}$ that depend on the size of $g' + g_i$, $\forall g_i \subseteq L_i(g)$ and $g' \subseteq g \setminus g_i$ such that Eq. (25) holds.

The next axiom is the axiom of efficiency (*Eff*), that is, for each $v \in V\mathcal{M}g$, $\sum_{i \in N} Y_i(g, v, \boldsymbol{\xi}) = v(g)$.

Definition 16 An allocation rule $Y(g, v, \boldsymbol{\xi}) : G^N \times V\mathcal{M}g \to \mathbb{R}^n$ satisfies *Eff* if

$$
\sum_{i \in N} Y_i(g, v, \boldsymbol{\xi}) = v(g)
\tag{32}
$$

Let $\xi = \sum_{i=1}^{n} \xi_i$. Thus we have the following lemma.

Lemma 5 *If* Y (g, v, ξ) *satisfies* **Lin, MA, Mon, AN,** *and* **Eff,** *then for every* $v \in V\mathcal{M}g$ *and* $i \in N \setminus M$ *there exist real constants* $\delta_{l(g') + l(g_i)}(g)$ *where* $l(g_i) = 1, 2, \ldots, l_i(g)$, $g_i \subseteq L_i(g)$ *and* $l(g') = 0, \ldots, l(g \setminus g_i)$, $g' \subseteq g \setminus g_i$ *such that*

$$
Y_i(g, v, \xi) = \begin{cases} \displaystyle\sum_{\varnothing \neq g_i \subseteq L_i(g)} \sum_{g' \subseteq g \setminus g_i} \delta_{l(g') + l(g_i)}(g) \Big[v(g' + g_i) - \eta_{l(g') + l(g_i)} v(g') \Big], & \text{if } i \in N \setminus M \\ \xi_i v(g), & \text{if } i \in M \end{cases}
\tag{33}
$$

where $\sum_{i \in N \setminus M} \sum_{\varnothing \neq g_i \subseteq g} \delta_{l(g)}(g) = 1 - \xi$ and $\sum_{i \in N \setminus M} \sum_{\varnothing \neq g_i \subseteq g} \delta_{l(g')}(g) - \sum_{i \in N \setminus M} \sum_{\varnothing \neq g_i \subseteq g \setminus g'} \delta_{l(g_i) + l(g')}(g) \eta_{l(g') + l(g_i)} = 0$ *for all* $g' \subset g$.

Proof. From *Eff* and Lemma 4, we have

$$
v(g) = \sum_{i \in N} Y_i(g, v, \xi)
$$

$$
\Rightarrow v(g) = \sum_{i \in M} \xi_i v(g) + \sum_{i \in N \setminus M} \sum_{\varnothing \neq g_i \subseteq L_i(g)} \sum_{g' \subseteq g \setminus g_i} \delta_{l(g') + l(g_i)}(g) \Big[v(g' + g_i) - \eta_{l(g') + l(g_i)} v(g') \Big]
$$

$$
\Rightarrow \left(1 - \sum_{i \in M} \xi_i \right) v(g) = \sum_{i \in N \setminus M} \sum_{\varnothing \neq g_i \subseteq L_i(g)} \sum_{g' \subseteq g \setminus g_i} \delta_{l(g') + l(g_i)}(g) \Big[v(g' + g_i) - \eta_{l(g') + l(g_i)} v(g') \Big]
$$

$$
= \sum_{\varnothing \neq g' \subseteq g} v(g') \left(\sum_{i \in N \setminus M} \sum_{\varnothing \neq g_i \subseteq g'} \delta_{l(g')}(g) - \sum_{i \in N \setminus M} \sum_{\varnothing \neq g_i \subseteq g \setminus g'} \delta_{l(g_i) + l(g')}(g) \eta_{l(g') + l(g_i)} \right)
$$

For $\eta \in (1, \infty)$ and $g' \subseteq g$, define the game $\tilde{v}_{g'}^{\eta}$ as follows.

$$
\tilde{v}_{g'}^{\eta}(g_1) = \begin{cases} \eta & \text{if } g' = g_1 \\ 0 & \text{otherwise} \end{cases}
$$

Then we have $\sum_{i \in N \setminus M} \sum_{\varnothing \neq g_i \subseteq g} \delta_{l(g)}(g) = 1 - \xi$ and $\sum_{i \in N \setminus M} \sum_{\varnothing \neq g_i \subseteq g'} \delta_{l(g')}(g) - \sum_{i \in N \setminus M} \sum_{\varnothing \neq g_i \subseteq g \setminus g'} \delta_{l(g_i) + l(g')}(g) \eta_{l(g') + l(g_i)} = 0$ for all $g' \subset g$.

Combining Lemmas 1–5, we have the following theorem.

Theorem 9.1 *If* Y (g, v, ξ) *satisfies* **Lin, MA, Mon, AN,** *and* **Eff,** *then for every* $v \in V\mathcal{M}g$ *there exist real constants* $\delta_{l(g') + l(g_i)}(g)$ *where* $l(g_i) = 1, 2, \ldots, l_i(g)$, $g_i \subseteq L_i(g)$ *and* $l(g') = 0, \ldots, l(g \setminus g_i)$, $g' \subseteq g \setminus g_i$ *such that*

$$
Y_i(g, v, \xi) = \begin{cases} \displaystyle\sum_{\varnothing \neq g_i \subseteq L_i(g)} \sum_{g' \subseteq g \setminus g_i} \delta_{l(g') + l(g_i)}(g) \Big[v(g' + g_i) - \eta_{l(g') + l(g_i)} v(g') \Big], & \text{if } i \in N \setminus M \\ \xi_i v(g), & \text{if } i \in M \end{cases}
$$

where

$$
\sum_{i \in N \setminus M} \sum_{\varnothing \neq g_i \subseteq g} \delta_{l(g)}(g) = 1 - \xi \text{ and}
$$

$$
\sum_{i \in N \setminus M} \sum_{\varnothing \neq g_i \subseteq g'} \delta_{l(g')}(g) - \sum_{i \in N \setminus M} \sum_{\varnothing \neq g_i \subseteq g \setminus g'} \delta_{l(g_i) + l(g')}(g) \eta_{l(g') + l(g_i)} = 0 \ \forall g' \subset g
\tag{34}
$$

Let us call the allocation rule Y for the network g, $v \in V\mathcal{M}g$ and IF ξ defined in Theorem 9.1, the *Network Middlemen Efficient value* (NME value). In view of the foregoing discussions, we conclude that Theorem 9.1 gives the existence and uniqueness of a parametric family of allocation rules with parameter ξ.

Theorem 9.1 works as the benchmark solution form for the rest of the chapter. But, before we proceed further, the following examples show that the requirement that an allocation rule for a $v \in V\mathcal{M}g$ satisfies *Lin, MA, Mon, AN,* and *Eff* together sufficiently restricts the domain of $V\mathcal{M}g$.

Example 1 Let $N = \{1, 2, 3, 4, 5\}$, $M = \{3\}$, and $g = \{12, 23, 34, 45\}$. If the corresponding Y (g, v, ξ) for $v \in V\mathcal{M}g$ and any $\xi \in [0, 1)^5$ with $\xi_3 = 0$ satisfies *Eff*, we must have from Eq. (34)

$$
\begin{aligned}
&8 \times \delta_4 = 1 - \xi_3; 5 \times \delta_3 - 2 \times \delta_4\eta_3 = 0; 4 \times \delta_3 - 2 \times \delta_4\eta_3 = 0; 6 \times \delta_3 - \delta_4\eta_3 = 0 \\
&7 \times \delta_3 - \delta_4\eta_3 = 0; 2 \times \delta_2 - 4 \times \delta_3\eta_2 - \delta_4\eta_2 = 0; 3 \times \delta_2 - 3 \times \delta_3\eta_2 = 0 \\
&4 \times \delta_2 - 3 \times \delta_3\eta_2 = 0; 3 \times \delta_2 - 3 \times \delta_3\eta_2 - \delta_4\eta_2 = 0; 3 \times \delta_2 - 3 \times \delta_3\eta_2 = 0 \\
&4 \times \delta_2 - 2 \times \delta_3\eta_2 = 0; \delta_1 - 5 \times \delta_2\eta_1 = 0; 2 \times \delta_1 - 4 \times \delta_2\eta_1 = 0 \\
&2 \times \delta_1 - 2 \times \delta_3\eta_1 - 3 \times \delta_2\eta_1 = 0; \delta_1 - 6 \times \delta_2\eta_1 - 2 \times \delta_3\eta_1 = 0
\end{aligned}
\tag{35}
$$

It follows from Eq. (35) that the only possibilities for a solution to exist is $\delta_i = 0$, for all i, which is against our assumption. Therefore, the efficiency of Y for $v \in V\mathcal{M}g$ and IF $\xi \in [0, 1)^n$ with $\xi_i = 0 \; \forall \; i \in N \setminus M$, is not consistent with the axioms *Lin, MA, AN,* and *Mon.* Following theorem gives a necessary and sufficient condition for an efficient allocation rule that satisfies *Lin, MA, AN,* and *Mon* together.

Theorem 9.2 *An allocation rule that satisfies* Lin, MA, Mon, AN, *and* Eff *on* g *for any* $v \in V\mathcal{M}g$ *and IF* ξ *if and only if* g *is a star network where the middleman is in the center.*

Proof When g is a star network where the middleman i is in the center, from Theorem 9.1 for each $j \in N \setminus i$ we have

$$
Y_j(g, v, \xi) = \sum_{g' \subseteq g \setminus ij} \delta_{l(g')+1}(g)\left[v(g' + ij) - \eta_{l(g')+1}v(g')\right]
$$

where

$$
\delta_{l(g')}(g) = \frac{l(g')!(n - l(g') - 2)}{(n-1)!}(1-\xi)\prod_{k=l(g')+1}^{n-1}\eta_k
$$

Thus the efficiency of Y is consistent with the axioms *Lin, MA, AN,* and *Mon.*

For the converse part, define a function $n_k : G^N \to \mathbb{N}$ such that $n_k(g)$ denotes the number of nodes in g having k links, where $k \in \{1, 2, ..., \max_{i \in N \setminus M} l_i(g)\}$. For any $g', g'' \subseteq g$ such that $l(g') = l(g'')$, let $g_1 = g \setminus g'$ and $g_2 = g \setminus g''$. The system of linear equations given by Eq. (34) is consistent if $n_k(g_1) = n_k(g_2)$, for all k. This holds if g is a star network with the central node as middleman.

Remark 1 For the game $v \in V\mathcal{M}g$ where g is a star network with the middleman at the central node, $v(g') = 0$ for all $g' \subseteq g$. Thus the NME value makes little sense to any $v \in V\mathcal{M}g$.

The above finding renders the findings of Theorem 9.2 of not much use as the only feasible cases turn out to have zero value in aggregate. This motivates us to identify some axioms other than efficiency that would yield practically useful solution concepts.

4 The NMMI Value for the Class $V\mathcal{M}g$

In Section 3, we have seen that the efficiency of an allocation rule Y for $v \in V\mathcal{M}g$ and IF ξ is consistent with the axioms *Lin*, *MA*, *AN*, and *Mon* only when g is a star network with the central node as middleman. Thus we propose an alternative to NME value in the following. In this value we replace *Eff* by the axiom of multilateral interactions (*MI*) due to Borkotokey et al. [10]. After replacing *Eff* we obtain a unique allocation rule Y for any $v \in V\mathcal{M}g$ and IF $\xi \in [0, 1)^n$ with $\xi_i = 0 \ \forall \ i \in N \setminus M$, that satisfies *Lin*, *MA*, *Mon*, *AN*, and *MI*.

For our next axiom *MI* we need the following definitions. First, we define a reduced game (originally defined for Cooperative games by Harsanyi [13]).

Definition 17 Let $v \in V\mathcal{M}g$ be a game on the network g. Fix a player i, $g_i \subseteq L_i(g)$. The reduced game with respect to g_i is a game denoted by $v_{[g_i]}^{g \setminus g_i + [g_i]}$ defined on the network $g \setminus g_i + [g_i]$ of $l(g) - l(g_i) + 1$ links, where $[g_i]$ indicates a single hypothetical link such that as if i is connected to the network $g \setminus g_i$ only through this link. We call the new network $g \setminus g_i + [g_i]$ the reduced network of g for g_i. The reduced game is defined as for every $g' \subseteq g \setminus g_i$,

$$v_{[g_i]}^{g \setminus g_i + [g_i]}(g' + [g_i]) = v(g' + g_i)$$

$$v_{[g_i]}^{g \setminus g_i + [g_i]}(g') = \eta_{g' + g_i} v(g')$$

(36)

Recall from Definition 17 in a reduced game $v_{[g_i]}^{g \setminus g_i + [g_i]}$ with respect to the link set g_i, player i is connected to him/her peers through a single hypothetical link and the value generated through this will be the same as that in the original game when he/she links up through all him/her links in g_i separately. The value for any $g' \subseteq g \setminus g_i$ will be multiplied by the SIA offered to the subnetwork $g' + g_i$, that is, $\eta_{g' + g_i}$ with the value in the original game. We consider each value of $l(g_i)$ as the level of interactions of player i through him/her links in g_i.

Our next axiom *MI* ensures that the total power of a player in the network is measured by summing all him/her powers stemming out from him/her possible multilateral interactions at each level.

Definition 18 An allocation rule Y is said to admit the Position value for the game $v \in V\mathcal{M}g$ at each level of interactions if for each $i \in N \setminus M$, it can be expressed as,

$$Y_i(g, v, \xi) = \sum_{\emptyset \neq g_i \subseteq L_i(g)} Y_i\left(g \setminus g_i + [g_i], v_{[g_i]}^{g \setminus g_i + [g_i]}, \xi\right)$$

(37)

where for each $\emptyset \neq g_i \subseteq L_i(g)$,

$$Y_i\left(g \setminus g_i + [g_i], v_{[g_i]}^{g \setminus g_i + [g_i]}, \xi\right) = Y_i^{NPV}\left(g, v_{[g_i]}^{g \setminus g_i + [g_i]}\right)$$

(38)

Definition 19 An allocation rule Y is said to satisfy the axiom *MI* if it admits the Position value for any Network game v at each level of interaction.

Theorem 9.3 *An allocation rule* Y *satisfies the axioms* Lin, MA, Mon, AN, *and* MI *if and only if for all* i $\in$ N $\setminus$ M *it can be expressed as follows.*

$$Y_i(g,v,\xi) = \begin{cases} \displaystyle\sum_{\varnothing \neq g_i \subseteq L_i(g)} \sum_{g' \subseteq g\setminus g_i} \frac{1}{2}\frac{(l(g)-l(g_i)-l(g'))!\,l(g')!}{(l(g)-l(g_i)-1)!}\Big(v(g'+g_i)-\eta_{l(g')+l(g_i)}v(g')\Big), & \text{if } i\in N\setminus M \\ \xi_i v(g), & \text{if } i\in M \end{cases}$$
(39)

Proof. From *MI* and Lemma 4, we have

$$Y_i(g,v,\xi) = \sum_{\varnothing \neq g_i \subseteq L_i(g)} Y_i^{NPV}\Big(g\setminus g_i + [g_i], v_{[g_i]}^{g\setminus g_i + [g_i]}\Big)$$

$$= \sum_{\varnothing \neq g_i \subseteq L_i(g)} \sum_{\varnothing \neq h_i \subseteq L_i(g\setminus g_i + [g_i])} \sum_{h' \subseteq (g\setminus g_i + [g_i])\setminus h_i} \frac{1}{2}\frac{(l(g)-l(g_i)-l(g'))!\,l(g')!}{(l(g)-l(g_i)-1)!}$$
$$\Big(v_{[g_i]}^{g\setminus g_i + [g_i]}(h'+h_i)-v_{[g_i]}^{g\setminus g_i + [g_i]}(h')\Big)$$

From Eq. (9), we have

$$Y_i(g,v,\xi) = \sum_{\varnothing \neq g_i \subseteq L_i(g)} \sum_{g' \subseteq g\setminus g_i} \frac{1}{2}\frac{(l(g)-l(g_i)-l(g'))!\,l(g')!}{(l(g)-l(g_i)-1)!}\Big(v(g'+g_i)-\eta_{l(g')+l(g_i)}v(g')\Big)$$
(40)

Comparing the coefficients of Eqs. (27), (40) we obtain the desired result.

We call the value defined in Eq. (39) the *network middlemen multilateral interaction value* (or NMMI value). This is the alternative benchmark solution form to that found in Theorem 9.2. This will be used now on.

Remark 2 The NMMI value defined in Eq. (39) is not efficient. Thus this value can be normalized in the line of van den Brink and van den Lann [14, 15], which distributes the worth of the network proportional to the NMMI value among the players. However, as in [14, 15] after normalization our value also will not satisfy *Lin* and *MA*. Therefore, we can consider the NMMI value as a representative of the power or influence of the players in generating the grand worth in the line of Borkotokey et al. [10].

In what follows next we present two further examples to illustrate that it is not always the case that each beneficiary receives a nonnegative NMMI value.

Example 2 Consider the game $(\{1,2,3,4,5\}, v)$ with $M=\{3\}$, $g=\{13,23,34,45\}$, $\eta_1=1.4$, $\eta_2=2.1$, $\eta_3=1.8$, and $\eta_4=2$, given by $v(\{13\})=v(\{23\})=v(\{34\})=0$, $v(\{45\})=2$, $v(\{13,23\})=v(\{13,34\})=v(\{23,34\})=0$, $v(\{13,45\})=v(\{23,45\})=v(\{34,45\})=4.2$, $v(\{13,23,34\})=0$, $v(\{13,23,45\})=v(\{13,34,45\})=v(\{23,34,45\})=3.6$, $v(g)=4$. Take for example, $\xi=(0,0,0.3,0,0)$. Thus the NMMI value for v is $Y(g,v,\xi)=(-8.76,-8.76,1.2,11.87,17.7)$.

Example 3 Let $(\{1,2,3,4\}, v)$ be the game with $M=\{3\}$, $g=\{12,13,23,34\}$, $\eta_1=2$, $\eta_2=1.5$, $\eta_3=1.2$, and $\eta_2=2$ so that $v(\{13\})=v(\{23\})=v(\{34\})=0$, $v(\{12\})=2$, $v(\{12,13\})=v(\{12,23\})=v(\{12,34\})=3$, $v(\{13,23\})=v(\{13,34\})=v(\{23,34\})=0$, $v(\{13,23,34\})=0$, $v(\{13,23,12\})=v(\{13,34,12\})=v(\{23,34,12\})=2.4$, $v(g)=4$. Take for example, $\xi=(0,0,0.4,0)$. Then the NMMI value for v is $Y(g,v,\xi)=(24.9,24.9,2.4,-2.4)$.

In Example 2, players 1 and 2 get negative NMMI value. Similarly player 4's NMMI value is also negative in Example 3. In both examples we have seen that a beneficiary's NMMI value is always negative when he/she has only links with the middlemen. In fact we prove the following lemma.

Lemma 6 *If a beneficiary can have access to him/her network only through the middlemen with respect to a $v \in V\mathcal{M}g$, then him/her NMMI value is always negative for all IF ξ*

Proof. Consider $i \in N \setminus M$ has only one connection with middleman $j \in M$ with respect to a $v \in V\mathcal{M}g$, and has no link with any other beneficiary. Then for each IF $\xi \in [0, 1)^n$ with $\xi_i = 0 \; \forall \; i \in N \setminus M$, it follows from Eqs. (40), (16),

$$
\begin{aligned}
Y_i(g, v, \xi) &= \sum_{g' \subseteq g \setminus ij} \frac{1}{2} \frac{(l(g) - l(g') - 1)! l(g')!}{(l(g) - 2)!} \left(v(g' + ij) - \eta_{l(g') + 1} v(g') \right) \\
&= \sum_{g' \subseteq g \setminus ij} \frac{1}{2} \frac{(l(g) - l(g') - 1)! l(g')!}{(l(g) - 2)!} \left(1 - \eta_{l(g')} \right) \eta_{l(g') + 1} v(g') < 0
\end{aligned}
\tag{41}
$$

Thus $Y_i(g, v, \xi) < 0$ for each IF $\xi \in [0, 1)^n$ with $\xi_i = 0 \; \forall \; i \in N \setminus M$.

Remark 3 Observe that if g has at least one beneficiary i who has only connections with the middlemen with respect to $v \in V\mathcal{M}g$ then v can never be monotonic. Thus Theorem 9.3 and Lemma 6 imply that i gets negative NMMI value for all such $v \in V\mathcal{M}g$. This idea is intuitive in the sense that when the beneficiary has access to the network only through the middlemen in a game it is quite likely that he/she will not be able to garner significant benefit from such networks as the middlemen can then extract a large share of the profit from their binding agreements. In international trade situations if middlemen refuse to trade with the beneficiary, he/she is rendered helpless. This may end up in a compromise with him/her payoff for the middlemen. Therefore, our NMMI value for him/her will be negative. Thus in the next, we introduce a property, which ensures each beneficiary a positive NMMI value. Basically it guarantees that if beneficiaries also have connections among themselves, such negative externalities and exploitations by middlemen can be avoided.

Definition 20 (Nonisolated Property). A network g satisfies the NIP with respect to a network game $v \in V\mathcal{M}g$ with middlemen if each of the beneficiaries having one link with a middleman has at least one more link connecting to another beneficiary, that is, for each middleman i, if there exists $j \in N \setminus M$ such that $ij \in g$ then there exists $k \in N \setminus M$ such that $jk \in g$.

Theorem 9.4 *If g satisfies NIP with respect to $v \in V\mathcal{M}g$ and the corresponding SIA $\{\eta_{g'} > 1 \mid \varnothing \neq g' \subseteq g\}$ is directly proportional to the size of each $g' \subseteq g$, then $Y_i(g, v, \xi) > 0$ for all $i \in N \setminus M$ and IF ξ*

Proof When g satisfies NIP with respect to $v \in V\mathcal{M}g$ for each $i \in N \setminus M$ then there exists a $j \in N \setminus M$ such that $ij \in g$. Thus from Eq. (40) it follows that

$$
\begin{aligned}
Y_i(g, v, \xi) &= \sum_{\varnothing \neq g_i \subseteq L_i(g)} \sum_{g' \subseteq g \setminus g_i} \frac{1}{2} \frac{(l(g) - l(g_i) - l(g'))! l(g')!}{(l(g) - l(g_i) - 1)!} \left(v(g' + g_i) - \eta_{l(g') + l(g_i)} v(g') \right) \\
&= \sum_{\varnothing \neq g_i \subseteq L_i(g) \,:\, g_i \neq \{ij\}} \sum_{g' \subseteq g \setminus g_i} \frac{1}{2} \frac{(l(g) - l(g_i) - l(g'))! l(g')!}{(l(g) - l(g_i) - 1)!} \left(v(g' + g_i) - \eta_{l(g') + l(g_i)} v(g') \right) \\
&\quad + \frac{l(g) - 2}{2} v(ij) + \sum_{\varnothing \neq g' \subseteq g \setminus ij} \frac{1}{2} \frac{(l(g) - l(g') - 1)! l(g')!}{(l(g) - 2)!} \left(v(g' + ij) - \eta_{l(g') + 1} v(g') \right) \\
&= \sum_{\varnothing \neq g_i \subseteq L_i(g) \,:\, g_i \neq \{ij\}} \sum_{g' \subseteq g \setminus g_i} \frac{1}{2} \frac{(l(g) - l(g_i) - l(g'))! l(g')!}{(l(g) - l(g_i) - 1)!} \left(v(g' + g_i) - \eta_{l(g') + l(g_i)} v(g') \right) \\
&\quad + \frac{l(g) - 2}{2} v(ij) + \sum_{\varnothing \neq g' \subseteq g \setminus ij \,:\, g_k \subseteq g' : g_k \subseteq g|_M} \frac{1}{2} \frac{(l(g) - l(g') - 1)! l(g')!}{(l(g) - 2)!} (\eta_{l(g') + 1} - \eta_{l(g')}) v(g' \setminus g_k)
\end{aligned}
\tag{42}
$$

The result follows immediately.

Note that in Theorem 9.4, the condition which says that the SIA $\{\eta_{g'} > 1 \mid \varnothing \neq g' \subseteq g\}$ is directly proportional to the size of each $g' \subseteq g$ is intuitive in the sense that more worth will be generated when the number of links among players increases. However, it is worth mentioning here that this condition is weaker than the condition of monotonicity.

5 Empirical Illustration

In what follows we next present two examples to show the application of our model.

Example 4 (International Trade[2]). International trade is the exchange of goods and services across national borders. In recent times the United States (USA) and China are two of the biggest traders in the world. In 2017, USA has the world's largest economy and China the second largest. For the purpose of illustration, we select a small set of six top ranking (in terms of value of trade) countries $N = \{$Mexico, USA, China, Hong Kong, Germany, the UK$\}$. We consider the real trade data among countries. We look at the net-export as a fraction of total value of trade for each of them. The countries for which this is small are natural candidates for middlemen. We finally choose $M = \{$USA, China$\}$, comprising of the two biggest traders. The trade network between countries is as follows (Fig. 1 and Table 1):

Construct the network

$$g = \{\text{Mexico} - \text{USA}, \text{USA} - \text{China}, \text{China} - \text{Hong Kong}, \text{China} - \text{Germany}, \text{USA} - \text{UK}, \text{UK} - \text{Germany}\}.$$

Then we define the game as follows:

$$v(g') = \begin{cases} 0, & \text{if } g' \subseteq g \backslash \{\text{UK} - \text{Germany}\} \\ \text{scaled total trade among them}, & \text{otherwise} \end{cases} \tag{43}$$

The subnetwork values are given by the scaled trade values between these pairs and are given in Table 2.

The values for the relevant parameters of our model η's are also estimated by solving Eq. (16) using the trade data. We decide that the value of ξ's as the rate of increase of trade in the game due to the presence of a middleman. These are given in Table 3.

Then the NMMI values are computed form the above data, yielding

$$Y(N, v, \boldsymbol{\xi}) = (-1.746, 1.55, 1.55, -23.451, 63.80255, 59.986)$$

Mexico and Hong Kong have only connections with middlemen; therefore, their payoffs are negative. UK and Germany have a link between them and thus they get positive NMMI value.

Example 5 (Internet Server Traffic Data[3]). Internet is omnipresent in our lives nowadays. Topology of the internet, particularly peer-to-peer network has become an active

---

[2]This data is from World Integrated Trade Solutions (WITS). We are grateful to Dr. Bibek Ray Chaudhuri of IIFT, Kolkata for his help.

[3]This data is from CAIDA Public IPv4 Macroscopic Topology Data Archive from the Archipelago Measurement Infrastructure. The data is on IPV4 DNS traffic for 1 day between servers. We are grateful to Dr. Susmita Ruj and Mr. Soumojit Das of ISI Kolkata for their help.

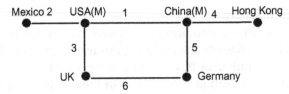

FIG. 1 The network *g* (with links numbered for referencing below).

Table 1   The Trade Network (Scaled Values)

Countries	China	Germany	United Kingdom	Hong Kong	Mexico	USA	Total Export
China		0.295		0.624		0.925	2.051
Germany	0.344		0.260				0.971
United Kingdom		0.253				0.200	0.634
Hong Kong	0.463						0.554
Mexico						0.855	1.013
USA	1.000		0.169		0.813		2.318
Total import	2.076	0.870	0.588	0.723	0.921	2.363	7.542

Table 2   Values of the Subnetworks (Nonzero Only)

Subnetworks	Value	Subnetworks	Value	Subnetworks	Value	Subnetworks	Value
{6}	0.513	{1,2,6}	4.106	{1,2,3,6}	4.475	{1,2,3,4,6}	5.562
		{1,3,6}	2.807	{1,2,5,6}	4.747	{1,2,3,5,6}	5.114
{1,6}	2.438	{1,4,6}	3.525	{1,2,4,6}	5.193	{1,2,4,5,6}	5.832
{2,6}	2.181	{1,5,6}	3.077	{1,3,4,6}	3.894	1{,3,4,5,6}	4.533
{3,6}	0.882	{2,3,6}	2.55	{1,3,5,6}	3.446	{2,3,4,5,6}	4.276
{4,6}	1.6	{2,4,6}	3.268	{1,4,5,6}	4.164		
{5,6}	1.152	{2,5,6}	2.82	{2,3,4,6}	3.637	{1,2,3,4,5,6}	6.201
		{3,4,6}	1.969	{2,3,5,6}	3.189		
		{3,5,6}	1.521	{2,4,5,6}	3.907		
		{4,5,6}	2.239	{3,4,5,6}	2.608		

Table 3   Estimates of Relevant Parameter Values

		Country	ξ_i	Y_i
η_2	1.719	China (M)	0.25	1.55025
η_3	1.754	Germany		
η_4	1.453	United Kingdom		
η_5	2.236	Hong Kong, China		
η_6	1.194	Mexico		
		USA (M)	0.25	1.55025

area of research. For our numerical illustration, we take one day's DNS traffic data (July 1, 2008). For the sake of computational feasibility, we collapse the data into that between clusters of IP addresses, creating only six clusters, which are numbered as {0, 1, 2, 3, 4, 5}. These are the nodes or players of our game. The total volume of traffic between each pair of node is the value of a link. We look at net (incoming-outgoing) as a fraction of total volume of traffic for each of them. The clusters for which this is small are natural candidates for middlemen. We finally choose $M = \{1, 3\}$, comprising of the two biggest clusters. The DNS traffic network between clusters is given in Fig. 2 (Table 4).

Then we define the game as follows:

$$v(g') = \begin{cases} 0, & \text{if } g' \subseteq g \setminus \{e\} \\ \text{scaled total volume of traffic among them,} & \text{otherwise} \end{cases} \tag{44}$$

The subnetwork values are given by the scaled traffic values between these pairs and are given in Table 5.

The values for the relevant parameters of our model η's are also estimated from the traffic data. We decide on a reasonable values of ξ's also. These are given in Table 6.

Then the NMMI values are computed from the above data, which is

$$Y(N, v, \xi) = (-17.21179547, 0.4854, -17.23280539, 0.4045, 5.523549879, 2.294841605)$$

As before we again see that the two isolated clusters, 0 and 2, who has connections only with middlemen, receive negative payoffs. Clusters 4 and 5 have a link between them and thus they get positive NMMI value.

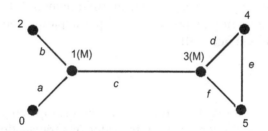

FIG. 2 The network *g* (with links numbered for referencing below).

Table 4   The Scaled Traffic Values

Node	0	1	2	3	4	5	Outgoing
0					0.064		0.064
1				0.071		0.124	0.195
2					0.030		0.030
3		0.019				0.067	0.086
4	0.103		0.137			0.358	0.598
5		0.200		0.186	0.259		0.645
Incoming	0.103	0.218	0.137	0.257	0.353	0.550	1.618

Table 5   Values of the Subnetworks (Nonzero Only)

Subnetworks	Value	Subnetworks	Value	Subnetworks	Value	Subnetwork	Value
{e}	0.089	{a,b,e}	0.422	{a,b,c,e}	1.0397	{a,b,c,d,e}	1.364
		{a,c,e}	0.874	{a,b,d,e}	0.7461	{a,b,c,e,f}	1.129
{a,e}	0.256	{a,d,e}	0.580	{a,b,e,f}	0.5115	{a,b,d,e,f}	0.836
{b,e}	0.255	{a,e,f}	0.345	{a,c,d,e}	1.1977	{a,c,d,e,f}	1.287
{c,e}	0.707	{b,c,e}	0.873	{a,c,e,f}	0.9631	{b,c,d,e,f}	1.286
{d,e}	0.413	{b,d,e}	0.579	{a,d,e,f}	0.6696		
{e,f}	0.178	{b,e,f}	0.345	{b,c,d,e}	1.1968	{a,b,c,d,e,f}	1.618
		{c,d,e}	1.031	{b,c,e,f}	0.9621		
		{c,e,f}	0.796	{b,d,e,f}	0.6686		
		{d,e,f}	0.503	{c,d,e,f}	1.1202		

Table 6   Estimates of Relevant Parameter Values

		Node	ξ_i	Y_i
η_2	2	0		
η_3	1.94	1 (M)	0.3	0.4854
η_4	2.963	2		
η_5	4.840	3 (M)	0.25	0.4045
η_6	3.756	4		
		5		

Thus in both the examples, even though the middlemen ({USA, China} and {1, 3}) increase the worth, it does not guarantee that all participating countries will benefit. To ensure positive payoffs, we need NIP.

6 Conclusion

The role and importance of middlemen in many relationships are manifested. In particular, situations where middlemen augment the value of a transaction but which does not benefit all parties concerned is a matter of great interest to economists, political scientists, and network architects alike. In this chapter we proposed a new model for Network games involving middlemen. The proposed NME value as a solution for this class of games is characterized using the axioms of linearity, middlemen, monotonicity, anonymity, and efficiency. We then show that, unfortunately, the efficiency of the NME value is consistent for a very narrow class of networks along with the other four axioms. Thus we proposed an alternative allocation rule replacing the axiom of efficiency by multilateral interactions to cover many possible networks and called this allocation rule as the NMMI value. However, the NMMI value is not efficient. Thus we can normalize the NMMI value in the line of van den Brink and van den Lann [14, 15]. The normalization and characterization of the NMMI value is kept for our future study.

But the NMMI value does not guarantee that concerned parties will all benefit (i.e., get positive payoffs). To make that happen, we actually need the players to have links with other (beneficiary) players. When the middleman realizes that trade is possible only through him/her intermediary activities it is natural that he/she shows monopolistic behavior leading to a negative payoff to those involved in him/her network. But if the beneficiaries also have direct connections among themselves, their bargaining capabilities increase and so the middleman cannot show monopolistic behaviors. This feature we characterize as our NIP. We finally show that NIP indeed guarantees that all parties benefit strictly from the presence of a middleman. Using international trade and DNS internet server traffic data we create two numerical illustrations to highlight and substantiate our theoretical findings.

Acknowledgments

This work was supported in part by UKIERI (184-15/2017(IC)). The authors acknowledge the inputs and comments from Rajnish Kumar.

References

[1] L.P. Bucklin, A theory of channel control, J. Market. 37 (1973) 39–47.

[2] L.E. Gadde, I. Snehota, Rethinking the Role of Middlemen, Paper for IMP, BI, Oslo, 2001, pp. 9–11.

[3] M. Christopher, Logistics & Supply Chain Management, Pearson, UK, 2016.

[4] E. Kalai, A. Postlewaite, J. Roberts, Barriers to trade and disadvantageous middlemen: nonmonotonicity of the core, J. Econ. Theory 19 (1979) 200–209.

[5] A. Rubinstein, A. Wosinky, Middlemen, Q. J. Econ. 102 (1987) 581–594.

[6] A. Yavas, Middlemen in bilateral search markets, J. Labor Econ. 12 (1994) 406–429.

[7] A. Johri, J. Leach, Middleman and the allocation of heterogeneous goods, Int. Econ. Rev. 43 (2002) 347–361.

[8] A. Arya, C. Löffler, B. Mittendorf, T. Pfeiffer, The middleman as a panacea for supply chain coordination problem, Eur. J. Oper. Res. 240 (2015) 393–400.

[9] A. van den Nouweland, M. Slikker, An axiomatic characterization of the position value for network situations, Math. Soc. Sci. 64 (3) (2012) 266–271.

[10] S. Borkotokey, S. Sarangi, R. Kumar, A solution concept for network games: the role of multilateral interactions, Eur. J. Oper. Res. 243 (3) (2015) 912–920.

[11] M.O. Jackson, A. Wolinsky, A strategic model of social and economic networks, J. Econ. Theory 71 (4) (1996) 44–74.

[12] M.O. Jackson, Allocation rules for network games, Games Econ. Behav. 51 (2005) 128–154.

[13] J.C. Harsanyi, A simplified bargaining model for the n-person cooperative game, Int. Econ. Rev. 4 (2) (1963) 194–220.

[14] R. van den Brink, G. van der Laan, Axiomatizations of the normalized Banzhaf value and the Shapley value, Soc. Choice Welf. 15 (4) (1998) 567–582.

[15] R. van den Brink, G. van der Laan, The normalized Banzhaf value and the Banzhaf share function, in: L. Petrosjan, V. Mazalov (Eds.), Game Theory and Applications, vol. 4, Nova Science, New York, NY, 1998, pp. 11–31.

10

The Interplay of Identity and Social Network: A Methodological and Empirical Study

Anirban Ghatak*, Abhishek Ray[†], Diganta Mukherjee[‡]

*Indian Institute of Management Visakhapatnam, Visakhapatnam, India [†]BCS Technology, Gurgaon, India [‡]Sampling and Official Statistics Unit, Indian Statistical Institute (ISI), Kolkata, India

1 Introduction

Social network analysis is a widely used tool to understand various kinds of social structures with the use of network theory and graph theory. Analysis of social structures is used in order to understand a variety of interactive network structures such as network of kinship, network of scientific collaboration, propagation of contagious or sexually transmitted diseases, propagation of news or advertisement, among many other. In social network analysis, each agent of an interaction can be considered as a node, and each interaction can be considered as an edge in a network. Every interaction structure can be modeled as a network and network theory can be applied onto the network in order to understand the pattern of interaction, propensity of propagation, clustering of importance, and so on.

Social network analysis has emerged to be a key tool in computational sociology [1]. Also, there are extensive uses of social network analysis in economics [2], history [3], communication studies [4], development studies [5], anthropology [6], biology [7], computer science [8], among other disciplines. Social network analysis is also used as a primary tool in security industry where identification of communication cluster is often used for identifying security threats.

There are four principal approaches to carry out a social network analysis in an interactive structure: namely, structural approach, resource-based approach, regulatory approach, and dynamic approach [9]. The structural approach primarily looks at the weight of the interaction edges between the nodes and the geometry of the structure is the key parameter in this approach. Resource-based approach deals with attracting resources through exploiting the position in a network. Resource-based approach talks about individual resources and differentiating the access to individual resources based on the relative location of individuals in a resource-based network. The regulatory approach studies the change in the behavior of the agents due to various changes in the norm, rules, or sanctions within a network. Regulatory approach deals with the questions of information dissipation, influences in a network, importance of an agent in a network, and so on. This approach depends on successful simulation or modeling of societal or organizational roles in order to understand the process of information flow within the network. Dynamic approach of social network analysis assumes that the agents, their behaviors, and their interaction patterns change over time. The questions of how new links are made, how old rituals become obsolete are answered using the dynamic approach of social network analysis.

Social network analysis uses different kinds of models and algorithms to solve different problems pertaining to the network. While graph models can be used for understanding the economic and communication links between people, use of centrality measures and other local graph properties can be used to identify the hub of information flow, or the mapping of important nodes within a network [10]. The specific research question drives the choice of model and algorithm for analysis the network. The method of community detection and analysis of subgroups allows one to study the stability of a subgroup within a larger network. Structural equivalence of participants, role algebras, detection of diads, and triads are some other important models and algorithms of social network analysis, which are used frequently.

In this chapter, we attempt to understand the pattern of human social connection. We have observed that in the daily run of life, people always choose their fellow travelers in some way or other. We hypothesize that such a choice of connection is not random, rather it follows a well-defined dynamic process. As examples, in a public transport, when someone is choosing a seat among many available, or when an undergraduate student is deciding on the supervisor for her graduate studies, or when a child goes to school and instantly makes friend with a certain section of children and not all, it suggests a manifestation of a specific preference of connecting to some kind of people over the others. We, in this chapter, present the results of a survey that was done in order to understand the preference structure that determines the pattern of human social connections.

We show that the identity of a human being who is choosing her acquaintances, protégées, seat-neighbors, and other connections is of supreme importance in order to understand the nature of the prevailing preference structure. We study the relationship between human activity of building connections and her identity through an extensive survey in this chapter. While the identity of human beings can have various meanings based on the context of discussion, we try to collate every single identifier of a human being to form its identity, as a specific and unique identifier of its self. These can be religious identity, caste identity, economic identity, professional identity, historical identity, gender identity, sexual identity, and many more such identities describing a person's current and previous states of being. Our notion of identity combines every such identities together to form any individual's "Identity vector" of which each identity mentioned earlier will be a member. The identity vector will be used to identify each individual in order to find out if there is any specific observable and testable pattern of connecting to other people with respect to that identity, or any of its variables. Our model of using identities to explain social and economic activities takes its cue from Akerlof and Kranton [11].

We chose to observe the network that forms around any person due to her past and present being, through her familial ties, societal relationships, personal relationships, and professional acquaintance. The people and individual connect to during all such either obligatory or strategic environments make her network. We record the nature of this network through the perception of the individual around whom the network is developed in order to find out the revealed preferences of the individual while connecting to other people in its life. We also record the identity characteristics of each member of the individual's network, as observed by the individual concerned. Thus, we find out the identity categories that remain unknown to the individual about a member of its network. The knowledge (or the lack of it) reveals the awareness level regarding to that specific identity category. For example, if we find that an individual does not know the caste of its close friend, we derive that caste was not instrumental in sustaining that particular edge of its friendship network. We also look at certain "openness" feature observed through the networks. We observe the character of a person's network and create a metric of the person's openness based on the number of persons dissimilar with its self. We will discuss more about the construction of these metrics later. We observe a number of individuals from various strata of the society to gather the data of their networks and the identities of the members of those networks as perceived by them. The revealed preferences regarding the decisions of their strategic connections combined with their own identity variables enable us to find a definite linkage between identities and the conscious choice of agents in one's network.

Our argument about the importance of one's identity being the primary decision maker behind one's social network originates from the economic understanding of the sociological concept of "Cultural Capital" [12], which is the qualitative characteristics of a human being that enables the person to access certain amenities provided by the society. Religion, race, caste, gender, sexuality, educational level, economic level, and all such characteristics of a person's identity contributes to the person's cultural capital that enables a person to be in a certain agentive position in the society. According to Bourdieu, cultural capital can be embodied, objectified or institutionalized. We are concerned about the embodied cultural capital in building our argument. The embodied form of cultural capital is not a static identifier of a person. A person can acquire cultural capital through various means of "self-development."

> *Most of the properties of cultural capital can be deduced from the fact that, in its fundamental state, it is linked to the body and presupposes embodiment. The accumulation of cultural capital in the embodied state, that is, in the form of what is called culture, cultivation, building, presupposes a process of embodiment, incorporation, which, insofar as it implies a labor of inculcation and assimilation, costs time, time which must be invested personally by the investor.*
>
> *Bourdieu [12]*

Cultural capital and economic capital give birth to another kind of capital that is "Social Capital" [12, 13]. Social capital, according to Bourdieu, is

> ...the aggregate of the actual or potential resources which are linked to possession of a durable network of more or less institutionalized relationships of mutual acquaintance and recognition—or in other words, to membership in a group—which provides each of its members with the backing of the collectively-owned capital, a "credential" which entitles them to credit, in the various senses of the word.

Thus, the appropriation of social capital enables oneself to aim for another network or institution that embodies even more resource and hence, increases the person's cultural capital. We hypothesize that the activity of network building observed in human beings is entirely driven by the urge of acquiring cultural capital through "a durable network of more or less institutionalized relationships of mutual acquaintance and recognition." Moreover, once the person is assured of the membership of the institutionalized network, that membership in turn increases further opportunities for enhancing the person's cultural capital. We believe that the process of human network building continues through this route of appropriation and re-appropriation of cultural capital through building one's own network.

The concept of Cultural Capital has been widely used in various disciplines of social sciences and humanities, as a theoretical tool to investigate and define various locations of sociocultural and political marginalization within the power structure. For example, studies have been done on how Cultural Capital plays a crucial role in the domain of education system [14–21]. Sometimes, the concept of Cultural Capital has also been critiqued for its deterministic nature [22, 23]. However, whereas Cultural Capital, as a theoretical tool of defining identity, talks extensively about its relation with other forms of capital, especially Economic Capital, it has been little used in Economics as a defining tool of socioeconomic relationship in a society, though the use of the term Cultural Capital has been exported to Economics with varied connotations [24, 25]. Social capital that gets enabled by cultural capital and economic capital is the ability of individuals or groups to access resources that are indigenous to their network. Social capital can give birth to other forms of capital such as human capital in terms of favor or intellectual capital in terms of new information or expansion of knowledge [26]. Lin et al. [27] defines social capital as "investment in social relations with expected returns in the marketplace." According to this framing, social capital is created through the interactions in the social networks a person creates and the expectations of the future resources that the network embeds in itself. Social capital can be of two types, "bridging" and "bonding" [28, 29]. Bridging capital is often associated with the ties, which connect two different clusters in a network that felicitates propagation of novel information [30]. Bonding capital, on the other hand, is generated by strong ties within a cluster through repetitive interaction and that is characterized with higher levels of trust, support, and intimacy. Weaker ties (such as a friend of a friend) are more likely to be bridging ties and thus provide access to novel information [31] and diverse perspectives (associated with bridging social capital). We deal with both types of ties here in the terms of filial and affilial relationships. The cultural capital acquired through filial ties, we assume, is either impossible or tough to change, and the utility acquired from such ties remains more or less constant. On the other hand, the affilial ties are the ones that a person can choose in order to maximize the cultural capital of one's own.

We divide the chapter in the following sections. In the next section the theoretical ground of the analysis is established using the concept of openness and awareness. Section 3 presents the details of the survey and the questionnaire. The mathematical definition and formulation of openness and awareness metrics are presented in Section 4. We discuss the outcome of the survey with tables and figures in Section 5, and subsequently conclude in Section 6.

2 Openness and Awareness

In order to understand the nature of the connection between people, it is imperative to understand their own identity as well as the identity of everyone in their network. Taking the cue from Akerlof and Kranton [11], we modeled the identity of a person in a form of an identity vector. Identity of a person has many components, a combination of which makes the unique identifier of a person. For the ease of modeling, we have started with four identity categories by which we are defining a person. The four identity categories are religion, income group, caste, and gender. We understand that there are many more identity categories, such as language, area of residence, occupation, education level, migration history, and so on, that build the unique identity of a person. But for the sake of convenience, as a starting point, we are trying to show the pattern of connection between people using the four aforementioned categories.

In each of the categories, we start with various identities that form a mutually exclusive and collectively exhaustive list of components to that category. For the category religion, we have considered Hindu, Buddha, Jain, Christian, Muslim, and others. For the category of income group, we have considered four identities as four income groups, namely, 0–5000 INR per month, 5000–10,000 INR per month, 10,000–40,000 INR per month, and more than 40,000 INR per month. In the caste category we have considered four sections, namely, general caste (GC), scheduled caste (SC), scheduled tribe (ST), and other backward classes (OBC). While analyzing, we have also noticed that many people did not disclose their caste, or people from non-Hindu religion were confused about the category. We have created another caste identity as undisclosed (UD) for those respondents. For the category gender, we consider male (M), female (F), and third gender (TG) for our analysis.

Building on the base of identity categories and identities within those categories, we form each person's category as a vector of identities, each belonging to one category. Thus, a person will be denoted as (R, I, C, G), where R will denote the religion, I will denote the income group, C will denote the caste, and G will denote the gender of the person.

In order to understand the pattern of connection between people, it is essential to understand the interconnection between the identities while the network is forming. To understand the pattern of the interconnection between the identities within each identity category and between the identity categories, we have defined the concept of openness. Openness will denote how open one identity is to incorporate other identity within that identity category into her/his network. For example, a behavior of having an SC friend in the network of a GC person is a manifestation of an "open" behavior, while the presence of an SC person in an SC person's network is considered as "closed." We measure openness using the proportion of people present in one's network who are from a dissimilar identity within that identity category. Thus, we can measure religion openness, income openness, caste openness, and gender openness. We compare these values of openness between the identities within the same category in order to understand the pattern of connection. Thus, we compare the caste openness between GC and non-GC respondents, income openness between high- and low- income respondents, and so on. The mathematical formulation of openness is presented in Section 4.

Apart from openness, another concept that we wish to deal with is called awareness. Openness, as we described earlier, is a matter of informed choice. A person decides whether to connect with another person based on her/his knowledge of the identity of the other person. But it is also possible that while connecting, one is not interested to know "all" the identities of the person to whom they are connecting. Thus, a question of awareness about some identities of the other person also defines a pattern of connection where we can try to find out which identities matter for whom, and which identities are not worth knowing about. For example, if a person does not know her friend's salary (range) but still recognizes the friend as a part of her connection, it can be said that the income group of the friend did not play any part in creating the connection. As this calls for a distinct measure of connection properties that is different from the informed choice measure of openness, we have defined the concept of awareness based on this behavior. The measure of awareness is also defined similar to the measure of openness. We find out the proportion of the network or subnetwork the respondent is aware about regarding to a specific identity, and from there, we prepare an awareness metric. Thus we can find out the caste awareness, gender awareness, and so on. The mathematical formulation of awareness is presented in Section 4.

3 Survey Details

Our survey was carried out during the months of November 2014 to June 2015. We had surveyed a total of 191 individuals spread over various social and economic strata. The respondents of our survey were mostly located in and around Kolkata, India primarily for the economic and locational feasibility as the surveyors and the researchers both were based in Kolkata. We consciously tried to achieve as much variation as possible in the social, economic, and cultural backgrounds of the people surveyed in our sample in order to maximize the diversity in the pool of identities we gather to observe their behavior.

We had adopted a two-tier sampling scheme where in the initial phase we had divided our target population into various strata and then within those strata, we did either a simple random sampling or a snowball sampling. We had stratified our population based primarily on their occupation. The strata those we had identified before doing a random sampling within them were

   (i) university student,
  (ii) university teaching staff,
 (iii) university nonteaching staff,
  (iv) information technology sector workers (white collar),
   (v) industrial blue-collar workers,
  (vi) industrial white-collar workers,
 (vii) unorganized sectors' workers,
(viii) beauty workers (both employed and self-employed),
  (ix) sex workers,
   (x) people with nonnormative sexuality (lesbian/gay/bisexual/transsexual—LGBT),
  (xi) auto rickshaw drivers, and
 (xii) cycle rickshaw drivers.

We had adopted a snowball sampling method for sampling from the sex workers and the LGBT population due to their constitutionally unrecognized existence in the society, while the rest were sampled by the method of simple random sampling.

Our respondents, who were randomly selected from the various strata mentioned earlier, were asked a set of questions regarding their various categories of identities like religion, caste, gender, sexuality, language, income, educational background, migration history, parents' details, and so on. They were also asked the same questions regarding their spouse (if any), children (if any), siblings (if any), and five most important persons in each of the three affiliative networks "Friends," "Colleagues," and "Neighbor" to have an idea about the identity of the agents that is formed centering the respondent. In this way, we got information about the various identities of 191 persons and their knowledge about the identities of their network consisting of 2305 persons.

The importance of this methodology of designing the questionnaire centers around the idea of revealed preference. We did not want to get "accurate" information about the persons in the network of the respondent. Rather, we asked the respondent about them, in order to understand what the respondent knows/thinks about them. This helped us in understanding the critical perceptions about the identity of the neighbors, colleagues, and friends by virtue of which they were selected by the respondent. Also, upon matching the identity categories of the persons in one's network with that of the respondent's, we can identify steady patterns of connections between various identities in the society. In our questionnaire, we have tried to incorporate as many components of identity as possible, but for the sake of the analysis, we have used only three of those components, namely, gender, caste, and income group, in the later section of this chapter.

4 Openness and Awareness Metric

In this section we will define the theoretical background that we use to find the relationship between identity and network formation. Using the data on the person's Caste, income, religion, and gender, one of our primary interests will be to know if a person mingles more in its own group according to these four categories, or is more "open" in its social behavior.

To understand the nature of the connections between various identities, we frame our variables as follows. We start with labeling the identity categories caste, income, religion, and gender as 1, 2, 3, and 4, respectively. We create some qualitative response variables like $I_j^{i=1} = GC, SC, ST, OBC$, where $i = 1$ denotes the category caste and j the person concerned. We create similar variables for each category.

Now, we define

$$d_{jl}^{i=1} = \begin{cases} 0 & \text{if } I_j^{i=1} = I_l^{i=1} \\ 1 & \text{otherwise} \end{cases} \tag{1}$$

Then the *unscaled measure of openness* is put forward as

$$M_j^{i=1} = \sum_l d_{jl}^{i=1} \tag{2}$$

We also get the following variables from the data collected through the survey (details follow):

$$F_j = \text{Total number of friends reported by the person } j \tag{3}$$

$$N_j = \text{Total number of neighbors reported by the person } j \tag{4}$$

$$C_j = \text{Total number of colleagues reported by the person } j \tag{5}$$

From these variables, we compute $Total_j = F_j + N_j + C_j$. Now the *openness index* for the person j with respect to caste can be defined as

$$O_j^{i=1} = \frac{M_j^{i=1}}{Total_j} \tag{6}$$

Clearly this "openness" index lies within 0 and 1.

In the next step, we build an *awareness index* for our analysis. Awareness index measures the level of awareness about various identities of the people creating a person's network. We assume that if a person is unaware of some identity of any member of the network, it means that specific identity did not carry any importance toward creating that specific connection. The overall awareness index with respect to any identity measures the "importance" of that identity in building one's network.

We create the following indicator variables for the person j and one of his acquaintances k.

$$A_{jk}^{i=1} = \begin{cases} 1 & \text{if } j \text{ knows the caste of } k \text{ and} \\ 0 & \text{otherwise} \end{cases} \tag{7}$$

$$A_{jk}^{i=2} = \begin{cases} 1 & \text{if } j \text{ knows the income of } k \text{ and} \\ 0 & \text{otherwise} \end{cases} \tag{8}$$

$$A_{jk}^{i=3} = \begin{cases} 1 & \text{if } j \text{ knows the religion of } k \text{ and} \\ 0 & \text{otherwise} \end{cases} \tag{9}$$

Then, $A_j^{i=1} = \Sigma_{k=1}^{N} A_{jk}^{i=1}, A_j^{i=2} = \Sigma_{k=1}^{N} A_{jk}^{i=2}$, and $A_j^{i=3} = \Sigma_{k=1}^{N} A_{jk}^{i=3}$.

So an *overall awareness index* for person j with respect to caste can be

$$a_j^{i=1} = \frac{A_j^{i=1}}{Total_j} \tag{10}$$

Also, as we have defined the distance function d we can define the relative distance function Rd as follows:

$$Rd_{jl}^{i=1}\big|_{j=SC} = \begin{cases} 0 & \text{if } I_l^{i=1} = GC \text{ or } SC \\ 1 & \text{otherwise} \end{cases} \tag{11}$$

Then relative openness can be formulated as:

$$RO_{j=SC}^{i=1} = \frac{\sum_l Rd_{jl}^{i=1}\big|_{j=SC}}{Total_j} \tag{12}$$

and likewise for other categories.

5 Results and Discussion

5.1 Descriptive Statistics

We present various descriptives in Tables 1–6 for a detailed understanding of the outcome of the survey.

In Table 1, we have presented the outcome of the survey by segregating our population by caste. We have seen that a sizable portion of the respondents did not choose to reveal their caste. This can be attributed to mainly three reasons. Some of the respondents might want to not associate their identity with their caste, and hence, they chose to not report

Table 1 Descriptives of the Sample by Caste

Characteristics	General	OBC	SC	ST	Undisclosed	Grand Total
Married	52	3	15	2	39	111
Avg. children	1.37	1.5	1.87	1.67	2.89	1.94
Avg. other caste	0.75	3	2.39	1.8		1.17
Avg. age	36.26	32.66	36.26	25.6	42.66	37.71
Avg. income	1.28	0.66	0.68	0.6	1.39	1.2
Avg. neighbor	2.16	0.5	2.4	1.8	4.44	2.84
Avg. friend	2.44	0.5	2.41	1.8	4.66	3.04
Avg. colleague	2.06	2.5	1.77	1.66	4.58	2.82
Total	99	3	25	5	51	183

Table 2 Descriptives of the Sample by Gender

Characteristics	Male	Female	Third Gender	Grand Total
Married	92	17	2	111
Avg. children	1.86	2.68	0.1	1.94
Avg. other caste	1.27	0.66	2.57	1.17
Avg. age	40.64	32.04	29.90	37.71
Avg. income	1.27	0.95	1.45	1.2
Avg. neighbor	2.74	2.6	4.81	2.84
Avg. friend	2.89	3	4.81	3.04
Avg. colleague	2.68	2.60	5	2.82
Total	124	48	11	183

Table 3 Descriptives of the Sample by Income

Characteristics	0	1	2	3	Grand Total
Married	26	25	40	20	111
Avg. children	2.36	2.6	1.26	1.3	1.94
Avg. other caste	1.58	0.88	1.81	0.16	1.17
Avg. age	32.45	38.23	39.65	45.90	37.71
Avg. neighbor	3.26	2.14	3.60	1.71	2.84
Avg. friend	3.42	2.30	3.87	1.90	3.04
Avg. colleague	2.92	2.45	3.60	1.61	2.82
Total	58	51	53	21	183

their caste. Another reason of not disclosing their caste is the discomfort of disclosing their caste due to various social conditions prevailing in the society. Also, as caste system is primarily a Hindu construct, it is not hard to imagine that the population from non-Hindu religion may choose to stay out of that. We can see that the income distribution is significantly skewed in terms of caste. Respondents who belong to the general caste category, and who chose not to reveal their caste has a significantly higher average value compared to the socially backward castes. Here we have defined four income groups, 0, 1, 2, and 3. 0 denotes the monthly income from 0 to 5000 INR, 1 denotes a monthly income of 5000–10,000 INR, 2 denotes a monthly income of 10,000–40,000 INR, and 3 denotes a monthly income above 40,000 INR. Another significant observation that can be made from the table is the average number of affiliative connections (i.e., friends, colleagues, and neighbors), who are from a different caste category from the respondent's. This is presented in the "Avg. other caste" row of the table. We can see that there is a significant difference in this parameter between various caste categories. We observe that people from lower caste category has much higher tendency to make connections with people from other caste categories while people from general caste category mostly tend to keep a tightly bound caste-based network around them. Here, connections are not seen as a two-way activity as our way of collecting the data only presents one way of a network

Table 4 Descriptives of the Sample by Caste and Gender

Caste	Gender	Married	Avg. Children	Avg. Other Caste	Avg. Age	Avg. Income	Avg. Neighbor	Avg. Friend	Avg. Colleague	Total
General	M	52	1.37	0.75	36.26	1.28	2.16	2.44	2.066	99
	F	39	1.19	1	40.35	1.45	1.75	1.98	1.65	57
	TG	12	2.08	0.37	30.71	0.97	2.25	2.71	2.13	35
OBC	M	1	0	0.66	30.71	1.42	4.71	4.71	5	7
	F	3	1.5	3	32.66	0.66	0.5	0.5	2.5	3
	TG	2	1.5	3	38.5	1	0.5	0.5	2.5	3
		1			21	0				2
SC	M	15	1.875	2.39	36.26	0.68	2.4	2.41	1.77	25
	F	14	2.26	1.68	37.77	0.55	2.5	2.36	1.68	20
	TG	1	0.5	3	31.75	1	1.25	2	1	4
		0	0	14	27	2	5	5	5	1
ST	M	2	1.66	1.8	25.6	0.6	1.8	1.8	1.66	5
	F	1	2	1.75	26	0.75	2	2	2.5	4
	TG	1	1	2	24	0	1	1	0	1
UD	M	39	2.89		42.66	1.39	4.44	4.66	4.58	51
	F	36	2.5		43.85	1.43	4.30	4.57	4.47	41
	TG	2	6.14		41.57	1.14	5	5	5	7
		1	0.33		29	1.33	5	5	5	3
	Total	111	1.94	1.17	37.71	1.2	2.84	3.04	2.82	183

Table 5   Descriptives of the Sample by Income and Caste

Income	Caste	Married	Avg. Children	Avg. Other Caste	Avg. Age	Avg. Neighbor	Avg. Friend	Avg. Colleague	Total
0		26	2.36	1.58	32.45	3.26	3.42	2.92	58
	General	7	1	0.95	26.96	2.5	2.77	1.42	30
	OBC	1			21				1
	SC	6	2.5	2.54	35	3.36	3.63	2.7	11
	ST	2	2.5	2.66	27	2.33	2.33	2.5	3
	UD	10	3.83		45.30	4.69	4.61	4.91	13
1		25	2.6	0.88	38.23	2.14	2.30	2.45	51
	General	13	2.33	0.75	36.96	2.16	2.48	2.625	29
	OBC	2	1.5	3	38.5	0.5	0.5	2.5	2
	SC	7	1.36	0.88	37.72	1.36	0.9	0.7	11
	ST	0		0	21	1	1		1
	UD	3	5.37		45.62	3.75	4.12	4.12	8
2		40	1.26	1.81	39.65	3.60	3.87	3.60	53
	General	15	0.7	1.11	39.77	2.73	3	2.75	22
	SC	2	1.66	6.33	34.5	2.66	3	2.5	3
	ST	0	0	1	26	1	1	0	1
	UD	23	1.72		40.44	4.48	4.83	4.51	27
3		20	1.3	0.16	45.90	1.71	1.90	1.61	21
	General	17	1.11	0.16	46.33	1.16	1.38	1.05	18
	UD	3	2.33		43.33	5	5	5	3
Total		111	1.94	1.17	37.71	2.84	3.04	2.82	183

Table 6   Descriptives of the Sample by Income and Gender

Income	Gender	Married	Avg. Children	Avg. Other Caste	Avg. Age	Avg. Neighbor	Avg. Friend	Avg. Colleague	Total
0		26	2.36	1.58	32.45	3.26	3.42	2.92	58
	M	22	2.7	2.09	37.63	3.48	3.51	3.33	39
	F	3	1.14	0.84	21.64	2.5	3.08	0.85	17
	TG	1	1	0	26	4	4	5	2
1		25	2.6	0.88	38.23	2.14	2.30	2.45	51
	M	22	1.73	1.13	40.06	1.46	1.55	1.53	30
	F	3	4.23	0.27	35.89	2.94	3.17	3.62	19
	TG	0	0	1.5	33	5	5	5	2
2		40	1.26	1.81	39.65	3.60	3.87	3.60	53
	M	31	1.5	1.41	41.05	3.57	3.84	3.5	37
	F	8	1.37	1.33	41.44	2.5	3	2.71	9
	TG	1	0	3.75	30.14	5	5	5	7
3		20	1.3	0.16	45.90	1.71	1.90	1.61	21
	M	17	1.35	0.2	47.16	1.77	1.94	1.72	18
	F	3	1	0	38.33	1.33	1.66	1	3
Total		111	1.94	1.17	37.71	2.84	3.04	2.82	183

connection. A person from a scheduled caste category might think that a person from general caste category is her favorite colleague, but that is not necessarily true for the other person. Thus, the revealed preference toward connecting or aspiring to connect to other caste category is much higher in lower caste than in upper caste. If we look at the average number of neighbor, friend, and colleague reported by people from each caste, we can see that those who have chosen to not disclose their caste identity has the highest number of affiliative connections reported. The average number of colleagues reported is also indicative of the social mobility to an extent as working in pubic spaces and getting exposed to people in general comes with certain extent of entitlement and social capacity.

In Table 2, we have divided the population by gender and has presented the descriptives based on gender. The pool of respondents is a predominantly male one as can be seen from the table. Also, the percentage of married respondents is much higher in men than in women and understandably, than in the third gender category. The average number of connections from the other caste category is also significantly different between men and women. The table shows that if we divide the population by gender, we will observe that men have much more loosely bound social community in terms of caste than women. Interestingly, the average number of connections from the other caste category is significantly high in the third gender category. One possible explanation for this fact can be that their social marginalization probably does not leave much space to bother for caste when it comes to make social connections. Also, the average income is higher for the men than the women in the population. The fact that the highest average income is seen for the third gender category may be for the fact that most of our respondents from the third gender category were from the entertainment industry. In terms of reporting of neighbors, friends, and colleagues, there is not much difference between men and women, whereas the third gender category has reported the maximum number of such affiliative connections. This is indicative of a larger community structure for the people from third gender.

In Table 3, we divide our sample into four different income groups and observe the characteristics of them. As mentioned earlier, we have defined four income groups, 0, 1, 2, and 3. 0 denotes the monthly income from 0 to 5000 INR, 1 denotes a monthly income of 5000–10,000 INR, 2 denotes a monthly income of 10,000–40,000 INR, and 3 denotes a monthly income above 40,000 INR. We can observe from the table that a lower income respondent has more number of children in average than a higher income individual. There is a significant difference in the number of people from other castes in the respondent's network between the highest income group and the rest. It shows that respondents earning more than 40,000 INR per month tend to belong in a community that is defined by caste to a large extent, while the others show increased level of openness toward having people from other castes in their network. In terms of average number of affiliative connections reported, it is observed that the highest income group has reported the lowest number of connections, while the rest are consistent about the reporting. This shows that the community of the economically elite community is thinner than the community of the people from the economically lower strata.

In Table 4, we show the two-way classification of the sample as we divide the sample based on caste and gender. This table shows that the openness toward other caste members between different genders vary between different castes. For example, within the general caste, openness toward other caste is much pronounced in the male population than in the female population, whereas within the scheduled caste community, openness toward other caste is more pronounced within women than within men. Similar observation can be drawn regarding average income too. Within general caste category, male members have significantly higher earning than female members, while within scheduled caste category, female members' average earnings are better than male members'. In case of listing favorite colleagues, friends, and neighbors, in most of the identity combinations, male and female respondents showed similar behavior, except one case. In the general caste category, the number of affiliative connections reported by men is significantly lower than that reported by women. As mentioned earlier, the number of such connections can be used to understand the sociability of an identity, in a broad sense, and it also denotes the community strength and size. While we find upper caste women having least number of people from other caste in their network, we can also see that they have a fairly large network around them. Scheduled caste women have very high openness toward other caste, but they have really small network around them, and the lack is more pronounced in the number of colleagues reported. The low number of colleagues reported by scheduled caste women can be indicative of their low presence in organized employment sector.

Table 5 refers to the survey outcome divided by income and caste. From this table, we see that the number of connections reported from the affiliative networks differs heavily between the people from very high income who are from general caste category and the people from other categories. In Table 1, we had seen how the openness toward people from other caste differs between higher caste and lower caste people. From this table we can see that most of such a difference is contributed by the respondents from the mid-high income, and from the lowest income. Also, from the significant difference of reporting of friends, colleagues, and neighbors between those who have disclosed their caste and those who have not, it can be seen that those who does not like to reveal their caste identity belongs to a bigger social network than others. Also it can be observed that those who did not disclose their caste identity, throughout all the income groups, have a larger family than others. One of the few probable reasons for the group of undisclosed caste having larger family is the fact that some Muslim people and Christian people may not have reported their caste position. As it is seen in this country than Muslim families are on an average larger than the others, the family size of the group who did not disclose their caste may have gone up for that.

In Table 6, we present the data in the identity combination of income group and gender. We can observe from this table that there is a significant difference in the openness of having people from other caste in the affiliative network between men and women of lower income group. Men and women from higher income groups do not show much difference in the caste openness. In the lowest economic group, the number of colleagues reported by women is significantly lower than men. The number of average friends and neighbors between men and women in this economic group is comparable. This hints at low presence of women in the lowest grade of organized employment.

5.2 Interaction Pattern

Apart from the descriptive tables, another way of understanding the properties of the networks around the respondents is to look at the interaction percentages between various identities reported by the respondents. Table 7 summarizes the interaction percentages of the respondents to various identities. Here we have considered income group, gender, and caste as the three defining variables in order to construct the identity of a person. For the sake of easier presentation and understanding, we have reduced the number of identities in each identity category to two. In the nomenclature presented in Table 7, every identity is denoted by a three-digit number. The first digit represents the income group, the second digit represents the gender, and the third digit represents the class. Income group is divided into two parts, 0 and 1. 0 denotes the group of people having 0–20,000 INR of income per month and 1 denotes the group of people having more than 20,000 INR of income per month. Gender is divided into two groups as male and others. 0 in gender denotes the nonmale category while 1 denotes male. Caste is also reduced to two sections where 0 denotes the nongeneral caste category and 1 denotes the general caste category. Thus, an identity 101 refers to the identity of an upper class, nonmale, upper caste person and an identity 010 refers to a lower class, male, lower caste person, and so on.

Table 7 gives us an idea about the importance of the various identity categories and very broadly presents us with the relative importance of those. In each row, the highest interaction percentage is highlighted, and from that we can see that caste seems to be the primary agent of building a social network for the respondents in our survey. Similarly, we can see that income group, or economic strata are the most fluid element of the network, where movement across income groups is a frequent phenomenon. Gender resides somewhere between caste and income group and if we look at the second largest value at every row, we can find out that after caste, gender is the parameter where "homophily" is observed.

Table 7 Interaction Percentages

	111	101	011	001	010	000	100	110
111	0.0366	0	0.1466	0.7958	0.0105	0.0052	0.0052	0
101	0.1596	0.0213	0.6489	0	0.1064	0.0638	0	0
011	0.1389	0.6528	0.0278	0.0694	0	0	0.1111	0
001	0.6243	0.221	0.0994	0.0221	0	0.0055	0.011	0.0166
010	0.0182	0	0	0	0.0182	0.0727	0.8	0.0909
000	0.0889	0.0111	0	0	0.0222	0	0.1556	0.7222

5.3 Distribution of Openness

We have generated the histograms of the openness indices for each of the identity category we have dealt with. The histograms tell us the way in which the subpopulations within any identity category are different in openness toward that specific identity category. Fig. 1A and B shows us the difference in gender openness between male and nonmale subgroups

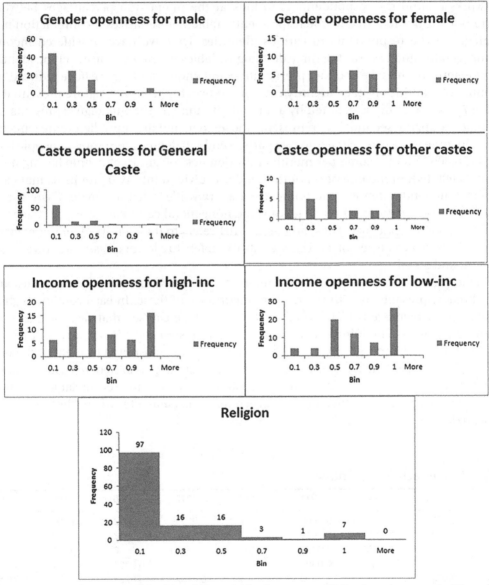

FIG. 1 Histograms of openness of identities within each identity category. (A) Gender openness: male; (B) gender openness: female; (C) caste openness: general caste; (D) caste openness: other castes; (E) income openness: high; (F) income openness: low; (G) religion openness.

of the population. It can be clearly seen that the males are much less open than their female or other counterparts as long as allowing people of other gender identities into one's network is concerned. Similarly, in Fig. 1C and D, we see that the people who belong to the general caste category are much more reluctant than the people of other caste category to mingle with people belonging to some caste category that is other than their own. In religion, we did not have enough non-Hindu population to compare the histogram between Hindu and non-Hindu people, but from Fig. 1G, we can see that overall religious openness is severely low throughout the population. As far as openness toward income group is concerned, Fig. 1E and F tells us that there is a distinct difference in the behavior of the low-income group people and their high-income group counterparts. The high-income group people are tending to be less tolerant in allowing low-income group in their network, while low-income group people are slightly better in accommodating high-income group people in their network. Although, this difference in the case of income group is not statistically significant within our sample population.

6 Conclusion

In this chapter we have, for the first time, quantified the essentially qualitative sociological concepts like openness and awareness regarding identity from an individual's point of view. Our survey data allowed us to make a detailed analysis of these measures.

A common trend that we can essentially locate from the histograms and the descriptive tables is—in a society that is dominated by Hindu, upper caste, upper class male representatives—the further people are from such normative combination of identities, the more accommodative they are in including their "socially higher" counterparts within their network. As for the case of gender, historically the "second sex," that is, females, and the "third sex," that is, LGBT population are seen to be more open in including males into their network whereas males are quite reluctant in "diluting" their all-male network. Similarly for the case for caste and income group. We believe there is a distinct and characteristic dynamics for such behavior of low openness of "higher" identities and high openness for "lower" identities. We are working toward formalizing the dynamics.

Moreover, as we have asked our respondents to identity five most important persons in their friendship, professional, and neighborhood network, it is evident that the persons who are most "open" are naturally alienated from the network comprised of people of its own identity. Hence, as Granovetter [31] showed, there is a high probability that this abundance of weak links in that person's network will change the affiliative identity of that person by virtue of being in the network of people with "higher" identity. For example, being in a group of highly influential persons increases the probability of getting a better job than others who do not belong in that network. It increases the probability of shifting the identity within the income group category. This way, the network a person forms, in turn also changes the identity of the person.

Thus, it can be concluded from the histograms and the descriptives that the identity of a person essentially and decisively determines the network built around that person and the role of identity in shaping the nature of the network is not at all random, rather quite systematic. We will be formulating an Evolutionary game in our future work to substantiate our claim of the systematic interaction between societal hierarchy of identities and human social network formation.

Acknowledgments

The authors thank the Government of West Bengal for a project grant which made the survey possible. The authors are grateful to the students and scholars who meticulously executed the survey for us. A special thanks goes to Dr. Nandita Dhawan for critical help in organizing the survey and to Ms. Malabika Biswas for her critical inputs regarding the sociology scholarship. The workshop participants at IIT Ropar and IGIDR Mumbai have contributed to the work at its various formative stages with comments and suggestions. The usual caveat applies.

References

[1] J. Scott, Social network analysis, Sociology 22 (1) (1988) 109–127.

[2] S.P. Borgatti, A. Mehra, D.J. Brass, G. Labianca, Network analysis in the social sciences, Science 323 (5916) (2009) 892–895.

[3] P. Pierson, Politics in Time: History, Institutions, and Social Analysis, Princeton University Press, Princeton, NJ, 2011.

[4] N.M. Tichy, M.L. Tushman, C. Fombrun, Social network analysis for organizations, Acad. Manag. Rev. 4 (4) (1979) 507–519.

[5] M. Barrera, I.N. Sandler, T.B. Ramsay, Preliminary development of a scale of social support: studies on college students, Am. J. Commun. Psychol. 9 (4) (1981) 435–447.

[6] S. Wasserman, Advances in Social Network Analysis: Research in the Social and Behavioral Sciences, Sage, Thousand Oaks, CA, 1994.

[7] M. Girvan, M.E.J. Newman, Community structure in social and biological networks, Proc. Natl Acad. Sci. USA 99 (12) (2002) 7821–7826.

[8] B. Wellman, Computer networks as social networks, Science 293 (5537) (2001) 2031–2034.

[9] T.V. Batura, Methods of social networks analysis, Vestnik of Novosibirsk State Univ. Ser. Inform. Technol. 10 (4) (2012) 13–28.

[10] M. Newman, Networks: An Introduction, Oxford University Press, Oxford, 2010.

[11] G.A. Akerlof, R.E. Kranton, Economics and identity, Q. J. Econ. 115 (3) (2000) 715–753.

[12] P. Bourdieu, The forms of capital (1986), in: Cultural Theory: An Anthology 2011, pp. 81–93.

[13] J.S. Coleman, Social capital in the creation of human capital, Am. J. Sociol. 94 (1988) S95–S120.

[14] M. Emirbayer, E.M. Williams, Bourdieu and social work, Soc. Serv. Rev. 79 (4) (2005) 689–724.

[15] R.D. Stanton-Salazar, S.M. Dornbusch, Social capital and the reproduction of inequality: information networks among Mexican-origin high school students, Sociol. Educ. 68 (1995) 116–135.

[16] S.A. Dumais, Cultural capital, gender, and school success: the role of habitus, Sociol. Educ. 75 (2002) 44–68.

[17] M. Emmison, J. Frow, Information technology as cultural capital, Aust. Univ. Rev. 41 (1) (1998) 41–45.

[18] A. Sullivan, Cultural capital and educational attainment, Sociology 35 (04) (2001) 893–912.

[19] P. DiMaggio, Cultural capital and school success: the impact of status culture participation on the grades of US high school students, Am. Sociol. Rev. 47 (1982) 189–201.

[20] N.D. De Graaf, P.M. De Graaf, G. Kraaykamp, Parental cultural capital and educational attainment in the Netherlands: a refinement of the cultural capital perspective, Sociol. Educ. 73 (2000) 92–111.

[21] R. Harker, Education and cultural capital, in: R. Harker, C. Mahar, C. Wilkes (Eds.), An Introduction to the Work of Pierre Bourdieu: The Practice of Theory, Palgrave MacMillan, UK, 1990.

[22] A. King, Thinking with Bourdieu against Bourdieu: a "practical" critique of the habitus, Sociol. Theory 18 (3) (2000) 417.

[23] J.H. Goldthorpe, "Cultural Capital": some critical observations, Sociologica 1 (2) (2007) 0–0.

[24] R. Fryer, An Economic Approach to Cultural Capital, University of Chicago, Chicago, 2003.

[25] D. Throsby, Cultural capital, J. Cult. Econ 23 (1–2) (1999) 3–12.

[26] P. Resnick, Beyond bowling together: sociotechnical capital, HCI New Millennium 77 (2001) 247–272.

[27] N. Lin, K.S. Cook, R.S. Burt, Social Capital: Theory and Research, Transaction Publishers, New York, 2001.

[28] R. Putnam, Bowling Alone: The Collapse and Revival of Community in America, vol. 389, Simon and Schuster, New York, NY, 2000, pp. 378–390.

[29] D. Williams, On and off the net: scales for social capital in an online era, J. Comput.-Mediat. Commun. 11 (2) (2006) 593–628.

[30] R.S. Burt, Structural Holes: The Social Structure of Competition, Harvard University Press, London, 2009.

[31] M.S. Granovetter, The strength of weak ties, Am. J. Sociol. 78 (1973) 1360–1380.

11

Social Networks and Their Uses in the Field of Secondary Education

Pablo-César Muñoz-Carril*, Isabel Dans-Álvarez-de-Sotomayor†,
Mercedes González-Sanmamed‡

*Department of Pedagogy and Didactics, University of Santiago de Compostela, Lugo, Spain
†Department of Specific Didactics, University of Vigo, Pontevedra, Spain ‡Department of
Pedagogy and Didactics, University of A Coruña, A Coruña, Spain

1 Introduction

Social networks have become one of the preeminent forms of digital communication and collaboration among young people and adolescents. The gradual increase in its use has been influenced, among other aspects, by the intensive use of mobile technology, under which smartphones are particularly important [1] since they allow ubiquitous, fast, and flexible access to content and information.

Despite being a relatively recent phenomenon, the use of social networks among young people has given rise to a good number of research studies which address various issues, such as: the frequency and type of use that young people make of social networks [2–5]; the explanatory factors and the existing motivations to use this type of technology [6–9]; the dangers and risks arising from abusive and inappropriate use [10–12]; the influence on behavior [13] or adolescents' digital identity in virtual situations [14], among others.

The adoption and inclusion of social network systems at educational levels is, unquestionably, a growing phenomenon; and the scientific literature offers results of great interest such as those related to the positive impact of their implementation in teaching processes and educational practice [15] or the formative benefits they are able to provide students with as an educational resource [16–19]. However, despite having more and more empirical evidence focused on the broad *dyad social networks-education*, studies focused on the use of this technology in secondary education are still meagre [35], since as Hew [20] states, most of this research has focused on the university stage.

Despite this, studies on how to support and reinforce learning through social networks at secondary education levels have been carried out in different parts of the world. Along the same lines, several research studies can be mentioned: Wodzicki et al. [21] in Germany; Al-Kathiri [22] in Saudi Arabia; Kim et al. [23] in Korea; [35] in Macao (China); Ribeiro and Pereira [24] in Portugal; or Ballesta et al. [25] in Spain. The results show that the use of this technology is linked to innovative, more student-centered methodologies that encourage active and collaborative learning. On the other hand, in Israel, Asterhan and Rosenberg

[26] revealed that the use of social networks in secondary education had a positive impact on the classroom climate and social cohesion. Almu and Alhaji [27] emphasize the importance of key figures, such as teachers and parents, in protecting and guiding the actions of minors in social networks.

In the following sections, these studies will be commented in detail, and some of the most outstanding results will be exposed. From these results, the need to investigate in depth the uses—both personal and educational—of social networks among secondary school students, is underpinned. Literature reviews by various authors ([20, 28–32]) have helped us to identify the most relevant publications in this field, to unveil the concerns that are trying to be answered from the perspective of a systematic and rigorous inquiry, as well as to evaluate, at different levels, proposals that should be promoted in order to take advantage of the social networks' potential in promoting and improving educational processes. Thus, Hew [20] analyzes students' attitudes toward Facebook, the uses they make of this social network and the effects it produces (e.g., the time students spend on Facebook each day, students' motives for using Facebook, as well as the effects of Facebook self-disclosure on teachers' credibility, the effects of Facebook on students' social presence and discussion, and the effects of Facebook on students' academic performance). Among its conclusions, it highlights a low use of Facebook in the school environment and a predominant use for connecting with acquaintances. Yang et al. [32] also review 21 studies in which the use of Facebook is analyzed in teaching-learning processes and conclude that although this social network's potential to favor learning can be discerned, they suggest it is still the beginning of a trend that will increase in the future. Aydin [28], after comparing the uses of Facebook in Turkey and globally, also commits to an increase in the use of social networks in educational environments. The following year, a new review was published: this time, 23 articles presenting empirical studies on the use of Facebook in educational environments were analyzed. The authors of this chapter, echo certain discrepancies about the educational potential of this social network, but their conclusions are clear when they state that the educational possibilities of Facebook have only been partially used. They point out that there are certain obstacles that need to be neutralized in order to take better advantage of the opportunities offered by social networks: modifying institutions traditional training methodologies, motivating and training teachers and students to use them effectively, and overcoming cultural limitations.

Gao et al. [29] analyzed 21 studies on the use of microblogging in education that have been published between 2008 and 2011. Although the research was conducted in various contexts and under unique characteristics, the contributions of microblogging are perceived as favorable about participation, commitment, reflective thinking, and collaborative learning in formal education settings. These authors recommend broadening the research perspectives, taking into account other learning environments, developing longitudinal studies to assess whether there is progress and, above all, identifying the most effective approaches to integrate these tools.

Greenhow et al. [30], after recognizing that research on social networks' educational possibilities is still incipient, propose an analysis of the psychological, social and educational aspects linked to the use of these tools among adolescents (between 12 and 17 years of age). In the review carried out between 2010 and 2014, they find three types of uses of social networks: in the development of informal learning, as support for formal learning, and as a platform aimed at developing a greater ethical and academic commitment to the students. Any of these three options demands attention from teachers, educators, and researchers. Taking into account the importance of social networks in the lives of young people, these authors highlight their possibilities of connecting school and life, allowing the integration between social and academic aspects.

In the last of the reviews cited [31], they analyzed 62 articles published between 2008 and 2013, assessing the results derived from the integration of social networks. They classify the studies consulted into 5 categories: 44 articles address the use of social networks as educational tools, 12 analyze other uses among students, 3 allude to their institutional use, 2 cite their academic use, and 1 features the design of social networks. Within the category related to the use of social networks as an educational tool, they include four types of articles: the way they influence on teaching-learning processes, identifying both the positive aspects and the limitations that may arise; the changes in social relationships produced in educational contexts; the assessment of various educational agents—teachers and students—regarding the benefits, potentialities, and attitudes they arouse and the analysis of their ethical implications. As the authors rightly conclude, the educational integration of social networks has motivated an important number of research studies which show the interest this topic arouses among the scientific community. Taking advantage of the role that social networks play in adolescents' and young people's world, it is a great challenge for teachers, designers, and researchers who commit to their effective integration in the educational field.

On the basis of these considerations, this chapter will be structured into three sections in which the progressive use of social networks worldwide, in secondary education, will be first addressed; in addition to its limitations and its potential for improvement in training processes. Next, the main findings about the use of social networks, derived from a cross-sectional research based on the survey method, will be explained [33]; in this research a sample of 1144 students in the fourth year of secondary education distributed among 29 public, state-subsidized, and private educational centers in the city of A Coruña (Spain) was studied.

Finally, a series of conclusions and reflections on the lights and shadows of the adoption of technological systems supported by social networks as a complement to teaching and learning situations will be considered.

2 Social Networks in Secondary Education: A Critical Look From a Triple Multilevel View

The so-called Web 2.0 has become an important breeding ground that has led to the rapid increase and development of especially enriching technological tools in the educational field. Such is the case of social networks which are aligned with the philosophy, principles, and features of the applications born under the cover of the social web, among which these can be highlighted: the strengthening of collective intelligence, the development of participative architecture, the possibility of interacting with multidevice systems, the trend toward the simplicity of technological use, the improvement of the user experience, etc. [34].

Under this perspective, social networks represent an optimal resource for channeling pedagogical actions based on socio-constructivist and connectivist learning processes, since these applications may facilitate the process of knowledge construction, as well as the profound transformation of teaching and learning practices, guiding them toward a significant, open, collaborative, and social perspective, where understanding is strengthened vs memorization [35, 36]. In this sense, social networks stand out as powerful allies for students, making them able to access specialized information, at the right time, based on the connections they created and on the way they articulate their networks and contacts, modifying the mere information into knowledge hybridization, starting from a co-construction of meanings resulting from the dialogic interaction with other people's content [37, 38]. It is clear that under this conception, the figure of the teacher becomes especially relevant as a professional capable of adopting various roles and competencies that allow him or her to design, systematize, moderate, motivate, guide, facilitate, manage, and assess learning, that often roams in an increasingly blurred way, between school curricular and formal conventions versus more open, flexible, and informal environments. Precisely authors like Greenhow et al. [30] highlight how various studies emphasize the students' demand for fun and participatory learning spaces, inviting communication and connection between peers, reflecting in this way a good part of what they understand to be characteristics of the spaces based on social network systems.

Fortunately, the specialized literature shows that, in the last decades, teachers and educational institutions are making an important effort to adopt active methodologies, where social networks (together with other ICT tools) begin to gain special importance in the instructional processes [28]. However, metaanalysis—such as those carried out by Rodríguez-Hoyos et al. [31]—highlight that the vast majority of research on social networks and education, focuses on the university stage, with few studies setting the turning point in the field of secondary education. Despite this circumstance, the adoption and inclusion of social network systems at the secondary education stage is not an isolated or atypical event, but there are more and more centers and teachers throughout the world who are prone to incorporating this type of technology in their curricular programming. In this sense, the scientific literature offers some examples that attest and corroborate—in the form of experiences, of good practices and, of course, of research results—the formative benefits of the use of this type of technological tools.

Taking these aspects into consideration and not intending to perform an exegesis on the state of this question, a brief compilation analysis of the main trends related to the use of social networks in secondary education will be presented further. The discourse, in line with Manca and Ranieri [36] and the category system articulated by Zawacki-Richter and Anderson [39], will be structured in three levels of analysis: microlevel, mesolevel, and macrolevel.

2.1 Microlevel: Uses of Social Networks for Teaching and Learning

One of the most fruitful lines of research in the study of social networks, and one of the greatest experiences developed at the secondary and university educational levels, is the one that deals with assessing the educational impact of these tools and, in particular, their impact on the teaching-learning processes in the classrooms. One of the main concerns has been how to measure and assess the degree of effectiveness of learning through social networks. These research studies have led to assessing the methodologies, learning contents, interactions, and other elements to be taken into account in any design process and curriculum development. But the informal learning that takes place outside the school, the support for formal learning, and the connections between both types of learning, which are promoted thanks to social networks, have also been analyzed. In addition to these central studies, at this microlevel perspective, the research referring to students' and teachers' perceptions regarding the use of social networks and their educational impact is included.

Research related to the use of social networks in the classrooms shows their influence on the enhancement of creativity [40], collaboration [41], literacy [42], thinking skills [43], or the improvement on connection among students, or between students and teachers [44].

Alias et al. [40] conducted a comparative study between two groups that were developing a course on Islamic studies. Using a pretest and posttest questionnaire and a creativity test, they found that the group that had used Facebook achieved better scores in the creativity measures, in both the writing and the problem-solving sections.

In the research carried out by Khan et al. [41] on 690 high school students, the factors that influence the possibility of academic collaboration through Facebook (e.g., their grade, their skills using the Internet and the instrumental support) are identified; but either way, they recognize the social network as a natural mechanism to establish relationships and collaborations with friends. Casey and Evans [45] also found that the Ning social network promoted collaboration and coproduction culture among students, while allowing them to develop their own ideas.

Regarding the development of thinking skills, Callaghan and Bower [43] insist on the importance of the teacher setting the learning expectations intended for the use of social networks; and that beyond motivation and the development of literacy, they can promote high-level skills, as found in the research they conducted among students in Sydney, in which the results were measured by applying Bloom's taxonomy.

The study conducted by Veira et al. [42] also highlights the fact that 283 high school students take advantage of access to online discussion groups through Facebook as a complement to Biology classes, and to improve their literacy, and to expand connection with their peers and with teachers, both inside and outside the school. The research conducted by Hershkovitz and Forkosh-Baruch[44] also analyzes the possibilities of communication between students and teachers through Facebook. Students who took part in this study declared that they preferred to keep the social network as a private space, and they were not inclined to use it to connect with teachers; nevertheless, some recognized that using a social network familiar to them such as Facebook promoted relationships and allowed them to connect with teachers from real life.

The incidence of the use of social networks allows connecting internal and external spaces to the classroom. From a similar perspective, Wodzicki et al. [21] found that those German students who spent the most time on StudiVZ (one of the most prominent social networks in the Teutonic country), were those who were more willing to participate in activities related to school learning.

Other studies, such as those carried out in Sokoto (Nigeria), conclude that social networks are suitable and appropriate tools for the development of learning activities for secondary school students, but it emphasizes the importance of key figures such as teachers and parents in order to protect and guide the virtual actions of minors [27].

In Israel, Asterhan and Rosenberg [26] investigated the type of interactions resulting from the use of Facebook among teachers and secondary school students. Their findings show that those teachers who did use this social network not only improved the relationship with their students, but also achieved a positive impact on the classroom climate and group cohesion. Likewise, the study concludes that the teacher-student relationships developed through Facebook are essential for students' psychopedagogical, social, emotional, and academic consolidation.

In other parts of the world such as Saudi Arabia, Al-Kathiri[22] implemented a quasiexperimental design among secondary students, through which he was able to confirm the positive effects of the use of Edmodo as a social platform for learning English as a foreign language. Specifically, students' ratings showed the benefits of this social network in meeting their learning needs. More specifically, the success of applying this type of technology resided in the possibility of fostering a social, collaborative, and active learning, centered on the student, and where teachers could develop innovative methodologies and effective practices, complementary to face-to-face education systems.

Other parts of the world have also joined the trend of analyzing the adaptation and incorporation of social network systems in secondary schools as an element for improving student learning and socialization. Thus, we can cite relevant studies such as Kim et al. [23] in Korea; Ribeiro and Pereira [24] in Portugal; or Ballesta et al. [25] in Spain.

Despite these results, uncertainty persists and also concerns about how to integrate social networks effectively into educational proposals in both secondary and university classrooms [46]. As Selwyn [47] warned, there are still differences in how technology is used, and how it is theoretically expected to be used, under favorable circumstances. Fewkes and McCabe [48] warn about the paradox between the usually expressed favorable vision regarding the possibilities of social networks, and reality, where only a few teachers are integrating this technology into their classes.

In addition to the research carried out in the formal framework of the classrooms, studies have also been accomplished to assess the scope of social networks from the perspective of informal learning. The key concept that is used to assess the contributions of social networks is *social capital*. Indeed, various authors place the use of social networks within the framework of informal spaces for socialization and development [49, 50] and show their contribution to improving relationships at school, to their integration in the group, and to their well-being. In this sense, the conclusions obtained by Greenhow and Robelia [51] are significant in mentioning the benefits of social networks: they provide the necessary emotional support to sustain relationships, and provide a platform to channel self-expression; the social network can be used for several functions, and among them is helping to carry out school tasks; and it allows the users to get involved in diverse and complex communication and relationship situations. Furthermore, it should be noted that in the framework of social networking sites usage, diverse studies (such as the ones carried out by Acharjya and Anitha [52] or Kamal et al. [53]) have focused their attention on the development of tools that enable the implementation of learning analytics and that involve not only the record of all the activities performed by students, but also the possibility to understand and improve the teaching and learning processes. In this sense, teachers can use analytical tools as well as data mining and then infer the level of acquisition and development of thinking skills in their students.

In this way, teachers can benefit from the use of the current ICT tools to test the efficiency of learning analysis through aspects such as:

- Visualizing interaction graphs.
- Knowing the network density and the intensity of collaboration among students in the framework of collaborative tasks or debates.
- Analyzing the centrality of a node, identifying its importance in the social network based on the relationships it establishes with other nodes.
- Analyzing the semantic content of the diverse tasks performed in the social network, which can recognize aspects such as the relevance of each word, its frequency, etc.
- Identifying when student participation is more representative, etc.

In short, the better use of the potential of social networks in the educational field requires a change in teachers' and students' mentalities, beliefs, and routines, so that traditional teaching-learning practices can be suspended, and access can be given to new ways of thinking and acting in teaching.

2.2 Mesolevel: Institutional Uses of Social Networks

This category mainly includes those studies that have focused their analysis on how educational centers and institutions have used social network systems as communicative resources. Research framed at this level suggests that until now the integration of tools based on social networks has not been developed efficiently, using them more as diaries than as a way of interacting, not seeming to have a clear strategy for their integration within the institutional means of communication. According to Osborn and LoFrisco [54], educational centers use social networks mainly to recruit students, to promote their events or facilities, as well as to give miscellaneous information about their academic activity.

Along the same line, the study by Iong [35], on 851 students in the Chinese region of Macao, is an example. According to this author, secondary education institutes need to have technologies which provide practical solutions to address issues related to accessing information and to the ability to communicate with members of the educational community. One solution to this question is the use of social networks, since, as this expert says, secondary schools do not have the same resources and infrastructure as universities.

Apart from the economistic aspects, Iong's research [35], developed through complex statistical regression techniques, demonstrates the strong positive relationship between the academic benefit perceived by students and their partaking in online activities such as raising questions to teachers and colleagues, or participating in debates related to the topics of study.

On the other hand, research results such as those developed by Fentry et al. [55] reflect a significant relationship between the use of social network systems and the social integration of students, as well as the improvement regarding their institutional commitment.

Pilot studies, such as those implemented by Barbour and Plough [56] at the Odyssey Charter High School (Nevada, United States), show evidence that supports the importance of using social networks in schools, at the organizational level. However, these researchers raise relevant issues that school administrators should take into account, such as maintaining a high degree of safety and minors' data protection; granting the necessary permissions from the students' parents or legal guardians; or the possibility of seeking volunteering teachers who can help with the supervision of groups, conversations, and student interactions to maintain a positive and safe environment.

In another order of things, at this mesolevel we cannot forget about the institutional responsibility implied in supporting those teachers who wish to implement innovative pedagogical actions based on the use of social networks. As Manca and Ranieri [36] point out, these teachers' initial motivation often turns into apathy when they do not possess the necessary knowledge and digital skills to design and implement educational activities based on the use of social networks. In this respect, designing proper institutional strategies for teachers training, guidance, and support are essential to encourage them to rethink the ways they teach; and also as a mechanism to stimulate the time they spend actively taking part in educational communities or school virtual networks. There is a clear example of this in the European E-Twinning program [57].

In addition, several research studies such as those developed by Wong [58] or Hughes et al. [59] highlight that taking part in online school networks provides various benefits such as: the rapid exchange of information, which is important for organizational development; the opportunity to break with isolation and cooperate with other professionals, to improve certain skills; the ability to identify new trends, connecting with other educators, sharing and receiving ideas, building relationships, and shaping a teacher's profile capable of identifying both the formative possibilities, as well as those other darker aspects of new technologies.

2.3 Macrolevel: Policies That Promote the Development of Digital Skills and the Incorporation of Information and Communication Technologies in the Education System

A broader look is directed at the institutions that regulate norms and formative designs, at the service of digital literacy. The teacher training policies are in the center, according to the competency-based model. The European Commission identifies five areas of digital competence (information and data literacy, communication and collaboration, digital content creation, safety, and problem solving), which favor lifelong learning. The knowledge, skills, and attitudes necessary to be functional in a digital environment are subject to digital competence today, according to the Common Digital Competence Framework for Teachers [60]. It concerns educating in a creative, critical, and safe use of Information and Communication Technologies to develop these new capacities.

The skills developed by this training in competencies require a methodological renewal, a curricular restructuring, to adjust the educational system. The use of technologies does not ensure school success, as seen in the OECD study [61]. There is a very high percentage of equipment in the centers, but there is no improvement in school performance. Millennials cannot live without their mobile phones [61a], but how this habit becomes an educational object is a matter of debate. Distance education and the use of mobile phones in schools as a BYOD system are some of the current controversies. Ahn [62] states that 70% of schools block access to devices, and Spanish regulations, among others, prohibit use during school hours. The construction of *social capital* in the connected educational network, as a place of participation, restrains the regulations of the centers themselves.

The Spanish digital agenda (2013) includes among its objectives the connectivity in social networks and services, together with the promotion of inclusion and digital literacy, and the training of new ICT professionals among which are students and teachers. To this end, initiatives are being implemented to install ICT tools and equipment, to promote the use of the Internet in classrooms, and to design spaces for the generation of shared digital knowledge. The evaluation of the technological plans of teacher training in Portugal points to curricular integration and teacher adhesion problems [63].

Special attention must be paid to training in school mediation, to prevent risks and solve conflicts with minors. Part of the official efforts focuses on safety. The European Network and Information Security Agency (ENISA) coordinates research and proposals to protect the network. In Spain, security forces conduct awareness campaigns in schools for families, teachers, and students. Other training levels are carried out by data protection agencies, and public and private collaborating entities. The social network companies themselves provide spaces for educators, perhaps because of the controversy that their "terms of use" raise, and the limited legal regulation [64]. These studies by Patchin and Hinduja [65], Livingstone and Haddon [66], Litt and Hargittai [67], and Bartsch and Dienlin [68] suggest that training is essential, over the risks of social networks: the more the training, the less the risk. It is committed to a greater investment in privacy, from a technical and ethical point of view [69, 70]. From a technical point of view, authors such as Yamin and Abi Sen [71] have shown that it is possible to develop new ways to improve privacy and efficiency in location-based services, which frequently expose users' information to malicious attacks.

3 Analysis of the Use Made of Social Networks Among Students in the Fourth Year of Secondary Education

The results obtained in a cross-sectional, nonexperimental and ex post facto research, based on the survey method [33], are presented further.

It is important to note that the survey method is the most frequently used in education and it has allowed us to translate the variables, on which, we wished to obtain information on particular questions about real life. In this sense, the techniques associated with this type of research are the questionnaire and the interview.

The consideration of our discussion under study, along with our claim to gather information in a short period of time and the large number of research participants, suggested the questionnaire technique as the most advisable tool for data compilation. In addition to these reasons, we mention the fact that the questionnaire is considered a respectable and valid inquiry technique, and if appropriately constructed and applied, it can be a suitable strategy to obtain information as it allows to quantify the specific data previously determined by the evaluators [33].

However, the decision to use the questionnaire as a means to gather information was supported by a revision of the specialized scientific literature, which allowed us to observe the possibilities and advantages that the use of the questionnaire as a data compilation tool offered.

One of the goals of the study was to examine the opinion and self-perception among adolescents in the fourth year of compulsory education, in the city of A Coruña (Spain), in relation to the social networks they ordinarily use, and what kind of uses they make of them. More specifically, the established objectives were the following:

Objective 1: Identifying the degree of awareness of various social networks among students in the fourth year of secondary education.
Objective 2: Knowing what type of use adolescents make of social networks.
Objective 3: Comparing whether gender influences the type of uses made of social networks.
Objective 4: Analyzing whether academic performance is a variable that shows a statistically significant relationship with the use made of social networks.

To achieve this, a questionnaire was crafted. It consisted of 251 items structured into 5 thematic blocks: identification of the participants' data; uses of the internet and other technologies; use of social networks; possibilities of use of social networks for school learning, and dangers and advantages of social networks. In this case, the statistical results analyzed in this section correspond to the block related to the use of social networks.

Note that during the design of the questionnaire, special care was taken in complying with key psychometric aspects. In this sense, the instrument was evaluated by a panel of five experts specialized in research methodology and educational technology. A pilot test was also carried out; after which various questionnaire items were readjusted and deleted, with the aim of improving its content and the construct validity. Likewise, the reliability obtained through the Cronbach alpha internal consistency index yielded a very high result, estimated at 0.937.

Regarding the participants' data—among a population of 1792 students in the fourth year of secondary education, distributed throughout 31 educational centers (public, private and state subsidized)—it is noteworthy that all of them, a total of 1144 surveys from 29 institutions, were collected during school hours (previously granting permission from the educational centers' principals and their teachers).

Among the main sociodemographic characteristics of the sample, we can point out that, as of gender, 47.2% ($n = 540$) were men and 52.8% ($n = 604$) women. As of age, 41.8% ($n = 478$) were students of 15 years of age, 45.2% ($n = 517$) of 16 years of age, 10.6% ($n = 121$) of 17 years of age and, finally, 2.4% ($n = 28$) of 18 years of age.

On the other hand, in regard to study time (see Table 1), 11.6% of the students surveyed devote >3 h a day, on weekdays, to studying or doing homework, which can be considered a high occupation at the secondary school level. A total of 37.8% of them devote between 2 and 3 h to studying and doing homework, and 31.7% devote 1 h a day. Almost 2 out of 10 students devote from half an hour to none, to daily study.

In terms of academic performance, Table 2 shows that the percentage of high-performing and average students is balanced, noting that 44.6% of the students get high and average grades, whereas 54.9% perform low. Perhaps, the most relevant fact is that >30%—this is, 3 out of 10 students—failed in 3 or more subjects, which means very low academic performance.

In order to meet the objectives established in the research, the analysis complies with descriptive and nonparametric statistics (since the distributions do not follow the principles of normality and homoscedasticity).

Descriptive analysis intended to collect, describe, organize, and synthesize the observed data, especially focusing on basic aspects such as central tendency and dispersion [71a,72].

Table 1 Frequency and Percentage of the Variable Study Time

	Frequency	Percentage
DK/NA	9	0.9
None	45	3.9
30 min	161	14.1
1 h	363	31.7
Between 2 and 3 h	433	37.8
Over 3 h	133	11.6

Table 2 Frequencies and Percentages of the Students' Academic Performance

	Frequency	Percentage
DK/NA	7	0.5
I passed all my subjects with high grades	256	22.4
I passed all my subjects with average grades	254	22.2
I failed 1–2 subjects	257	22.5
I failed 3–4 subjects	178	15.6
I failed over 4 subjects	192	16.8
Total	1144	100.0

Regarding nonparametric analysis, the aim has been to identify significant differences between the variables under study. For this, bivariate analysis has been conducted using the Mann-Whitney U test for dichotomous variables and Kruskal-Wallis for polytomous variables.

Addressing the first objective—identifying the degree of awareness on various social networks among students in the fourth year of compulsory education—Table 3 shows a compilation of the percentages obtained according to students' awareness and use of various social networks.

As shown in Table 3, the most used social network is Tuenti (90.6%), followed by Twitter (55.3%), YouTube (55.3%), and Facebook (44.5%). These data are similar to those obtained in other research studies such as the one by García-Jiménez et al. [73].

Table 3 Percentages According to the Awareness and Use of Social Networks

	DK/ NA	Never Heard About It	Heard About It, But Don't Have an Account	Know It, But Don't Have an Account	Have an Account	Have an Account, and I Use It
Facebook	0.6	1	3.6	20.7	29.6	44.5
Tuenti	0.6	0.6	1	3.5	3.7	90.6
Hi5	2.1	55.9	18.7	14.6	6.9	1.8
Myspace	1.7	6	42.7	38.8	8.2	2.6
Orkut	1.7	78.3	9.3	6.7	1.5	2.5
Twitter	1.3	1.3	6.3	24.8	11	55.3
Messenger	1.3	1.1	1.8	6.6	56.5	32.7
Youtube	1.6	2.5	1.9	28.7	14.9	50.4
Ning	2.8	87.2	4.3	4.6	0.5	0.6
Diigo	2.5	82.7	9.6	3.9	0.8	0.5
Flickr	1.9	62.9	16.8	15.2	1.6	1.6
Slideshare	2	78.2	11.1	7.0	1.0	0.7
Edmodo	1.9	88.5	4.5	3.9	0.6	0.6
Grou.ps	1.9	87.9	4.3	4.3	0.6	1
Google+	1.8	17.5	20.8	28.3	11.5	20.1
Metroflog	2.1	13.7	16.9	30.4	32.2	4.7

Likewise, a large part of the students are not aware of very popular and useful networks in the training field, including: the network of images and videos, known as Flickr (62.9%); services to share presentations, such as Slideshare (78.2%); social markers, such as Diigo (82.7%); or platforms for the management of learning contents, such as Edmodo (88.5%) and Groups (87.9%). From these data, and given the nature of the social networks consulted, it is inferred that the students mainly use these tools as an *add-on* to their leisure time, instead of a feasible educational resource.

Regarding the second objective—knowing the type of use that adolescents make of social networks—Table 4 shows that the main use focuses on communicative and relational aspects, specifically: "Message-sending," "Photographs exchange," "News-reading," "Videos," "Search for information and music." The item "Connecting with current friends" (4.24) reaches the highest average score, followed by "sending of messages" (4.02), while the lowest average obtained refers to "connecting with teachers" (1.41). These data warn about how young people prioritize connecting with friends and family over the possibility of doing so with teachers. Thus, social networks are not used to connect with teachers, but they are used to connect, to a limited extent, with the other major educational support: the family. The rejection to connect with strangers (1.63) is also highlighted.

Regarding the third objective—finding out whether gender influences the type of uses made of social networks—the Mann-Whitney *U* test, shown in Table 5, reflects that there are many differences. Specifically, women make a greater use of social networks than men in aspects such as "Search for information," "Sending messages," "Sharing music,"

Table 4   Types of Use of Social Networks

	Mean	Standard Deviation
Search for information	3.03	1.598
Sending messages	4.02	1.228
Sharing music	3.33	1.364
Reading comments and news	3.51	1.313
Viewing/sharing photos	3.84	1.266
Viewing/sharing videos	3.35	1.372
Creating events	2.27	1.272
Watching offers and promotions advertising	1.71	1.122
Playing games online	2.00	1.296
Creating/maintaining a blog personal	2.05	1.387
Connecting with old friends	3.31	1.298
Connecting with current friends	4.24	1.259
Connecting with strangers	1.63	1.097
Connecting with teachers	1.41	0.924
Connecting with relatives	2.60	1.313
Following a topic of interest	2.91	1.402
Following the actions and/or opinions of people I am interested in	2.87	1.459
Other	0.56	1.230

Table 5   Differences in the Use of Social Networks According to Gender

		N	Mean Rank	Sum of Ranks	Mann-Whitney U	Wilcoxon W	Z	Sig. Asympt. (Bilateral)
Search for information	Men	512	489.39	250,570.00	119,242.000	250,570.000	−5.794	0.000[a]
	Women	574	591.76	339,671.00				
	Total	1086						
Sending messages	Men	521	523.76	272,881.50	136,900.500	272,881.500	−4.360	0.000[a]
	Women	593	587.14	348,173.50				
	Total	1114						
Sharing music	Men	522	522.69	272,846.50	136,343.500	272,846.500	−3.454	0.001[a]
	Women	587	583.73	342,648.50				
	Total	1109						
Reading comments and news	Men	521	526.96	274,548.50	138,567.500	274,548.500	−3.172	0.002[a]
	Women	590	581.64	343,167.50				
	Total	1111						
Viewing/ sharing photos	Men	523	489.20	255,851.50	118,825.500	255,851.500	−8.294	0.000[a]
	Women	592	618.78	366,318.50				
	Total	1115						
Viewing/ sharing videos	Men	521	523.50	272,743.00	136,762.000	272,743.000	−3.379	0.001[a]
	Women	588	582.91	342,752.00				
	Total	1109						
Creating events	Men	522	553.68	289,021.50	152,518.500	289,021.500	−0.372	0.710
	Women	591	559.93	330,919.50				
	Total	1113						
Watching offers and promotions advertising	Men	523	573.40	299,887.50	146,754.500	322,282.500	−2.161	0.031[a]
	Women	592	544.40	322,282.50				
	Total	1115						
Playing games online	Men	523	627.58	328,226.50	116,323.500	289,489.500	−8.769	0.000[a]
	Women	588	492.33	289,489.50				
	Total	1111						
Creating/ maintaining a blog personal	Men	521	543.11	282,959.50	146,978.500	282,959.500	−1.459	0.145
	Women	589	566.46	333,645.50				
	Total	1110						
Connecting with old friends	Men	523	520.18	272,056.00	135,030.000	272,056.000	−4.071	0.000[a]
	Women	594	593.18	352,347.00				
	Total	1117						
Connecting with current friends	Men	521	525.60	273,837.50	137,856.500	273,837.500	−4.793	0.000[a]
	Women	591	583.74	344,990.50				
	Total	1112						
Connecting with strangers	Men	524	579.82	303,826.50	143,931.500	319,459.500	−3.244	0.001[a]
	Women	592	539.63	319,459.50				
	Total	1116						
Connecting with teachers	Men	523	559.84	292,797.00	152,276.000	326,031.000	−0.558	0.577
	Women	589	553.53	326,031.00				
	Total	1112						

Table 5 Differences in the Use of Social Networks According to Gender—cont'd

		N	Mean Rank	Sum of Ranks	Mann-Whitney U	Wilcoxon W	z	Sig. Asympt. (Bilateral)
Connecting with relatives	Men	521	514.03	267,810.00	131,829.000	267,810.000	−4.391	0.000[a]
	Women	590	593.06	349,906.00				
	Total	1111						
Following a topic of interest	Men	519	554.79	287,936.00	152,996.000	287,936.000	−0.073	0.941
	Women	591	556.12	328,669.00				
	Total	1110						
Following the actions and/ or opinions of people I am interested in	Men	520	530.91	276,071.00	140,611.000	276,071.000	−2.266	0.023[a]
	Women	584	571.73	333,889.00				
	Total	1104						

[a]Statistically significant differences (*P*-value <.05).

"Reading comments and news," "Viewing/sharing photos," "Viewing/sharing videos," "Connecting with old friends," "Connecting with current friends," "Connecting with relatives," and "Following the actions and/or opinions of people I am interested in."

Men, on their side, show differences in use when compared with women in topics such as "Watching offers and promotions advertising," "Playing online games," and "Connecting with strangers."

Thus, given these data, the impression is that women have a more collaborative and communicative profile than men since the latter tend to develop behaviors that follow a remarkably more ludic and entertainment line. Studies such as the one by Sánchez and Frutos [74] identify similar results.

Addressing the fourth objective—analyzing whether academic performance is a variable that shows a statistically significant relationship with respect to the use adolescents make of social networks—the number of variables to be analyzed has been reduced using factor analysis, in order to contribute to a better interpretation of the data.

In order to verify the conditions of applicability of factor analysis by principal components, Bartlett's sphericity test and KMO measure of sampling adequacy were used. As shown in Table 6, the Bartlett output (*P*-value = .000) informs us that the null hypothesis of incorrect initial variables is not significant; therefore, it makes sense to apply factor

Table 6   KMO and Bartlett's Test

Kaiser-Meyer-Olkin measure of sampling adequacy		0.802
Bartlett's test of sphericity	Approx. Chi-Square	3537.581
	Df	136
	Sig.	0.000

Table 7 Total Variance Explained by Principal Component Analysis

Component	Initial Eigenvalues			Extraction Sums of Squared Loadings		
	Total	% of Variance	% Cumulative	Total	% of Variance	% Cumulative
1	3.853	22.664	22.664	3.853	22.664	22.664
2	2.260	13.292	35.956	2.260	13.292	35.956
3	1.215	7.145	43.101	1.215	7.145	43.101
4	1.053	6.193	49.294			
5	1.001	5.890	55.184			
6	0.927	5.453	60.637			
7	0.874	5.139	65.777			
8	0.805	4.733	70.509			
9	0.752	4.426	74.935			
10	0.710	4.175	79.111			
11	0.635	3.737	82.847			
12	0.601	3.535	86.382			
13	0.547	3.216	89.598			
14	0.518	3.047	92.645			
15	0.475	2.793	95.438			
16	0.432	2.543	97.981			
17	0.343	2.019	100.000			

analysis. Likewise, the KMO statistic reaches a value of 0.802, a value very close to unity, which indicates a high adequacy of the data to a factor analysis model.

Taking these aspects into consideration, factor analysis tested through varimax rotation, identified a total of three components with a total explained variance percentage of 43.10%. Factor 1 explains 22.66% of variance, while factor 2 explains 13.29%, and the third factor, 7.14% (Table 7).

Table 8 displays the matrix of rotated components, where the distribution of the variables, regarding the uses of social networks, is based on the three identified components.

The first component refers to a socio-ludic use of networks with acquaintances; the second component is oriented toward connecting with unknown people and toward more individual than cooperative actions. Finally, the third component refers to their uses related to academic elements, such as the search for information, following topics and also people who can provide valuable opinions (highlighting family).

After identifying the aforementioned factors, a contrast was made between these and the students' academic performance, using the Kruskal-Wallis test. Table 9 reflects statistically significant differences, which are displayed in components 1 and 2. Specifically, the mean ranks show how students with the worst academic performance are those who make the greatest use of those functions, closest to entertainment and the ludic aspects that social networks offer.

These results are consistent with similar findings which displayed that a network built on the basis of friendship is not considered to influence student performance [75].

Table 8   Rotated Components Matrix

	Component		
	1	2	3
Viewing/sharing photos	0.809	0.009	−0.006
Viewing/sharing videos	0.755	0.211	−0.035
Sending messages	0.617	−0.180	0.160
Sharing music	0.588	0.172	0.204
Reading comments and news	0.584	0.008	0.257
Connecting with current friends	0.537	−0.345	0.096
Connecting with old friends	0.375	0.171	0.296
Watching offers and promotions advertising	0.049	0.697	0.115
Connecting with strangers	0.004	0.689	0.034
Connecting with teachers	−0.142	0.657	0.135
Creating events	0.435	0.517	−0.015
Creating/maintaining a blog personal	0.173	0.452	0.253
Playing games online	−0.001	0.434	0.095
Following a topic of interest	0.189	0.116	0.725
Search for information	−0.025	0.000	0.598
Following the actions and/or opinions of people I am interested in	0.337	0.180	0.597
Connecting with relatives	0.079	0.183	0.497

Table 9   Kruskal-Wallis Test. Grouping Variable: "Academic Performance"

	Academic Performance	N	Mean Rank	Test Statistics
Component 1	I passed all my subjects with high grades	247	522.97	Chi-Square: 23.359
	I passed all my subjects with average grades	252	545.37	Df: 4
	I failed 1–2 subjects	255	591.43	Asymp. Sig.: 0.000
	I failed 3–4 subjects	175	537.61	
	I failed over 4 subjects	189	603.28	
	Total	1118		
Component 2	I passed all my subjects with high	246	481.32	Chi-Square: 10.545
	I passed all my subjects with average grades	252	555.09	Df: 4
	I failed 1–2 subjects	255	578.95	Asymp. Sig.: 0.032
	I failed 3–4 subjects	175	581.21	
	I failed over 4 subjects	189	617.85	
	Total	1117		
Component 3	I passed all my subjects with high grades	247	530.13	Chi-Square: 3.075
	I passed all my subjects with average grades	252	560.00	Df: 4
	I failed 1–2 subjects	256	575.12	Asymp. Sig.: 0.545
	I failed 3–4 subjects	176	566.42	
	I failed over 4 subjects	188	572.64	
	Total	1119		

4 Discussion and Conclusions

In recent years, the rapid advances in technology, under cover of Web 2.0 tools, have led an exponential growth on the use of systems based on social networks, becoming one of the preeminent forms of communication and interaction among young people.

This new phenomenon has aroused the interest of academicians and researchers in the field of education, which has translated into the development of a wide range of heterogeneous studies in recent decades, that have sought to deepen (under different perspectives), both the advantages and potentialities, as well as the risks and problems, derived from the use of social networks.

However, although the research studies framed in the study of social networks are increasingly prolix, the truth is that there is an important bias toward higher education to the detriment of other stages, such as secondary education [20, 31]. Taking this fact into consideration, in this chapter, we have analyzed some of the main international trends on the uses of social networks in secondary education, framed in three inclusive and interrelated levels.

At the microlevel, this analysis shows how the main lines of research on social network systems delve into the study of the type of constructivist and connectivist methodologies used, the student participation processes and their implications regarding the classroom climate and group cohesion, the improvement of teacher-student educational relationships, the need for adult supervision of online processes, their complementary nature with face-to-face teaching, as well as their academic uses in both formal and informal situations.

At the mesolevel, social networks are studied as a communicative resource, problem solver, and factor that contribute to students' social integration. The educational centers also benefit at organizational levels, which include strong ethical components in regard to their use with adolescents, and to enhancing teacher training in order to promote appropriately the pedagogical uses of social networks.

Finally, the macrolevel stresses the importance of designing and developing national and supranational policies for an effective integration of information and communication technologies in schools, not only from the point of view of mere provision of infrastructure and equipment, but, above all, in relation to the implementation of measures aimed at improving students' and teachers' literacy and digital competence. A good example is found in the DIGCOMP, project promoted by the European Commission [76], which has led some countries, such as Spain, to make important efforts in order to establish a "Common Framework of Digital Competencies of Teachers" [60], where not only the need of technical training is addressed, but also in the pedagogical and social fields.

At this macrolevel, there is also an important concern in the school environment regarding the proper use of social networks in terms of safety and privacy, with valuable institutional efforts being made, and training programs being aimed at teachers, families, and students.

On the other hand, this chapter has provided some enriching results to understand the uses that high school students make of social networks. Specifically, the analysis presented in previous lines, on a group of 1144 students, incorporate data that may be relevant to expand the *corpus* of research on social networks in education.

Specifically, the results obtained through an ex post facto design, based on the survey method show that adolescents are aware and use social networks mainly with friends. Followed by family, leaving teachers virtually out from all online contact. Connection is a sub-element of digital competence, and it is interesting to note how this does not occur in student-teacher relationships, according to the data of this research. The variation by gender does show that there are differences between boys and girls in the use they make of social networks: the first ones are mainly oriented toward leisure and entertainment activities. Girls, however, use these tools more for communicative purposes, oriented toward social relationships. These differences by gender have also been widely addressed and documented in the scientific literature, confirming the trend of this type of uses (for more information see the research by Lenhart et al. [77] and Liu and Brown [78]). Besides, the results obtained in the current research are similar to those collected in the European Project EU Kids On-line relating to Spanish minors, as well as to other studies carried out by Rial et al. [79] with students in Secondary Education in the Autonomous Region of Galicia, Spain.

Regarding academic performance, the results obtained show an important fact: students categorized as "with a low level of school performance" make a more playful use of social networks, to the detriment of academic uses. Thus, this type of students fills their "virtual spaces" as a way of replacing other less reflective and enriching practices, although also necessary for their personal development. In this line, studies such as those developed by Liu et al. [80] point out the existence of a negative and significant relationship between the use of social network systems and academic performance; so students, who have a low academic performance are more likely to spend more time using social networks.

However, this information must be interpreted with caution, since the key lies with how and in what way social networks are being used. As confirmed by the results shown in previous sections, students with poor academic performance do not use social networks for academic purposes, but eminently for ludic ones. In addition, as Kirschner [81] states, students in their everyday life are not very aware of how to use social networks as learning and problem-solving mechanisms, so they rarely use these applications with an educational purpose. In this sense, the figure of the teacher is of paramount importance to design guided, organized and structured, rich and meaningful learning situations, aimed at benefiting students in making an optimal use of social networks as complementary tools to their academic training.

Acknowledgments

We thank Government of Spain (MINECO) for their support of our study under a research project entitled "How the best university teachers learn: impact on learning ecologies on quality of teaching" (Reference: EDU2015-67907-R).

References

[1] M. Salehan, A. Negahban, Social networking on smartphones: when mobile phones become addictive, Comput. Hum. Behav. 29 (6) (2013) 2632–2639.

[2] IAB, Estudio Anual Redes Sociales 2017, Retrieved from: http://iabspain.es/wp-content/uploads/iab_estudioredessociales_2017_vreducida.pdf, 2017.

[3] ONTSI, Las Redes Sociales En Internet, Retrieved from:http://www.ontsi.red.es/ontsi/sites/default/files/redes_sociales-documento_0.pdf, 2011.

[4] A. Sánchez, A.A. Martín, Generación 2.0 2011. Hábitos de uso de las redes sociales en los adolescentes de España y América Latina, Universidad Camilo José Cela, Madrid, 2012.

[5] R. Zheng, A. Cheok, Singaporean adolescents´ perceptions of on-line social communication: an exploratory factor analysis, J. Educ. Comput. Res. 45 (2) (2011) 203–221.

[6] P. Colás, T. González, J. De Pablos, Juventud y redes sociales: motivaciones y usos preferentes, Comunicar 40 (2013) 15–23, https://doi.org/10.3916/C40-2013-02-01.

[7] M. González, P.C. Muñoz, I. Dans, Factors which motivate the use of social networks by students, Psicothema 29 (2) (2017) 204–210, https://doi.org/10.7334/psicothema2016.127.

[8] T. Notley, Young people, online networks, and social inclusion, J. Comput.-Mediat. Commun. 14 (2009) 1208–1227.

[9] K. Subrahmanyam, P. Greenfield, Online communication and adolescent relationships, Futur. Child. 18 (1) (2008) 119–146.

[10] E. Christofides, A. Muise, S. Desmarais, Risky disclosures on Facebook: the effect of having a bad experience on online behaviour, J. Adolesc. Res. 27 (6) (2012) 714–731, https://doi.org/10.1177/0743558411432635.

[11] S. Livingstone, Taking risky opportunities in youthful content creation: teenager's use of social networking sites for intimacy, privacy and self-expression, New Media Soc. 10 (3) (2008) 393–411.

[12] E. Vanderhoven, T. Schellens, M. Valcke, Educating teens about the risks on social network sites. An intervention study in secondary education, Comunicar 43 (2014) 123–132, https://doi.org/10.3916/C43-2014-12.

[13] A. Hayta, A study on the effects of social media on young consumers buying behaviors, Eur. J. Res. Educ. 2013 (c) (2013) 65–74.

[14] M. Ruiz, A. de Juanas, Redes sociales, identidad y adolescencia: nuevos retos educativos para la familia, ESE: Estudios sobre Educación 25 (2013) 95–113, https://doi.org/10.15581/004.25.95-113.

[15] S. Hamid, J. Waycott, S. Kurnia, S. Chang, Understanding students' perceptions of the benefits of online social networking use for teaching and learning, Internet High. Educ. 26 (2015) 1–9, https://doi.org/10.1016/j.iheduc.2015.02.004.

[16] H. Bicen, H. Uzunboylu, The use of social networking sites in education: a case study of Facebook, J. Univ. Comput. Sci. 19 (5) (2013) 658–671.

[17] R. Junco, Student class standing, Facebook use and academic performance, J. Appl. Dev. Psychol. 36 (2015) 18–29.

[18] S. Jung-Lee, Online communication and adolescent social ties: who benefits more from internet use?, J. Comput.-Mediated Comm. 14 (2009) 509–531. Internet High. Educ., 26, 1–9, https://doi.org/10.1016/j.iheduc.2015.02.004.

[19] A.I. Vázquez-Martínez, J. Cabero, Las redes sociales aplicadas a la formación, Revista Complutense de Educación 26 (1) (2014) 253–272.

[20] K. Hew, Students' and teachers' use of Facebook, Comput. Hum. Behav. 27 (2011) 662–676.

[21] K. Wodzicki, E. Schwammlein, J. Moskaliuk, Actually, I wanted to learn: study-related knowledge exchange on social networking sites, Internet High. Educ. 15 (1) (2012) 9–14, https://doi.org/10.1016/j.iheduc.2011.05.008.

[22] F. Al-Kathiri, Beyond the classroom walls: edmodo in Saudi secondary school EFL instruction, attitudes and challenges, Engl. Lang. Teach. 8 (1) (2015) 189.204, https://doi.org/10.5539/elt.v8n1p189.

[23] J.H. Kim, D.J. Holman, S.M. Goodreau, Using social network methods to test for assortment of pro-sociality among Korean high school students, PLoS One 10 (4) (2015) 1–14, https://doi.org/10.1371/journal.pone.0125333.

[24] A.V. Ribeiro, M. Pereira, Representatividade das redes sociais no processo educacional: potencialidades dos grupos virtuais como ferramentas de ensino-aprendizagem no ensino médio, Revista Eletrônica Gestão & Saúde 4 (2013) 589–599. Retrieved from: http://gestaoesaude.bce.unb.br/index.php/gestaoesaude/article/view/606/pdf.

[25] F.J. Ballesta, J. Lozano, M.C. Cerezo, E. Soriano, Internet, redes sociales y adolescencia: un estudio en centros de educación secundaria de la región de Murcia. Revista Fuentes 16 (2014) 109–130, https://doi.org/10.12795/revistafuentes.2015.i16.05.

[26] C.S.C. Asterhan, H. Rosenberg, The promise, reality and dilemmas of secondary school teacher-student interactions in Facebook: the teacher perspective, Comput. Educ. 85 (2015) 134–148, https://doi.org/10.1016/j.compedu.2015.02.003.

[27] A. Almu, B. Alhaji, Effect of mobile social networks on secondary school students, Int. J. Comput. Sci. Inf. Technol. 5 (5) (2014) 6333–6335. Retrieved from: http://www.ijcsit.com/docs/Volume%205/vol5issue05/ijcsit2014050574.pdf.

[28] S. Aydin, A review of research on facebook as an educational environment, Educ. Technol. Res. Dev. 60 (6) (2012) 1093–1106, https://doi.org/10.1007/s11423-012-9260-7.

[29] F. Gao, T. Luo, K. Zhang, Tweeting for learning: a critical analysis of research on microblogging in education published in 2008–2011, Br. J. Educ. Technol. 43 (5) (2012) 783–801.

[30] C. Greenhow, B. Gleason, J. Li, Psychological, social, and educational dynamics of adolescents' online social networking, Media Educ. Studi, Ricerche, Buone Pratiche 5 (2) (2014) 115–130.

[31] C. Rodríguez-Hoyos, I. Haya, E. Fernández-Díaz, Research on SNS and education: the state of the art and its challenges, Australas. J. Educ. Technol. 31 (1) (2015) 100–111.

[32] Y. Yang, Q. Wang, H.L. Woo, C.L. Quek, Using facebook for teaching and learning: a review of the literature, Int. J. Contin. Eng. Educ. Life-Long Learn. 21 (1) (2011) 72–86.

[33] J. McMillan, S. Schumacher, Investigación Educativa, Pearson Addison Wesley, Madrid, 2005.

[34] F.I. Revuelta, L. Pérez, Interactividad de los entornos en la formación on-line, 2009. Barcelona: Editorial UOC.

[35] S. Iong, Extending social networking into the secondary education sector, Br. J. Educ. Technol. 47 (2) (2016) 721–733, https://doi.org/10.1111/bjet.12259.

[36] S. Manca, M. Ranieri, Implications of social network sites for teaching and learning. Where we are and where we want to go, Educ. Inf. Technol. 22 (2) (2015) 605–622, https://doi.org/10.1007/s10639-015-9429-x.

[37] C. Greenhow, E. Askari, Learning and teaching with social network sites: a decade of research in K-12 related education, Educ. Inf. Technol. 22 (2) (2017) 623–645, https://doi.org/10.1007/s10639-015-9446-9.

[38] G. Siemens, M. Weller, Higher education and the promises and perils of social network, Revista de Universidad y Sociedad del Conocimiento (RUSC) 8 (1) (2011) 164–170.

[39] O. Zawacki-Richter, T. Anderson, Online Distance Education. Towards a research agenda, AU press, Athabasca University, Alberta, 2014.

[40] N. Alias, S. Siraj, M.K.A.M. Daud, Z. Hussin, Effectiveness of facebook based learning to enhance creativity among Islamic studies students by employing isman instructional design model, Turkish Online J. Educ. Technol. 12 (1) (2013) 60–67.

[41] M.L. Khan, D.Y. Wohn, N.B. Ellison, Actual friends matter: an internet skills perspective on teens' informal academic collaboration on Facebook, Comput. Educ. 79 (2014) 138–147.

[42] A.K. Veira, C.J. Leacock, S.J. Warrican, Learning outside the walls of the classroom: engaging the digital natives, Australas. J. Educ. Technol. 30 (2) (2014).

[43] N. Callaghan, M. Bower, Learning through social networking sites–the critical role of the teacher, Educ. Media Int. 49 (1) (2012) 1–17.

[44] A. Hershkovitz, A. Forkosh-Baruch, Student-teacher relationship in the Facebook era: the student perspective, Int. J. Contin. Eng. Educ. Life Long Learn. 23 (1) (2013) 33–52.

[45] G. Casey, T. Evans, Designing for learning: online social networks as a classroom environment, Int. Rev. Res. Open Dist. Learn. 12 (7) (2011) 1–26.

[46] C. Crook, The 'digital native' in context: tensions associated with importing web 2.0 practices into the school setting, Oxf. Rev. Educ. 38 (1) (2012) 63–80.

[47] N. Selwyn, Looking beyond learning: notes towards the critical study of educational technology, J. Comput. Assist. Learn. 26 (1) (2010) 65–73.

[48] A.M. Fewkes, M. McCabe, Facebook: learning tool or distraction? J. Dig. Learn. Teacher Educ. 28 (3) (2012) 92–98.

[49] K. Erjavec, Aprendizaje informal a través de Facebook entre alumnos eslovenos. Comunicar 21 (41) (2013) 117–126, https://doi.org/10.3916/C41-2013-11.

[50] C. Greenhow, L. Burton, B. Robelia, Help from my Bfriends: ˆsocial capital in the social network sites of low-income high school students, J. Educ. Comput. Res. 45 (2) (2011) 223–245.

[51] C. Greenhow, B. Robelia, Old communication, new literacies: social network sites as social learning resources, J. Comput.-Mediat. Commun. 14 (4) (2009) 1130–1161.

[52] D. Acharjya, A. Anitha, A comparative study of statistical and rough computing models in predictive data analysis, Int. J. Ambient Comput. Intell. 8 (2) (2017) 32–51, https://doi.org/10.4018/IJACI.2017040103.

[53] S. Kamal, N. Dey, A.S. Ashour, S. Ripon, V.E. Balas, M.S. Kaysar, FbMapping: an automated system for monitoring Facebook data, Neural Netw. World 1 (2016) 25–57, https://doi.org/10.14311/NNW.2017.27.002.

[54] D.S. Osborn, B.M. LoFrisco, How do career centers use social networking sites? Career Dev. Q. 60 (3) (2012) 263–272, https://doi.org/10.1002/j.2161-0045.2012.00022.x.

[55] R.S. Fentry, T.F. Boykin, K.B. Vickery, Establishing a framework for successful social network site use in the community college, Commun. Coll. J. Res. Pract. 41 (12) (2017) 881–896, https://doi.org/10.1080/10668926.2016.1242440.

[56] M. Barbour, C. Plough, Odyssey of the mind: social networking in a cyberschool, Int. Rev. Res. Open Dist. Learn. 13 (3) (2012) 1–18. https://doi.org/10.19173/irrodl.v13i3.1154.

[57] R. Vuorikari, A. Gilleran, S. Scimeca, Growing beyond innovators—ICT-based school collaboration in eTwinning, in: C.D. Kloos, D. Gillet, R.M. Crespo García, F. Wild, M. Wolpers (Eds.), Towards Ubiquitous Learning. EC-TEL 2011. Lecture Notes in Computer Science, vol. 6964, Springer, Berlin, Heidelberg, 2011.

[58] T. Wong, Meeting needs: are you connected? School Library Monthly 29 (8) (2013) 33–34.

[59] J.E. Hughes, Y. Ko, M. Lim, S. Liu, Preservice teachers' social networking use, concerns, and educational possibilities: trends from 2008-2012, J. Technol. Teach. Educ. 23 (2) (2015) 185–212. Retrieved from: https://0-www-learntechlib-org.cataleg.uoc.edu/p/130448/.

[60] INTEF, Marco Común de Competencia Digital Docente, Retrieved from: http://aprende.educalab.es/wp-content/uploads/2017/11/2017_1020_Marco-Com%C3%BAn-de-Competencia-Digital-Docente.pdf, 2017.

[61] OECD, Students, Computers and Learning: Making the Connection, in: PISA, OECD Publishing, 2015 https://doi.org/10.1787/9789264239555-en.

[61a] Refuel Agency, Millennial Teens, Retrieved from: Refuel Agency, 2015. http://research.refuelagency.com/wp-content/uploads/2015/07/Millennial-Teen-Digital-Explorer.pdf.

[62] J. Ahn, The effect of social network sites on adolescents' social and academic development: current theories and controversies. J. Assoc. Inf. Sci. Technol. 62 (8) (2011) 1435–1445, https://doi.org/10.1002/asi.21540.

[63] B. Silva, M.J. Gomes, A. Silva, Avaliação de Políticas e Programas em TICE: análise do Plano Tecnológico da Educação em Portugal, in: J. Morgado, M.P. Alves, S. Selli Pillotto, M.I. Cunha (Eds.), Actas do 2° Congresso Internacional de Avaliação em Educação. *Aprender ao longo da vida: contributos, perspectivas e questionamentos do currículo e da avaliação.* Braga: CIEd, 2011, pp. 1256–1275.

[64] N. Baym, Social networks 2.0. En, in: M. Consalvo, C. Ess (Eds.), The Handbook of Internet Studies, John Wiley & Sons-Blackwell, Oxford, 2013.

[65] J.W. Patchin, S. Hinduja, Changes in adolescent online social networking behaviors from 2006 to 2009, Comput. Hum. Behav. 26 (6) (2010) 1818–1821, https://doi.org/10.1016/j.chb.2010.07.009.

[66] S. Livingstone, L. Haddon, EU Kids Online: Final Report. LSE, EU Kids Online, London, 2011. Retrieved from: www.eukidsonline.net.

[67] E. Litt, E. Hargittai, The imagined audience on social network sites, Soc. Media + Soc. 2 (1) (2016), https://doi.org/10.1177/2056305116633482.

[68] M. Bartsch, T. Dienlin, Control your Facebook: an analysis of online privacy literacy, Comput. Hum. Behav. 56 (2016) 147–154, https://doi.org/10.1016/j.chb.2015.11.022.

[69] Y. Feng, W. Xie, Teens' concern for privacy when using social networking sites: an analysis of socialization agents and relationships with privacy-protecting behaviors, Comput. Hum. Behav. 33 (2014) 153–162, https://doi.org/10.1016/j.chb.2013.09.012.

[70] A. Taneja, J. Vitrano, N.J. Gengo, Rationality-based beliefs affecting individual's attitude and intention to use privacy controls on Facebook: an empirical investigation, Comput. Hum. Behav. 38 (2014) 159–173, https://doi.org/10.1016/j.chb.2014.05.027.

[71] M. Yamin, A.A. Abi Sen, Improving privacy and security of user data in location based services, Ambient Comput. Intell. 9 (1) (2018) 19–42, https://doi.org/10.4018/IJACI.2018010102.

[71a] J.A. Gil, Estadística e informática (SPSS) en la investigación descriptiva e inferencial, UNED, Madrid, 2000.

[72] R. Vilà, R. Bisquerra, El análisis cuantitativo de los datos, in: R. Bisquerra (Ed.), Metodología de la investigación educativa, Editorial la Muralla, Madrid, 2004, pp. 259–271.

[73] A. García-Jiménez, M.C. López de Ayala, B. Catalina, The influence of social networks on the adolescents' online practices. Comunicar 41 (2013) 195–204, https://doi.org/10.3916/C41-2013-19.

[74] M. Sánchez, B. De Frutos, ¿Marca el género la diferencia? Adolescentes en las redes sociales, Telos: Cuadernos de comunicación e innovación 92 (2012) 50–59. Retrieved from: https://telos.fundaciontelefonica.com/url-direct/pdf-generator?tipoContenido=articuloTelos&idContenido=2012071612040003&idioma=es.

[75] M. Nkhoma, H. Pham, A. Bill, T. Lam, J. Richardson, R. Smith, J. El-Den, Facebook as a tool for learning purposes: analysis of the determinants leading to improved students' learning, Act. Learn. High. Educ. 16 (2) (2015) 87–101, https://doi.org/10.1177/1469787415574180.

[76] R. Vuoikari, Y. Punie, S. Carretero, L. Van den Brande, DigComp 2.0. The Digital Competence Framework for Citizens, Joint Research Center. European Comission, Sevilla, 2016. Retrieved from: http://publications.jrc.ec.europa.eu/repository/bitstream/JRC101254/jrc101254_digcomp%202.0%20the%20digital%20competence%20framework%20for%20citizens.%20update%20phase%201.pdf.

[77] A. Lenhart, A. Smith, M. Anderson, M. Duggan, A. Perrin, Teens, Technology and Friendships, http://www.pewinternet.org/files/2015/08/Teens-and-Friendships-FINAL2.pdf, 2015.

[78] D. Liu, B.B. Brown, Self-disclosure on social networking sites, positive feedback, and social capital among Chinese college students, Comput. Hum. Behav. 38 (2014) 213–219, https://doi.org/10.1016/j.chb.2014.06.003.

[79] A. Rial, P. Gómez, T. Braña, J. Varela, Actitudes, percepciones y uso de las redes sociales entre los adolescentes de la comunidad gallega (España), Anales de Psicología 30 (2) (2014) 642–655, https://doi.org/10.6018/analesps.30.2.159111.

[80] D. Liu, P.A. Kirschner, A.C. Karpinski, A meta-analysis of the relationship of academic performance and social network site use among adolescents and young adults, Comput. Hum. Behav. 77 (2017) 148–157, https://doi.org/10.1016/j.chb.2017.08.039.

[81] P.A. Kirschner, Facebook as learning platform: argumentation superhighway or dead-end street? Comput. Hum. Behav. 53 (2015) 621–625.

Further Reading

[82] C.M.K. Cheung, P.Y. Chiu, M.K.O. Lee, Online social networks: why do students use Facebook? Comput. Hum. Behav. 27 (4) (2011) 1337–1343.

[83] A. Ferrari, DIGCOMP: A Framework for Developing and Understanding Digital Competence in Europe, JRC-IPTS, Sevilla, 2013. Retrieved from: http://ipts.jrc.ec.europa.eu/publications/pub.cfm?id=6359.

[84] M. Garmendia, C. Garitaonandia, G. Martínez, M.A. Casado, Riesgos y seguridad en internet: los menores españoles en el contexto europeo, Universidad del País Vasco, Bilbao, 2011. EU Kids Online. Retrieved from: http://www.lse.ac.uk/media@lse/research/EUKidsOnline/EU%20Kids%20II%20(2009-11)/National%20reports/Spanish%20report.pdf.

[85] P.A. Kirschner, A.C. Karpinski, Facebook® and academic performance, Comput. Hum. Behav. 26 (6) (2010) 1237–1245, https://doi.org/10.1016/j.chb.2010.03.024.

12

NGOs' Communication and Youth Engagement in the Digital Ecosystem

M.C. García-Galera*, C. Fernández Muñoz[†], J. Del Olmo Barbero[‡]

*King Juan Carlos University, Madrid, Spain [†]Complutense University, Madrid, Spain [‡]King Juan Carlos University, Madrid, Spain

1 Introduction

With online media, networks, and social media, Internet is generally producing an unquestionable change in the world of business communication [1]. Digitalization—the mass adoption of Internet-connected digital technologies and applications by consumers, enterprises, and governments—is a global phenomenon that touches every industry and nearly every citizen in the world. For every organization, digitalization changes the way products are made, sold, and distributed, as well as how companies are managed, and how and with whom they compete. For many industries, digitalization is completely revolutionizing the way companies interact with their customers [2]. For an organization, to ignore social media in the 21st century would be the equivalent of turning away from radio and television in the second half of the 20th century [3]. Social networks and Web 2.0 as a whole still constitute a new ecosystem. An ecosystem is a community of living beings whose vital processes are interrelated. The development of these living beings occurs based on the physical factors of a shared environment.

If we transfer this concept to the digital environment, it can be said that a digital ecosystem reproduces the mechanisms of natural ecosystems in a virtual environment in which its members interact and share with each other online [4]. It is a metaphor used to exemplify the way in which the different elements and tools that form part of an organization's digital strategy are integrated and work together [5]. As López [6] points out, this ecosystem is composed of three main elements: digital technologies, new media or social media arising from these technologies, and finally, the public, which is an indispensable component in establishing interrelations in this ecosystem. Therefore, it seems that at the present time every organization lives in a unique relational ecosystem, different from that of past decades, in which there is now greater dynamism, interrelation, and mutual influences among the different agents, as opposed to the static, divided, and more independent character of the different players of the past.

As a consequence of this digitalization, the public is the specific element that has experienced greater change in the way it is perceived by organizations and in its way of relating.

Social Network Analytics. https://doi.org/10.1016/B978-0-12-815458-8.00012-8

Traditionally, corporate communication programs have only considered the groups to which their communication actions were addressed as final agents, a mere recipient of a specific message without any, or if it existed, very limited feedback, and there was even less of a structured personal relationship with the individuals who led or composed such groups. On many occasions, the difficulty in obtaining such feedback was because mass media, such as the print press, were used to convey the message. In others—as direct communication to investors or through newsletters or similar tools—the message was more adapted and further segmented, but there was no face-to-face or person-to-person dialogue based on mutual interests of the organization and individuals in that group.

Social networks have produced an unprecedented change. They impose a fast response, and additionally, they compel an organization to adopt a more conversational attitude [3]. The new channels of communication provide immediacy and the ability to reach many audiences that used to be much harder to contact, and took longer to reach as well. Now these audiences are more participatory and the organization needs to be able to converse with them [1]. According to Bernal [7], before the arrival of social networks, the media agenda was built only on the basis of what journalists considered newsworthy. Therefore, the reader could solely access one specific agenda (the media offered only that version, a version of reality according to its editorial line of thinking), passive, closed (it did not allow for participation in the choice of topics), and limited (it offered a single vision in which the source was also the medium).

Social networks have allowed for a transition to a multiple agenda in which there are as many options as users who have a profile on the network and who choose the person or organization that they follow. They are also active, in the sense that the user is the one who chooses and participates. They are open in the sense that even people who are not followed are capable of participating. Finally, social networks are collaborative as a consequence of participation and the options they offer of creating and sharing content. As Brennen and Kreiss [8] point out, many of these forms of engagement are premised on the use of data and analytics that are made newly possible with the explosion of digital 'trace data' that can provide real-time feedback on the actions and interactions of users. For example, David Karpf [9] has analyzed how digitally native civic organizations such as MoveOn.org rely on digital analytics as a form of "passive democratic feedback." These organizations work to assess what is important to their "membership," by tracking what they click. In an important way, the organizations' comparatively small leadership uses digital media to shape organizational strategy, set goals, prioritize tactics and actions, and ultimately, even provide members with a voice in the organizations' priorities. Even more broadly, Karpf shows how the same structures, processes, and forms of engagement have shifted given the informational affordances of digital media.

2 NGOs in the Digital Ecosystem

This digital ecosystem, as defined so far, still requires progressive adaptation by organizations, including nongovernmental organizations (NGOs). NGOs have a presence in social media with three purposes: to make themselves visible to the population, to raise awareness about the issues they defend, and third, to turn those media into conduits for channeling donations from citizens.

According to a study conducted by the University of Massachusetts in 2014, almost all of the charitable and nonprofit organizations in the United States were already present in social networks. Fully 98% used at least one social platform. Of all the social networks, YouTube was the most widely used social tool at 97%, followed by Facebook at 92%, Twitter with 86%, and Pinterest at 72% [10]. In that same study, 81% of NGO social network community managers ensured that the main purpose of using social networks was to make their organizations known, followed by the considerably lower percentage of 40% of organizations that claim they are on social networks to obtain donations.

Thus, in the 2.0 context, it is not that new situations, contexts, or communication objectives have appeared for third-sector organizations. What is happening is that social networks and platforms have become a useful and necessary tool that help these organizations to spread their messages, increase the number of donors, recruit volunteers, become authorities on a topic, generate relationship bonds, raise awareness about a subject, have an influence on public policy, or communicate with those who receive their messages, among others. As Anduiza et al. [11] point out, the emerging literature on online social media has so far mostly concluded that these networks complement rather than act as substitutes for traditional mobilization organizations such as unions, parties, or mass media [12–14].

Bimber et al. [14a] have detailed how civic engagement changes in an information environment defined by digitalization. These scholars argue that citizens now have radically different expectations and much greater ability and desire to shape their own participation. Whereas participation in a predigital era was mostly defined by the incentives and opportunities that organizations could provide to individuals to entice them to participate, in the digital era individuals have radically increased their choices. Therefore, organizations need to provide more open forms of engagement that enable individuals to define and act on their own definitions of membership and political action.

Digital communication seems to have changed the traditional way that NGOs operate and communicate as organizations pursuing the goal of social assistance, and they do so, on a nonprofit basis, independent of governments and administrations. The field of action of NGOs is increasingly difficult to classify, given the diversity of causes they advocate [15]. Meriläinen and Vos [16] define the role of these organizations as a counterforce to traditional dominance, which is carried out through the mobilization of public support and the presentation of issues sensitive to public opinion and politicians. For these same authors, as more people are attracted to or support a cause initiated by the organization, the organization will have more power with regard to those who make decisions.

Therefore, the public is the group who is able to develop or collaborate in a process of change [17], and for that reason, NGOs have always encouraged the participation of citizens, traditionally, by means of letters, signatures at petitioning tables, boycotts, or other communicative tactics [18]. As such, until recently, NGOs needed the traditional media due to that fact that it was the only instrument capable of reaching large audiences and achieving the social change proclaimed by the organizations. Currently, however, social networks and the digital world have provided NGOs with a new tool to reach their audience without intermediaries.

As Meriläinen and Vos [16] state, social networks have led to a change in communication strategies that invite citizens to participate directly, and have paved the way toward the so-called "social activism." The Global Report on Online Technology of NGOs [19] gathers information on the use that third-sector organizations make of social networks as a tool to reach their target audiences. According to what is stated on their website, it is the only annual research project dedicated to studying how NGOs use online technology on a global scale. In the latest edition, they have gathered information from 4907 NGOs from 153 countries around the world. Some noteworthy data show that 92% of NGOs have a profile on Facebook, 72% have the same on Twitter, and 39% are on Instagram [19].

Consequently, while the background and way of working of NGOs has not changed, digitization has produced a formula that facilitates globalized communication. It arrives easily, quickly, and without borders to all citizens of the planet, to all people who are ultimately capable of producing changes and making the impossible possible, thereby doing what governments cannot or will not do. The work carried out by Meriläinen and Vos [16] related to how digital communication has changed the way of reaching citizens by NGOs concludes the following: among other things, platforms are constantly updated, and social networks provide information almost immediately on their activities, inviting users to access their websites to obtain more detailed information. Digital communication allows NGOs to raise awareness among citizens regarding the issues that these organizations address, according to the subject matter, and to place them on the social agenda.

The study carried out by Lovejoy and Saxton [20] on communication in social networks by NGOs presents three objectives of this communication: to inform, to create a community, and to act. In their study of the 100 largest NGOs in the United States, they conclude that informing the target audience is important to these organizations, and platforms such as Twitter help in this endeavor quickly and efficiently with their traditional 140-character limit. Users, however, can decide how much they want to know by reading only the tweet or by clicking on the link to find out more.

The second objective, creating community, involves dialogue, and this is where true engagement begins when online networks are developed and users can join the conversation and provide feedback. The third category is action. In this category, the users not only feel that they are making a difference, but they begin to do something about it, whether participating in an event, signing a petition, or making a donation. Organizations at this level are completely committed to their supporters. Users want information and want to be part of the dialogue, but an organization fulfills its mission by compelling its followers do something for the cause it supports.

3 The Mobilization of Young People

Social networks have provided a world of infinite possibilities for their users: the ability to socialize, to be informed, to contribute socially with positive attitudes of solidarity and empathy, to be trained intellectually, etc. Young people no longer use traditional means of communication to know what is happening in the world. In fact, their main source of staying informed on current affairs is through social networks. In this sense, as Joaquin Moral states in the aftermath of the 2015 attacks in Paris, the incursion of social networks has radically changed the way people perceive these misfortunes. At the informative level with its immediate reach in real time with the capacity to show solidarity and rectify errors, as well as at the level of getting people involved [21].

In fact, when faced with events of a social or political nature that concern and have an impact on the general population, young people use social networks to inquire about the issue, participate, and mobilize [22]. This is done to such an extent that traditional media echo these same conversations due to the impact of online mobilization. Before the existence of social networks and the possibility of communication offered by the digital world, the need to involve the individual in collective social actions that helped achieve common solidarity goals had already been studied. The German sociologist Lorenz von Stein was the first to introduce the term "social movement" into academic discourse in the 1950s [23].

Although the number of authors who have approached the concept [23–26] has been significant since then, considering their approximations and their meanings (critical analyses and results), we can establish four key concepts in a possible current definition of social movement: social media, change, cooperation, as well as online and/or offline mobilization. Therefore, the situation is such that social media (online social networks and instant messaging) seeks the necessary collaboration of individuals to join forces in order to protest as a group for the purpose of trying to change or improve a given situation, and as a consequence these social media achieve online and/or offline mobilization from part of the population.

Recent studies have attempted to establish a relationship between social media and citizen activism [27–30]. In this sense, Ilten [31] considers clear that social movements and citizen involvement with causes have changed along with the development of information and communication technologies. However, according to this author, these changes have taken place in organizations that already exist, because the new technologies have made it possible for these institutions to contact citizens more effectively, an example being through the use of online platforms, and change has been less evident in the new social activism organizations that have emerged.

Participation in collective social actions can be considered a multidimensional phenomenon, while the motives that lead to involvement in one cause or another vary. A social movement can be defined as a voluntary, coordinated, collective action, organized around a cause or demand, which identifies an adversary to confront and a situation that a person wants to change (Neveu, 2002 quoted in Asún and Zúñiga [31a]). Some other authors argue that a social movement does not always want to change a situation but sometimes only seeks to express discomfort (Contreras-Ibáñez et al., 2005 cited in Asún and Zúñiga [31a]). It should be added that it is also a matter of expressing a feeling of solidarity with the cause, as this feeling is what impels citizens to decide whether or not to mobilize. More than discomfort, it is the empathy with the situation, especially "with the close proximity to the experiences we live with and how these experiences affect us [...]

It is more likely that when the need is close to us, we see more clearly how to attempt to solve the problem" (Porto Pedrosa [31b], p. 40).

González-Anleo [32, p. 59] affirmed more than 15 years ago that "in the majority of sociological investigations on Spanish youth, what stands out is their political apathy, low level of participation in social movements and groups, and the absence of civic ethics or culture, which are essential elements of what we call citizenship." Contrary to this pessimistic scenario, a more recent study carried out by the Youth Observatory of Spain [33] shows that the number of young people involved in activities related to associations and civic participation is increasing. Thus, the study shows that 38% of young respondents belonged to an association at the time of the survey, a 9% increase when compared with the data recorded by this same observatory in 2007.

It is true that associative spaces related to activities involving sports, festivities, and/or recreational activities are more important to young people than associations of a political or social nature [33], but we must not forget that the course of action of a civil society is identified with the social sphere. Associations are seen as the first "horizontal" alternative to political participation. It is interesting to note that the gender variable offers some differences regarding participation in associations. Thus, men participate more in sports, recreational and student associations, while women are more numerous in religious, cultural, and charitable groups.

The volunteering activities that interest Spanish youth most are those related to children and young people (17%), alleviation of poverty (12%), health and health-care services (11%), working with disabled people (10%), and ecology and the environment (8%). These are followed by aid to the Third World and countries in conflict (7%), aid to drug addicts and alcoholics (7%), help for the elderly (5%), support for women (4%), and activities related to culture and maintaining cultural heritage (4%). Between 2006 and 2014, when the economy was in crisis, there were changes in volunteering activities that became more attractive to young people, with an increased interest in activities related to poverty and health, as well as health-care assistance, with less interest in environmental activities and aid to the Third World. In associations, young people like to volunteer their time in activities they enjoy (40%), while the ultimate goal has less weight on their reasons for participation. To a lesser extent, among the motives that encourage young people to participate in an association are aspects such as "feeling useful in helping others" (12%), "enjoying being part of an association" (11%), the feeling of being included in a peer group "because my friends belong to the association" (10%), or "to be with people who think like me" (9%). Lastly, "to be able to defend rights and opinions (8.5%).

Interest in participating in associations is evidenced by the fact that one in four young people who have never belonged to an association declare that they would like to participate in one. Young Spaniards point out that one of the main advantages of being part of an association is to be able to talk, share ideas, and make new friends, which highlights the socialization aspect of belonging to youth associations. As for volunteering activities, young people also have high participation rates. Four out of ten young people in Spain state that they have been involved in volunteering activities. In all, 9% of the population surveyed stated that they were collaborating at that moment with a volunteer organization, a profile that corresponds more to women, young people with higher education, students, and singles.

The report by Injuve (Youth Institute) in 2014 also found that the number of young people who regularly collaborate with volunteer organizations has increased in recent years. Some of the main reasons why young people in Spain become volunteers are to perform social service for the community (90%), to feel useful (88%), for moral beliefs (82%), to interact with other people (79%), and for religious beliefs (60%). These attitudinal and behavioral patterns of young Spaniards are not far from those of other countries. To a certain extent, and in a way that is similar to what has happened with the new digital society in the last decade, the phenomenon of globalization is not foreign to the field of social and political mobilization of young people.

Thus, accusations that young people are politically apathetic and have somehow failed in their duty to participate in many democratic societies around the world have been refuted by a growing number of scholars over the past few years [34, 35]. In recent years, proposals for new ways of participating have emerged, characterized by a greater conciseness in the way people participate and in their objectives. Kallio and Häkli [36] point out that young people as well as other groups may be empowered to participate in matters that concern them and thereby become more important as members of their communities and societies if given the opportunity. Likewise, there are an increasing number of studies, such as the one by Yamamoto et al. [37], which point out that online political expression modifies the traditional panorama of civic participation, improving the effects of traditional media due to the mobilizing role of social networks in the development process of active digital citizenship among young people.

4 Methodology

The general objective of this research is to understand how NGOs use digital communication as a necessary means of mobilizing and involving young people. Regarding specific objectives, the study tries to recognize the successful actions of NGOs in the mobilization of young people, as well as the advantages and difficulties that these organizations find in the use of social networks as a tool to reach this target audience.

The research questions we are trying to answer are the following: (1) What actions do NGOs take in trying to mobilize young people and make them aware of their causes? (2) What advantages do NGOs have in social networks? and (3) What tactics have been successful in reaching and involving young people, and why? Given this methodological approach, the research hypothesis is that NGOs find in social networks a necessary ally for the involvement of young people in the actions of solidarity they undertake, not forgetting that offline actions must also be undertaken and require the involvement of young people in this type of mobilization to achieve the expected result.

Within this context, the focus group was chosen as the most adequate technique for obtaining information about the object of study. Focus group discussions fall within qualitative research tradition. The name of the method defines its key characteristics, in that it involves a focus on specific issues, with a predetermined group of people, participating in an interactive discussion, thereby a focus group discussion [38].

The method may be described as "an interactive discussion between six to eight preselected participants led by a trained moderator and focussing on a specific set of issues. The aim of a focus group discussion is to gain a broad range of views on the research topic over a 60–90 min period, and to create an environment where participants feel comfortable to express their views" (Hennink et al. [39, p. 136]). The goal of this technique is to collect as much information as possible at a preestablished time regarding the perceptions or attitudes of a diverse conglomerate of people represented by one particular group. Focus groups lead to a type of data that can hardly be obtained by other means, as the participants are placed in real, natural situations in which spontaneity is possible, and due to the lenient environment, opinions, feelings, and personal desires arise which would not be revealed in more rigidly structured experimental situations. Focus group discussions are able to produce "collective narratives" on the research issues that go on beyond individual perspectives to generate a group perspective on the issue discussed, which produces a different type and level of data from that gained in individual interviews (Hennink [38, p. 3]).

We have defined the selected target group as "representatives of Third Sector Organizations, or NonGovernmental Organizations" in Spain. Responding to the operational capacity of collection and analysis, as suggested by Hernández Sampieri et al. [40], we selected individuals who actively collaborated by developing communication actions within one of the following NGOs or web platforms: Greenpeace, UNICEF, Mauricio Garrigou Foundation, International Cooperation, the Spanish Association Against Cancer (AECC), and Change.org.

■ ■ ■ ▬▬▬▬▬▬▬▬▬▬▬▬▬▬▬▬▬▬▬▬▬▬▬▬▬▬▬▬▬▬▬▬▬▬

NGOs or Web Platforms

Greenpeace is an independent global campaigning organization that acts to change attitudes and behavior, to protect and conserve the environment, and, as they say in their webpage, to promote peace by: catalyzing an energy revolution to address the number one threat facing our planet: climate change; defending our oceans by challenging wasteful and destructive fishing, and creating a global network of marine reserves; protecting the world's ancient forests and the animals, plants, and people that depend on them; working for disarmament and peace by tackling the causes of conflict and calling for the elimination of all nuclear weapons; creating a toxic-free future with safer alternatives to hazardous chemicals in today's products and manufacturing; campaigning for sustainable agriculture by rejecting genetically engineered organisms, protecting biodiversity and encouraging socially responsible farming.

Greenpeace is present in more than 55 countries across Europe, the Americas, Asia, Africa, and the Pacific (www.greenpeace.org).

UNICEF promotes the rights and well-being of every child. UNICEF works in 190 countries and territories to translate that commitment into practical action, focusing special effort on reaching the most vulnerable and excluded children, to the benefit of all children. UNICEF was created with a distinct purpose in mind: to work with others to overcome the obstacles that poverty, violence, disease, and discrimination place in a child's path. UNICEF is part of the Global Movement for Children—a broad coalition dedicated to improving the life of every child. Through this movement and events such as the United Nations Special Session on Children, they encourage young people to speak out and participate in the decisions that affect their lives (www.unicef.com).

Fundación Garrigou (The Mauricio Garrigou Foundation) was set up in Spain in July 2012 to give children and young people with different capabilities or skills an education of the highest quality, attending to their specific needs and using the most avant-garde educational methods and best adapted to the uniqueness of each one. They talk about different capacities, not disability, because they know that these kids are capable (www.fundaciongarrigou.org).

Cooperación Internacional (International Cooperation NGO) is a Spanish nonprofit organization that has been working since 1993 "for a supportive youth." It carries out most of its activities in Spain and it also works in more than 30 countries in which they carry out cooperation projects for development, volunteer programs, and other initiatives in collaboration with various institutions. At the end of 2016, International Cooperation had 174 partners, of which 83 were civil associations, representing more than 2500 people (www.ciong.org).

The Spanish Association Against Cancer (AECC) was constituted on March 5, 1953 with the purpose of fighting against cancer in all known modalities. It is composed of volunteers, partners, and hired personnel that join the forces to achieve the objectives of the Association. Its aims: (1) inform and raise awareness: educate society on all measures and possible mechanisms to prevent the disease; (2) support and accompany: be close to the sick and their families, offering encouragement and support to reduce their suffering; (3) encourage oncological research: promote excellent oncological research, serving as a bridge between society and the scientific community (www.aecc.es).

Change.org was launched on February 7, 2007. Change.org is a petition website which claims to have more than 100 million users. The company helps people petition specific leaders on any issue. Change.org's stated mission is to "empower people everywhere to create the change they want to see" [41]. The platform, as its CEO declares, was built for micromovements: small, personal petitions replicated hundreds or thousands of times over across cities, states, even countries (www.change.org).

■ ■ ■

To begin with, the segmentation variables used in the selection of NGOs were organizations with websites and profiles on social networks in which participation in campaigns, donations, complaints, etc., were possible; second, organizations that belonged to the online or offline world, or both; and lastly, organizations with a scope of activity that could be local, national, and/or international.

The objective was to obtain rich, depth, and quality information, not just quantity or standardization. Participants presented their own views and experience, but they also hear from other people. It was a sample oriented to diverse qualitative research, or of maximum variation, that was used when trying to show different perspectives and to represent the complexity of the phenomenon studied, or for documenting diversity in order to locate differences and similarities, patterns, and distinct features [40].

The moderator was a university researcher specialist in focus groups. Every session took around 1 h and 45 min. During that time, the language that participants used, the emphasis they gave, and their general framework of understanding was audio recorded and later, transcribed for its analysis.

5 Results

According to Richie and Lewis [42], there are two main ways in which group data can be analyzed: (1) Whole group analysis which treats the data produced by a group as a whole without delineating individual contributions. The group therefore becomes the unit of analysis and will be treated in the same way as a unit of individual data. Additional information (in the form of notes) about group interactions or the balance of individual contributions may be added to the data as part of the evidence. (2) Participant-based group analysis where the contributions of individual participants are separately analyzed within the context of the discussion as a whole. This allows the information of each participant to be retained and for interactions between individual members to be noted as part of the recording of the group dynamic.

For the analysis of the focus group carried out with representatives of the NGOs, the participant-based group analysis has been used. The advantage of participant-based analysis over whole group analysis is that it allows more detailed evidence about the similarities and differences between group members to be determined. It also allows certain types of analysis (such as associative analysis) to take place at an individual as well as at a group level [42].

NGOs start from the assumption that young people are the ones who want to participate in social causes, but the organizations find it difficult to reach them and get them involved:

> We don't know how to give them valuable proposals that appeal to them, or we don't know how to reach them. I see it as more of a problem of the organizations. I don't think young people are not interested in getting involved. In fact, you see them participating in a lot of things...even more than previous generations, in my opinion. Collaborative consumption has become commonplace... I'm not so sure they are non-political or individualist.
>
> *Greenpeace*

> Yes, it really bothers them that politicians steal money. That interests them. The way they say it, or how they express it, is different from what we do. They might think voting is useless, but that doesn't mean they don't care or aren't interested in anything.
>
> *Fundación Garrigou*

Faced with this situation, NGOs see a world of possibilities in digital social communication, specifically in social networks, as a tool to reach and mobilize young people. Thus, among the advantages and valuations that emerge in their speeches are, in the first place, the role of information that social networks generally possess for the user, and second, the extent to which networks allow organizations to keep their communities and potential followers informed about their actions. Information regarding everything the organizations do, their campaigns, and their calls for participation:

> *And then they don't know, or in other words, the community doesn't know. What I mean is the community is not aware of many actions that the organization carries out if it is not done through Facebook, which is feeding them interesting topics every day. Our organizations do a lot of things. People have to know what we do, and social networks are an incredible tool for that.*
>
> *AECC*

In this way, social networks promote communication that is more effective insofar as they open a gap that allows organizations to move surreptitiously into the social networks of their audiences, to be among the content of the daily lives of their potential followers in their more personal and private daily activities:

> *I think it's also a way of opening the door so they can receive your message even more effectively than through a web or a traditional means of communication in the sense that you sneak a bit into their daily lives, their interests, and their friends. Internet is a source of almost daily consultation for other reasons, and they give you a window, or an opening, to appear among the contents of more personalized information related to what really interests them, and they set aside some time for you.*
>
> *Cooperación Internacional*

This quality brings another one. Organizations point out how fast some information can be spread. Social networks are very good tools for a call to participate in some social event, because it is really a very fast way to get thousands of people in a very little time:

> *The fact that any message can spread quickly is something very positive, whether it is through the organization's own site, as in our case, or whether your organization uses Internet to carry out their actions.*
>
> *Change.org*

Another quality that NGOs confer upon digital communication, specifically social networks, is direct and bidirectional communication. In other words, social networks additionally allow organizations to test the information they disseminate and assess their impact through direct feedback they receive from users in the form of opinions, evaluations, criticisms, or suggestions about the various initiatives and participation campaigns:

You can reach people, launch your message, or your campaign, and get immediate feedback. It also helps you evaluate the level of interest of your followers, or the interest of the people you have a relationship with. To the extent that you can obtain feedback and opinion, this is a barometer that let you see what they really like, and what really interests them. This is of enormous interest to these entities because it lets them evaluate what is actually reaching the people.

Unicef

For NGOs, social networks are also an important way of raising awareness and engaging young people in solving social problems. Awareness, information, and participation campaigns launched by organizations through online social networks aim to raise young peoples' consciousness at an early age.

These campaigns make them think, and help them to open their minds on social issues, empowering them to become engaged in changing the world and to face the serious problems that NGOs detect and that affect everyone:

We invest a lot of energy in educating people from childhood, because in the long run, what is not sown is difficult to reap.

Unicef

It's a breeding ground that will grow bigger later on. We don't care if they are in one or another NGO, whether it's for the environment, for cancer, for people who have individual causes or try to change the world. What I'm saying is that the important thing is for them to open their minds.

Greenpeace

This generation, Generation Z, is one that places high importance on values. What I mean is, it's more important to them than anything else. I'm talking about the values they have now, which are the values they will still have in five or ten years.

AECC

The actions of NGOs as well as web petition platforms are aimed at empowering young people, conveying trust and motivation, trying to get them involved, and making them leaders of social change:

Our work has to be more about empowerment, so they will know how to communicate the message in their own way, and through their own channels. More than communicating in the old way, the work needs to be more about empowerment.

Greenpeace

We also need to give them the confidence to know that they can be protagonists of change, and convey motivation so they understand that they can really do a lot.

Change.org

NGOs are also somewhat self-critical in recognizing their lack of knowledge of the new communicative situation of young people and of online social networks where young people meet and interact with each other and which are possibly different from those used by adults.

An effort is now being made by NGO leaders to understand these new uses and to learn the means through which young people establish online communication processes in order to understand what is occurring and how it works:

We want to be at their level, trying to understand what is happening: they don't watch television or listen to the radio. They watch YouTube, a world in which a YouTuber comes and asks you for three thousand Euros in exchange for mentioning you in a video. So we have to kind of understand how that works because you cannot become a YouTuber yourself.

Unicef

As far as we can see, yes, they are social beings. What is happening is that maybe they are not in the same networks as we are.

Greenpeace

The evidence also reflects the difficulty that organizations have in providing the youngest users with important proposals that appeal to them.

The only thing that needs to happen is…well, to reach out to them a bit. But of course, when they are offered something good, they take it, and they value it, I believe.

Cooperación Internacional

We don't know how to reach them.

AECC

They're not interested in things because of the way we explain them.

Unicef

How they say it and how they express it is, naturally, different from the way we do it.

Fundación Garrigou

But what I feel is that they don't care about things because of the way we explain them. It's not that they are not interested in them.

Greenpeace

5.1 NGO Communication Activities in Social Networks

Despite the difficulties, NGOs refer to the initiatives they promote on social networks that aim to encourage participation, and they also adopt different strategies and tactics to stimulate the involvement of young people. Among the initiatives mentioned by representatives of organizations are the following: first of all, a call for participation through actions or leisure and entertainment activities. It is a matter of adapting the campaign to the target audience: of raising awareness, promoting solidarity, and informing through participation that takes the form of action that young people see as related to play—gamification—and obtaining some compensation, result, prize, or gift.

It can be a game, a proposal of 'gamification,' sending content or any other action…

Unicef

Another of the activities is related to the launch of surveys through social networks, which serve as an attraction. In other words, they are associated with requests for solidarity or collaboration carried out by web platforms and NGOs. These questionnaires fulfill the purpose of stimulating the curiosity of users as a means of reporting a problem and trying to obtain citizen involvement:

For example, using Twitter surveys can raise awareness about a particular issue in a different way. You show three options and say, 'if you want to know the answer, you have it in the petition.' Then, many people just think, 'I'm going to try to guess', and they respond to the request. That tweet has an engagement that is fifteen or twenty times greater than a normal tweet. You get them to go to the petition to see the answer, and at the same time, if they are interested in the subject, they can sign.

Greenpeace

To encourage young people to participate, NGOs agree that it seems necessary to include the emotional dimension in the development of the stories that serve as the basis for participation campaigns.

In the opinion of NGOs, to turn at present to emotional storytelling—building a moving story—that touches a sensitive nerve of potential participants in their campaigns, is an action that has been working well in encouraging participation, especially among youth:

You have to tell a story that touches their sensitive side a bit, because it has always been like that. But in my opinion, I think things are going more in that direction – story-telling–.

Cooperación Internacional

This is a form of social marketing that tries to avoid the classic institutional message of organizations that in the past made direct calls for collaboration. This is a new narrative, which allows the public to identify with the problem presented through the use of emotions:

> *The 'we need your help' statement should come last. Before that, there is a long road to travel before touching the heart a bit with emotional stories that people can identify with.*
>
> *Unicef*

One of the problems posed by this strategy for NGOs is that the resource is being increasingly used to excess, both in the field of advertising as well as by petitioning web platforms:

> *There is increasing competition in this area. This has always been a classic feature of NGOs. It has always been our message, but is now being used increasingly in more sectors and in more media.*
>
> *Fundación Garrigou*

NGOs are in agreement when referring to the need to use universal values such as *leitmotiv* in their campaigns for the purpose of calling for commitment, volunteerism, and participation. This is about the transmission of messages in online campaigns that reflect universal values that everyone can identify with, such as honesty, transparency, the fight against corruption, or concern for others. These messages, in the opinion of the organizations, have strong echoes among potential participants. Their impact helps to achieve the objectives of raising awareness and the dissemination of information, since these are values that people want to identify with:

> *They reflect values that everyone can identify with, and that everyone is happy to adopt as their own, to transmit them to their contacts, because these are values that everyone can identify with.*
>
> *Unicef*

> *Everyone is thrilled to give you a retweet or to let people know you support such positive values.*
>
> *Greenpeace*

According to these organizations, it is particularly interesting to offer examples in these campaigns of testimonies of young people, ordinary people, of people who epitomize these values, and who young people can identify with:

> *It is necessary to show these values exemplified in other young people like themselves in order to serve as a reference to them.*
>
> *Cooperación Internacional*

These are average, ordinary people, with very attractive traits, real people. This is not an advertisement. You might meet the protagonist the day after tomorrow. She can tell you what she's doing and how happy she is; I believe a real example has considerable value.

Fundación Garrigou

Despite the importance they see in social networks in achieving youth mobilization for their causes, the campaign plan that combines offline and online actions is more effective than the one that uses only one of the two channels for its dissemination, in the opinion of NGOs and web platforms:

To us, the campaigns that have worked best are those that have combined both online and offline actions.

Greenpeace

In this respect, at the present time both channels are considered complementary when designing campaigns.

The work in both fields is complementary because the possibility of changing from one to the other, depending on the campaign, on the subject, on thousands of variables, is very high. At least we believe that the ability to move from one to the other is considerable.

Greenpeace

5.2 The Role of Influencers

In this digital and participatory context, the so-called "influencers" play a decisive role, either in a call to action offline or online. Resorting to leaders and opinion makers—YouTubers, bloggers—to inform young audiences in an alternative way about their campaigns and the problems they pose is very important. Some NGOs turn to YouTubers and bloggers, but also to famous artists—celebrities—as a formula for disseminating their campaigns and for getting their message to young people.

These opinion leaders are people who are trusted by young people, who have become role models for the prestige acquired in their online activity, which is endorsed, by thousands of followers registered in their accounts or YouTube channels. With these influential people, NGOs take advantage of the ability of these people to reach extensive youth audiences, which otherwise would be impossible to access through the institutional messages of these organizations:

We use several formulas, and the one that is working for us now is to collaborate with the so-called 'influencers'; what we are looking for are YouTubers.

Fundación Garrigou

We work with people who we believe have a special sensitivity; it is not enough for us to tell you something, but you need to hear it from someone you trust. A blogger you like, or an Instagrammer you follow.

Greenpeace

They have another way of communicating. Also, these people really do it like that, and they get five thousand clicks of 'I like it' with just a photo of them shaking their hair around. Yes, really, five thousand clicks on 'I like it'! Do you know what you have to do to get five thousand 'I like it' clicks? It's like building the El Escorial Palace complex, one of the Spanish royal sites built during the 16th and 17th centuries. Our NGO, as an organization, cannot tweet something and have the same impact on networks. At that level of response, and with those ages, there's no way!.

Cooperación Internacional

When choosing the protagonists for their campaigns, NGO leaders look for people with the following characteristics: first, they must be endowed with sensitivity, a special style, an ability to reach young people in a different way. Second, they need to be interested in the campaigns promoted by the NGO and be willing to offer their services without an interest in personal gain:

Zero euros, eh! We haven't paid even one single euro. They do it for free.

Greenpeace

However, this is not true in all cases. The recruitment by organizations of opinion leaders for their campaigns is not always possible on a volunteer basis, as some bloggers and You-Tubers demand economic compensation in exchange for their involvement:

In our case, the bloggers charge us. At least they want to charge us, but we don't pay them. That's why we don't have bloggers. But YouTubers, for example, collaborate and don't charge us for their services.

Cooperación Internacional

We try to put ourselves at their level, and also try to understand what is happening: they don't watch television or listen to the radio, but they use YouTube. It's a world where the YouTuber comes to you and asks for three thousand Euros for mentioning you in a video, and it's like noooo way!.

Unicef

In general, the communication they establish with young, potential participants in their campaigns is more effective if not only the organization sends the message, but also people of their generation. This people have a special and unique way of presenting their message, a narrative that allows for communication and connection with young people in their own language, with their values, concerns, problems, lifestyles, and their own way of speaking and acting:

> *They [the influencers] don't explain things the way we do; their language is not the same as ours. They have a way of expressing things, of reaching people. And only through them can it be done.*
>
> *Fundación Garrigou*

> *The way influencers communicate the message is nothing like other ways of presenting the issue. So what they are doing is [establishing special communication]: 'Hey, this is my lifestyle. Look how great it is! Adopt my way of life.*
>
> *Greenpeace*

6 Conclusions

NGOs have now entered fully into the digital ecosystem. These organizations have found in social networks a space for civic participation to report on their solidarity objectives, to expand their visibility, and even to increase the number of donors that keep the organizations alive. Thus, NGOs see in social networks a world of possibilities, such as those of informing, offering civic training, raising awareness about injustice, and providing citizen empowerment.

Moreover, they try to make the most of all of their attributes, not forgetting that they also encounter problems and obstacles in encouraging or promoting youth participation in their organizations.

Within this participatory and digital context, and in the search for an attitude of solidarity among young people, the work we present here has shown that NGOs are adjusting their strategies to become closer to young people in a more effective way.

Among these strategies, we would like to highlight their practice of hiring of young people for their communication network teams, the use of influencers, celebrities, YouTubers, and bloggers for their campaigns, and finally, their constant attempt to adapt to a digital environment. An environment that has overwhelmed them, but which they know is the right formula to use if they want to reach young people.

In addition, the feedback that NGOs and platforms receive from networks helps them focus their campaigns much more effectively by allowing them to analyze the impact of such campaigns and make changes, if necessary, to their approach.

The communication activities of NGOs are aimed at planting a seed in order to create participatory citizens in the future who will reflect and become involved in other social issues.

To this end, they use the most traditional ethical values that everyone can identify with, such as honesty, transparency, the fight against corruption, and concern for others. In this sense, NGOs are making a strong effort in offering civic and political education that is likely to deliver short-term results in creating participatory digital citizens.

References

[1] B. Berceruelo, Planificar en Internet. Online u offline: solo comunicación Empresarial, in: B. Berceruelo (Ed.), Comunicación Empresarial, Estudios de Comunicación, Madrid, 2016, pp. 281–283.

[2] O. Acker, F. Gröne, T. Lefort, L. Kropiunigg, The Digital Future of Creative Europe. The Impact of Digitization and the Internet on the Creative Industries in Europe, Booz & Company, Berlin, 2015.

[3] A. Mariñas, Las empresas frente al reto 2.0, in: B. Berceruelo (Ed.), Comunicación empresarial, Madrid, Estudios de Comunicación, 2016, pp. 283–284.

[4] Zafra, I. (2012). Ecosistema Digital. Recuperado en http://www.pmfarma.es/articulos/1143-ecosistema-digital.html (9 de mayo de 2017).

[5] Santa Laurín, L.F. (2015). Un acercamiento al concepto de ecosistema digital. Retrieved from: http://www.vallempresa365.com/articulos/marketing/un-acercamiento-al-concepto-de-ecosistema-digital (9 de mayo de 2017).

[6] G. López García (Ed.), El ecosistema digital: Modelos de comunicación, nuevos medios y público en Internet, Servei de Publicacions de la Universitat de Valencia, Valencia, 2005. Retrieved from:http://roderic.uv.es/bitstream/handle/10550/53701/El_ecosistema_digital_modelos_de_comunic.pdf?sequence=1.

[7] A.I. Bernal, Tecnología, redes sociales, política y periodismo. ¿Pluralidad informativa o efecto bumerán? Cuadernos.info (36) (2015), https://doi.org/10.7764/cdi.36.647.

[8] S. Brennen, D. Kreiss, Digitalization and digitization, in: Culture Digitally, 2014. Retrieved from: http://culturedigitally.org/2014/09/digitalization-and-digitization/.

[9] D. Karpf, The Move on Effect: The Unexpected Transformation of American Political Advocacy, Oxford University Press, 2012.

[10] Marketingdirecto.com (6 de julio de 2014). El 98% de las ONGs tienen presencia en las redes sociales. Retrieved from: www.marketingdirecto.com/digital-general/social-media-marketing/el-98-de-las-ongs-tienen-presencia-en-las-redes-sociales (5 de mayo de 2017).

[11] E. Anduiza, C. Cristancho, J.M. Sabucedo, Mobilization through online social networks: the political protest of the indignados in Spain, Inf. Commun. Soc. 17 (6) (2014) 20.

[12] V. Bekkers, R. Moody, A. Edwards, Micro-mobilization, social media and coping strategies: some Dutch experiences, Pol. Internet 3 (4) (2011) 1–29, https://doi.org/10.2202/1944-2866.1061.

[13] V. Bekkers, H. Beunders, A. Edwards, R. Moody, New media, micromobilization, and political agenda setting: crossover effects in political mobilization and media usage, Inf. Soc. 27 (4) (2011) 209–219, https://doi.org/10.1080/01972243.2011.583812.

[14] M.M. Skoric, N.D. Poor, Y. Liao, S.W.H. Tang, in: Online organization of an offline protest: from social to traditional media and back, Paper Presented at the 44th Hawaii International Conference on System Sciences, Hawaii, 2011.

[14a] B. Bimber, A.J. Flanagin, C. Stohl, Collective Action in Organizations: Interaction and Engagement in an Era of Technological Change, Cambridge University Press, New York, 2012, 240pp.

[15] J. Brinkerhoff, D. Brinkerhoff, Government—nonprofit relations in comparative perspective: evolution, themes and new directions, Publ. Admin. Dev. 22 (1) (2002) 3–18.

[16] N. Meriläinen, M. Vos, Human rights organizations and online agenda setting, Corp. Commun. Int. J. 16 (4) (2011) 293–310.

[17] S. Goss, Making Local Governance Work—Networks, Relationships and the Management of Change, Palgrave, New York, 2001.

[18] J.A. Scholte, Global Civil Society: Changing the World?, 1999. University of Warwick, CSGR Working Paper, 31.

[19] Nonprofit tech for good (2017). 2017 Global NGO. Online Technology Report. Retrieved from: http://www.techreport.ngo/english.html (9 de mayo de 2017).

[20] K. Lovejoy, G.D. Saxton, Information, community, and action: How nonprofit organizations use social media, J. Comput. Mediated Commun. 17 (3) (2012) 337–353.

[21] Cabanelas, L. (22 de noviembre de 2015) Redes sociales, el «arma de sofá» de las tragedias contemporáneas. ABC. Retrieved from: http://www.abc.es/internacional/abci-atentados-paris-redes-sociales-arma-sofa-tragedias-contemporaneas-201511222317_noticia.html.

[22] C. García Galera, C. Fernández Muñoz, L. Porto, Empoderamiento de los jóvenes a través de las redes sociales. Construcción de una ciudadanía digital comprometida, Comunicación y Sociedad (30) (2017) 129–140.

[23] C. Tilly, Social Movements, 1768–2004, Paradigm Publishers, London, 2004.

[24] J. Goodwin, J. Jasper, The Social Movements Reader: Cases and Concepts, Blackwell Publishing, Oxford, 2003.

[25] J. Lucas, Sobre desobediencia y democracia. La hora de la ciudadanía. Derechos y Libertades: Revista de Filosofía del Derecho y Derechos Humanos 31 (2014) 57–75, https://doi.org/10.1400/222449.

[26] S. Tarrow, Power in movement: Social movements, in: Collective Action and Politics, Cambridge University Press, New York, 1994.

[27] R. Caers, T. De Feyter, M. De Couck, T. Stough, C. Vigna, C. Du Bois, Facebook: a literature review, New Media Soc. 15 (6) (2013) 982–1002, https://doi.org/10.1177/146144481348806.

[28] C. Guo, G.D. Saxton, Tweeting social change: how social media are changing nonprofit advocacy, Nonprofit Volunt. Sect. Q. 43 (1) (2014) 57–79, https://doi.org/10.1177/0899764012471585.

[29] J.M. Sánchez Duarte, La red como espacio para la militancia política: tecnología y participación en campaña electoral, Commun. Soc. 29 (3) (2016) 33–47.

[30] K. Thorson, K. Driscoll, B. Ekdale, S. Edgerly, L.G. Thompson, A. Schrock, L. Swartz, E.K. Vraga, C. Wells, Youtube, twitter and the occupy movement, Inf. Commun. Soc. 16 (3) (2013) 421–451, https://doi.org/10.1080/1369118X.2012.756051.

[31] C. Ilten, Use your skills to solve your challenge!: the platform affordances and politics of digital micro-volunteering. Social Media Soc. 1 (2) (2015) 1–11, https://doi.org/10.1177/2056305115604175.

[31a] R. Asún, C. Zúñiga, Por qué se participa? Explicando la protesta social regionalista a partir de dos modelos psicosociales, Psicoperspectivas 12 (2) (2013) 38–50.

[31b] L. Porto Pedrosa, El futuro del emprendimiento y la participación social visto a través del discurso de los jóvenes, Revista de Estudios de Juventud 107 (2015) 29–44.

[32] J. González-Anleo, Jóvenes y valores cívico-políticos, Educación y Futuro (13) (2005) 59–70.

[33] Observatorio de la Juventud en España (2014). Jóvenes, satisfacción personal, participación asociativa y voluntariado. Retrieved from: http://www.injuve.es/sites/default/files/2016/04/publicaciones/informesondeo_2014-1.pdf

[34] B.D. Loader, Young Citizens in the Digital Age: Political Engagement, Young People and New Media, Routledge, Londres, 2007.

[35] B.D. Loader, A. Vromen, M.A. Xenos, The networked young citizen: social media, political participation and civic engagement, Inf. Commun. Soc. 17 (2) (2014).

[36] K.P. Kallio, J. Häkli, Children and young people's politics in everyday life, Space Polity 17 (1) (2013) 1–16.

[37] M. Yamamoto, M. Kushin, F. Dalisay, Social media and mobiles as political mobilization forces for young adults: examining the moderating role of online political expression in political participation, New Media Soc. 17 (6) (2015) 880–898, https://doi.org/10.1177/1461444813518390.

[38] M.M. Hennink, Focus Groups Discussions, Oxford University Press, 2014.

[39] M.M. Hennink, I. Hutter, A. Bailey, Qualitative Research Methods, Sage Publishing, London, 2011.

[40] R. Hernández Sampieri, C. Fernández Collado, P. Baptista Lucio, Metodología de la Investigación, McGraw-Hill, México, 2006.

[41] Kelly, M (May 7, 2013). Change.org CEO Shows How Online Petitions Change the Face of Health Care (Q&A). VentureBeat. Retrieved from: https://venturebeat.com/2013/05/17/change-org-health-petitions/

[42] J. Richie, J. Lewis, Qualitative Research Practice. A Guide for Social Science Students and Researchers, SagePublications, London, 2003.

Further Reading

[43] Arrieta, E. (2017). Change.org alcanza los 12 millones de usuarios en España. Expansión Recuperado en http://www.expansion.com/economia-digital/companias/2017/04/18/58f63935268e3e76658b45d2.html (22 de mayo de 2017).

[44] A. Casero Ripollés, R. Feenstra, The 15-M movement and the new media: a case study of how new themes were introduced into Spanish political discourse, Media Int. Aust. 144 (2012) 68–76. Recuperado en: http://repositori.uji.es/xmlui/bitstream/handle/10234/80466/53905.pdf?sequence=1.

[45] A. Kavada, Engagement, bonding, and identity across multiple platforms: Avaaz on Facebook, YouTube, and MySpace, J. Media Commun. Res. (52) (2012) 28–48.

[46] M. Otte, El crash de la información: Los mecanismos de la desinformación cotidiana, Ariel, Barcelona, 2010.

[47] J.M. Sabucedo, G. Seoane, M.J. Ferraces, M. Rodríguez, C. Fernández, La acción política en el contexto supranacional y los marcos de acción colectiva, Revista de Psicología Social Aplicada 6 (3) (1996) 103–120.

Index

Note: Page numbers followed by *f* indicate figures, *t* indicate tables, and *b* indicate boxes.

Printed in the United States
By Bookmasters